Master Drawings from The Courtauld Gallery

THE COURTAULD Gallery

THE FRICK COLLECTION

Master Drawings from The Courtauld Gallery

EDITED BY
Colin B. Bailey and Stephanie Buck

CONTRIBUTORS

Denise Allen
Julian Brooks
Mary Camp
Caroline Campbell
Chris Fischer
Susan Grace Galassi
Margaret Iacono
Nancy Ireson
Satish Padiyar

Stephanie Porras
David Solkin
Joanna Selborne
Katie Scott
Margret Stuffmann
Nathaniel Silver
Christopher White
Joanna Woodall
Zahira Véliz

THE COURTAULD GALLERY
AND THE FRICK COLLECTION
IN ASSOCIATION WITH
PAUL HOLBERTON PUBLISHING
LONDON

First published to accompany the exhibition

Mantegna to Matisse:
Master Drawings from The Courtauld Gallery

The Courtauld Gallery, London
14 June – 9 September 2012

The Frick Collection, New York
2 October 2012 – 27 January 2013

The Courtauld Gallery is supported by
the Higher Education Funding Council for England (HEFCE)

I S B N   978 1 907372 38 4 (paperback)
I S B N   978 1 907372 39 1 (cased)

British Library Cataloguing in Publication Data

A catalogue record for this book is
available from the British Library

Produced by Paul Holberton publishing
89 Borough High Street, London SE1 1NL, UK
www.paul-holberton.net

Designed by Philip Lewis

Origination and printing by E-graphic, Verona, Italy

Front: detail, cat. no. 11 (with stains retouched)
Back: detail, cat. no. 54
Frontispiece: detail, cat. no. 38
Page 9: detail, cat. no. 53
Pages 12 and 13: detail, cat. no. 15
Page 34: detail, cat. no. 45
Page 266: detail, cat. no. 34
Page 284: detail, cat. no. 12

Contents

Foreword

FOUNDED IN 1932, The Courtauld Institute of Art is renowned as one of the world's leading specialist centres for teaching and research in the history of art. Through The Courtauld Gallery it also cares for one of Britain's finest public collections. Within this celebrated collection, consisting of works on paper, paintings, sculpture and decorative arts, the Gallery's 7,000 drawings form an area of outstanding strength and vitality. Their chronological sweep gives a sustained account of the major national European schools of draughtsmanship. Alongside individual works of singular importance, numerous artists are represented in depth, including Rembrandt, Rubens, Guercino, Giovanni Battista Tiepolo, Turner and Cézanne. The Courtauld Gallery and The Frick Collection are proud to collaborate on this exhibition, which brings the collection to new audiences and, in its scholarly approach, aims to encourage its further use in international art-historical research.

The Courtauld Gallery last presented a comparable selection of its master drawings in 1991. Nowhere have the profound changes that the Gallery has undergone in the intervening two decades been more evident than in its stewardship of the drawings collection. Early digitisation and the handsome redevelopment of the study room provided the foundations for increasing public access and promoting the use of the collection for teaching and research. Since 2007 the collection has been in the hands of Stephanie Buck, Martin Halusa Curator of Drawings, and under her care it has assumed a central role in the life of The Courtauld. Major cataloguing and research projects, publications, a rich series of scholarly events, and international exchanges and museum partnerships have helped transform specialist engagement with the collection. The integration of conservation research on the material aspects of drawings has provided a further important dimension to this work, whilst an acclaimed programme of exhibitions and displays has brought the fruits of these many endeavours to a wider public.

With its particular scale and character, its reputation for scholarship and its exemplary record of drawings exhibitions, The Frick Collection is a natural partner for The Courtauld Gallery. The Courtauld Institute of Art's three founders – Samuel Courtauld, Sir Robert Witt and Lord Lee of Fareham – as well as its other great benefactor, Count Antoine Seilern, all enjoyed close professional and personal ties to the United States of America. Indeed, their founding vision for a new institution that would combine teaching and research with outstanding collections was closely informed by innovations in America, specifically at Harvard University's Fogg Art Museum. Sir Robert Witt, the largest single donor to The Courtauld's drawings collection, paid his first visit to the Fogg in 1920, in the company of Helen Frick, whose Art Reference Library was inspired by Witt's example.

From the selection of the individual works for the exhibition to the production of the catalogue, every stage of this project has been approached as a genuine collaboration. Led by Stephanie Buck at The Courtauld Gallery and Colin B. Bailey, Deputy Director and Peter Jay Sharp Chief Curator at The Frick Collection, the team also included numerous members of staff at each institution, who are thanked in the Acknowledgments. We are also greatly indebted to the specialist authors of this catalogue, many of whom have close ties to our two institutions. With their knowledgeable and illuminating contributions they have helped realise our shared ambition that this project should not just be a straightforward display of highlights but rather an opportunity to present fresh perspectives on important individual works and, collectively, an illustration of the rich diversity of approaches to the study of drawings. The collections held at The Courtauld Gallery are owned by the Samuel Courtauld Trust. We would like to record our gratitude to the Trust's Chairman, the Hon. Christopher McLaren, and its trustees for enabling us to show these drawings in London and New York.

The Courtauld's drawings collection has received major support from The International Music and Art Foundation, which has played an important role in the essential conservation of the collection as well as in the Gallery's programme of publications and exhibitions. For the presentation of this exhibition in London, The Courtauld Gallery has received vital additional support from the Friends of The Courtauld, The Tavolozza Foundation and The Doris Pacey Charitable Foundation. We are very grateful to them.

In New York, where the exhibition is supported by an indemnity from the Federal Council on the Arts and the Humanities, assistance for the presentation has been generously provided by Jean-Marie and Elizabeth Eveillard, The Christian Humann Foundation, The Peter Jay Sharp Foundation, the late Melvin R. Seiden in honor of Neil and Angelica Rudenstine, the Joseph F. McCrindle Foundation, Diane Allen Nixon and an anonymous gift in honor of Colin B. Bailey and in memory of Melvin R. Seiden.

ERNST VEGELIN VAN CLAERBERGEN
Head of The Courtauld Gallery

IAN WARDROPPER
Director, The Frick Collection

Exhibition Supporters

Support for the presentation of the exhibition in London
and the production of the accompanying catalogue is generously
provided by The International Music and Art Foundation,
Friends of The Courtauld, The Tavolozza Foundation, and
The Doris Pacey Charitable Foundation.

Support for the presentation in New York is generously
provided by Jean-Marie and Elizabeth Eveillard, The Christian
Humann Foundation, The Peter Jay Sharp Foundation, the late
Melvin R. Seiden in honor of Neil and Angelica Rudenstine,
The Joseph F. McCrindle Foundation, Diane Allen Nixon,
and an anonymous gift in honor of Colin B. Bailey and in
memory of Melvin R. Seiden. The exhibition is also supported
by an indemnity from the Federal Council on the Arts and
the Humanities.

Curators' Acknowledgements

MORE THAN FIVE YEARS have passed since our earliest discussions to mount an exhibition of master drawings from The Courtauld Gallery that could be shown in both London and New York. We wanted to represent each school with the finest examples available and to show the range of The Courtauld's holdings in a chronology that would also resonate with the permanent collection at the Frick. To arrive at a fitting florilegium, we spent several sessions reviewing the incomparable group of Old Master, nineteenth-century and early twentieth-century drawings now housed in their refurbished quarters. Given the strict oversight of loans by the Trustees of the Samuel Courtauld Trust and the desire, on the part of all involved, that our exhibition should also bring new insights and scholarship to these often published drawings, we were excited by the possibility of engaging specialists in both institutions (and some from outside) to study, review and catalogue each sheet. We are most grateful to Deborah Swallow, Märit Rausing Director of The Courtauld Institute of Art, Ernst Vegelin van Claerbergen, Head of The Courtauld Gallery, and Anne L. Poulet, Director Emerita at The Frick Collection, for their enthusiastic and crucial support of this ambitious project from its inception. Ian Wardropper, current Director of The Frick Collection, has also endorsed this undertaking wholeheartedly since his arrival in October 2011.

With twenty authors in several cities, the prospect of facilitating systematic study and inspection of every sheet was indeed a daunting one. We are most grateful to our colleagues working in The Courtauld's Prints and Drawings Study Room and its Paper Conservation Studio – and above all to Kate Edmondson – for welcoming both resident and visiting authors, for enabling close examination of each drawing and for granting access to curatorial files. Over the years many of The Courtauld's Print Room assistants worked with great commitment on the project. Julia Bischoff deserves special thanks for compiling the provenance of each drawing with meticulous care, often guided by Helen Braham, who most generously shared her immense knowledge of the Princes Gate collection and its archives. The curatorial staff at The Frick Collection is also indebted to research assistant Aimee Ng for her exceptional contribution.

We are proud of the variety of voices and approaches in the extended entries that comprise this catalogue, which we trust will stand as an introduction to the drawings collection at The Courtauld Gallery for years to come. We thank contributors Denise Allen, Julian Brooks, Mary Camp, Caroline Campbell, Chris Fischer, Susan Grace Galassi, Margaret Iacono, Nancy Ireson, Satish Padiyar, Stephanie Porras, Katie Scott, Joanna Selborne, Nathaniel Silver, David Solkin, Margret Stuffman, Zahira Véliz, Christopher White and Joanna Woodall.

The editing, coordination, design and publication of the catalogue was a task no less Herculean than the writing of it. Above all we are indebted to Elaine Koss, Julie di Filippo, Michael Bodycomb, Fronia Simpson and Pamela T. Barr. Paul Holberton and his staff deserve our warmest thanks as well as Philip Lewis for his beautiful design of the catalogue and Ezio Guerra for his commitment to the colour reproductions.

At The Courtauld we wish to thank in particular Graeme Barraclough, Julia Blanks, Sue Bond, Mary Ellen Cetra, Louisa Dare, Alexandra Gerstein, Kerstin Glasow, Henrietta Hine, Jack Kettlewell, Karin Kyburz, Katharine Lockett, Chloe Le Tissier, Belinda Moore, Alice Odin, Charlotte Oertel, Rachel Sloan, Hannah Talbot, Viyki Turnbull, Joff Whitten and Barnaby Wright.

At The Frick Collection we extend our warm thanks to Robert Goldsmith, Lynne Rutkin, Alison Lonshein, Rosayn Anderson, Heidi Rosenau, Alexis Light, Joseph Godla, Diane Farynyk, Allison Galea, Katie Steiner, Nicholas Wise, Rika Burnham and Adrienne Lei. We also acknowledge Mark Brady, Stephen Saitas and Anita Jorgensen.

In *Avant et Après* Paul Gauguin famously wrote, "A critic at my house sees some paintings. Greatly perturbed, he asks for my drawings. My drawings! Never! They are my letters, my secrets." Because of their inherently fragile nature, drawings in public collections will also remain hidden to a certain degree. Even with the great advances in on-line technology and digital reproduction, the experience of viewing and studying the actual sheet is one most often reserved for the scholar, the curator or the collector. We are delighted to extend that experience to a wider public, on both sides of the Atlantic, while encouraging those with an interest in graphic art to explore the deep and rich holdings of The Courtauld Gallery's collection in its permanent home at Somerset House.

STEPHANIE BUCK
Martin Halusa Curator of Drawings, The Courtauld Gallery

COLIN B. BAILEY
Deputy Director and Peter Jay Sharp Chief Curator, The Frick Collection

Mastery on Paper:
Drawings at The Courtauld Gallery

STEPHANIE BUCK

Author's note
I am very grateful to Julia Bischoff, Helen Braham,
Stephanie Porras and Ernst Vegelin van Claerbergen
for their help with the research for this essay and to
Pamela T. Barr and Ernst Vegelin van Claerbergen
for editing the text.

THE FIFTY-NINE WORKS discussed in this catalogue have been selected from the approximately seven thousand sheets in the collection of European drawings and watercolours at The Courtauld Gallery.[1] Dating from the fifteenth to the early twentieth century, they introduce the art of drawing in an exemplary manner. The works are executed in a broad variety of media, ranging from pen and ink, brush and wash, watercolour and bodycolour to metalpoint, graphite, charcoal and various coloured chalks. They vary greatly in their graphic character, some being predominantly linear, others more painterly. They range in function from preparatory studies for paintings and prints to complex, highly finished drawings prepared as works of art in their own right. Some capture movement and record anatomy, others space and light; some celebrate the expressive power of line, others explore subtleties of colour; some have a documentary purpose, others are purely an expression of the artist's imagination. All these diverse uniquely conceived and executed works are, however, united by their support – paper.

While it might be said that the act of drawing stands at the very beginning of any pictorial expression[2] – on canvas, wood, stone or parchment – paper has been intimately linked to drawing since the rise of the paper industry in the late fourteenth and fifteenth centuries.[3] As the material became more available and affordable, the types and functions of drawings became more diversified. Concomitant with these developments was the increase and variety of approaches to the appreciation, theoretical examination, connoisseurship and collecting of drawings.

Because of their sensitivity to light and relative fragility, drawings on paper require a high degree of protection, achieved by keeping them in albums, as was common during the early years of collecting,[4] or mounting them individually, which allows them to be stored in boxes and safely handled. When framed, mounted drawings can be displayed much like paintings, which distances them from the characteristically intimate viewing experience in a study room. While the necessity of only brief periods of display clearly limits the presentation of works on paper, the support has stimulated the production of many more drawings than works on other supports, as paper is not only comparatively inexpensive but also lightweight, easily transported and easily stored in great quantities. These properties explain the relatively large size of drawings collections. At the same time, the fragility of paper has contributed to the destruction or deterioration of many works, which may have been over-exposed, folded, torn or cut. Signs of such history cannot be concealed and remain apparent on every extant drawing subjected to such treatment (see, for example, cat. no. 24). This aspect of a sheet's physicality and material history strongly informs the perception of drawings. We also need to be particularly aware that most sheets have been trimmed – sometimes considerably – compromising or disturbing the original *mise-en-page*.

Beyond the issues of the physical condition, style, iconography, function or role of an individual drawing in the creative process, 'openness' fundamentally defines its practice, as Max Klinger argues in his treatise on painting and drawing:

> Drawing stands in a freer relationship to the representable world: it allows considerable leeway to the imagination in supplying the missing element of colour to the representation. It can treat those forms that do not immediately belong to the principal subject, and indeed this subject itself, with such freedom that the imagination must also participate to supply the missing elements.[5]

Continuing in this vein David Rosand summarises various aspects of 'drawing':

> By drawing we generally understand a pictorial structure more open than that of painting. Drawing tends to cover its supporting surface only incompletely; the ground retains its own participating presence in the image, just as the marks it hosts, and which so transform it, retain their autonomy. Ambivalence is an essential and functioning aspect of drawing. More insistently than the brush stroke in painting, the drawn mark resists surrender to the mimetic imperative, to pictorial illusion.[6]

Mark making stands not only at the heart of the act of drawing itself but is also intimately connected with the collecting of drawings. Owners have inscribed sheets with the names of artists who, for the most part, did not sign their work[7] and have often added their personal marks, whether discreetly on the verso or more visibly on the recto. The practice of linking a drawing to an owner can be traced to the early history of collecting. Famous examples are Albrecht Dürer, who noted names and ages of draughtsmen on the sheets he owned, and Giorgio Vasari, who collated and framed drawings on elaborate album sheets.[8] Numer-

FIG. 1 Detail of cat. no. 20 showing the marks of Sir Robert Witt and an unknown collector (E.A. Philips?) on the drawing's wash-line mount

Numerous drawings in the present selection bear the marks of former owners. Early inscriptions are the monogram *Ad* and the date *1508* added to Dürer's *Wise Virgin* (cat. no. 7), the name *Spagnoletto* on Ribera's *Man tied to a tree* (cat. no. 21), and *CAV. Bernini* on Bernini's *The Louvre, east façade* (cat. no. 30)[9] – all written by unknown hands. Besides these correct attributions, there are also misleading ones, which are nevertheless informative. For instance, *Barocci* is inscribed on Heintz's *Holy Family* (cat. no. 19), which, for stylistic reasons, had long been understood to be an Italian, rather than a Northern drawing, and Rubens's *Head of the Farnese Hercules* (cat. no. 23) was attributed to *AVDÿck*, which reveals the high regard in which the younger artist was held among collectors, particularly in England.

Other inscriptions, as well as printed marks, identify drawings as part of specific collections. Not only private collectors but also public institutions have placed such marks of ownership on works on paper, an important reason being that these works can easily be removed from a collection. The Courtauld, however, has never used a collector's mark; instead, inventory numbers are added on the mounts. This practice follows that of most individual collectors who gave or bequeathed their collections to The Courtauld; only Sir Robert Witt used a mark, stamped either on the mount or the verso of his drawings (fig. 1).[10]

The Formation of The Courtauld Gallery's Collection of Drawings

THE FORMATION AND CHARACTER of The Courtauld's collection of drawings is unusual when compared to holdings of similar size and art-historical importance, both in England and abroad.[11] Being part of a university art museum, it was created to some extent as a resource for the teaching and scholarly research of art history. This continues to form a vital part of the life of the collection in its home at The Courtauld Institute of Art. No less important is the mandate that it should be shared with a wider public audience. Given the exceptional quality of the collection, it is unusual that it was assembled exclusively in the twentieth and twenty-first centuries. Comparable university collections, such as those of Oxford's Ashmolean Museum or the Fitzwilliam Museum in Cambridge were long established when The Courtauld Institute of Art and its gallery were created in 1932.[12] Equally unusual is the fact that the drawings collection is almost entirely a collection of collections, and in this it mirrors the origins and character of The Courtauld Gallery's wider holdings, formed through a series of magnificent private gifts and bequests. The narrative begins with the three co-founders of The Courtauld Institute of Art, Viscount Lee of Fareham (1868–1947), Samuel Courtauld (1876–1947) and Sir Robert Witt (1872–1952), each of whom left substantial, and complementary, collections to the Gallery. Together with other collections that arrived during the following decades – most notably Count Antoine Seilern's unrivalled Princes Gate Collection in 1978 – The Courtauld's holdings of European drawings now encompasses most national schools and periods and provides an overview of the medium's history until World War I. Notwithstanding some important individual works, the account given of drawing through the middle decades of the twentieth century is more hesitant. However, it may be expected that the collection's breadth and chronological range will continue to develop and that it will also engage with contemporary draughtsmanship.

Our present selection reflects the collection's overall character. Italian drawings are superbly represented with examples dating from the mid fifteenth century to the second half of the eighteenth. Other particular strengths are sixteenth- and seventeenth-century Dutch and Flemish drawings, seventeenth-century Spanish drawings, eighteenth- and nineteenth-century British drawings, and eighteenth- to early twentieth-century French drawings. The German school is not well represented, despite two outstanding works by Dürer (cat. nos. 7, 8), and there are currently relatively few examples of the work of American draughtsmen.

The Courtauld Institute of Art was the embodiment of a shared vision of three very different men, each of whom had come to recognise that, whereas England had many of the world's finest art collections, it lacked the means to train the specialists who were to care for this heritage and to interpret it for the benefit of the public. The notion that the rigorous academic training of this new professional generation of art historians, curators, conservators, critics, museum administrators and lecturers should happen with immediate reference to representative works of art was informed substantially by the development of the new Fogg Art Museum. Robert Witt and Samuel Courtauld travelled separately to Cambridge, Massachusetts, in 1927 to meet Edward Forbes and Paul Sachs and study their 'art laboratory' very soon after it opened.[13] For Lord Lee the pedagogical purposes of the collection which he formed were always paramount. In an article announcing the establishment of The Courtauld, Lee stated:

The present writer has endeavoured to build up a small collection of works of art (principally pictures), which shall illustrate the chief developments of painting in Europe from the fourteenth to the eighteenth centuries, and which shall possess a definite educational value. His intention is ultimately to bequeath the bulk of this collection (or so much of it as is considered suitable) to the Courtauld Institute of Art, in order that it may play in connection therewith a similar part to that taken by the Fogg Collection at Harvard, and at the same time be accessible for the enjoyment of the general public.[14]

Lee collected mainly paintings and some applied arts for the new Institute, but he also left a small number of drawings – a series of cloud studies by Constable, which he gave in 1932, and Pieter Bruegel's *Kermis at Hoboken* (cat. no. 15), a sheet he acquired in 1944 that became part of his bequest in 1947.

While Lee bought drawings only in exceptional cases, Samuel Courtauld acquired works on paper alongside paintings, bequeathing more than eighty drawings to the institute which carries his name. The group includes about thirty British works, mostly by contemporary artists, notably Walter Sickert and Jacob Epstein, and only a few so-called Old Masters. There are close parallels between Courtauld's collecting of works on paper and the formation of the celebrated collection of French Impressionist and Post-Impressionist paintings for which the Gallery is now internationally renowned.[15] Major works by Cézanne, Degas, Manet, Seurat, Toulouse-Lautrec and Van Gogh (cat. nos. 51, 53–57) stayed in Courtauld's private collection until his death, when they came to the Institute with the 1948 bequest.

Courtauld's activity as one of Europe's major collectors of modern French art was confined largely to the 1920s. His acquisitions of drawings span that decade and the range of works he bought shows that he fully embraced drawings as a medium: the earliest acquisition in our selection is Toulouse-Lautrec's linear graphite drawing *Au lit*, purchased in 1922 (cat. no. 56), followed by Degas's sketchy pastel *Woman adjusting her hair* in 1923 – an extraordinarily evocative colour composition (cat. no. 53); in 1927 he bought Van Gogh's pen drawing *Tile factory* (cat. no. 55); in 1928 Seurat's large *Female nude*, finished to a high degree of complexity (cat. no. 54), as well as Manet's red-chalk sketch *La Toilette* (cat. no. 51), a preparatory study for a print that Courtauld also owned in two impressions; and in 1929 Daumier's elaborately finished watercolour *Le Malade imaginaire* (cat. no. 50). Although Courtauld drastically reduced his collecting activities in 1929 after the death of his wife Elizabeth, he bought Cézanne's superb still life *Apples, bottle and chairback* (cat. no. 57) in 1937 for £3,500, highlighting the importance he assigned to Cézanne's watercolours. The sheet was the last of three major acquisitions of works on paper by the artist alongside a collection of paintings which originally numbered some eleven canvases.[16]

Home House, the magnificent eighteenth-century townhouse designed by Robert Adam in London's Portman Square, was presented by Samuel Courtauld to the new Courtauld Institute of Art. An early guidebook lists among the works left on display Cézanne's watercolours *A shed* and *Montagne Saint-Victoire,* Daumier's *Le Malade imaginaire* and Degas's pastel *After the bath* (fig. 2).[17] Given the large number of drawings he owned, Courtauld probably did not display all of them framed on the wall; however, he certainly considered that to be the most appropriate way of viewing master drawings in both private and public collections. Photographs of his last London residence show Cézanne's *Apples, bottle*

FIG. 2 The 'Etruscan Room', Home House, with a display of Edgar Degas's pastel *After the bath*

FIG. 3 Samuel Courtauld's home in North Audley Street, London, with a display of paintings, a watercolour and drawings, including works by Cézanne (cat. no. 57) and Seurat (cat. no. 54)

and chairback as well as drawings by Forain and Guys hanging on the walls amongst his paintings (fig. 3); and Courtauld fully appreciated the educational power of the particularly intimate encounter with the medium, noting in a rare public statement about art:

> Many a private owner of a few drawings will gladly show them to a small appreciative group, and he will never be better pleased than when he can transmit a share of his enthusiasm to newcomers. Such an experience may very likely be more inspiring to young people than visits to public Galleries in the large regiments which one sometimes encountered before the war.[18]

Courtauld's collection provided the first generation of art-history students at the Institute with primarily modern and contemporary works as study material. One of the latest drawings in our selection, Matisse's *Seated woman* (cat. no. 59), dated 1919 and acquired by Courtauld in 1928 from the Leicester Galleries, had already been given during his lifetime, in 1935. It was only possible to study the rich and varied development of European drawings through original works when Robert Witt's collection of about three thousand drawings was bequeathed in 1952 along with his vast reference library of photographs of paintings and the approximately twenty thousand largely reproductive prints now held by The Courtauld Gallery. In the scale and depth of his bequest and in his ambitions for its use Robert Witt may properly be regarded as the founder of the drawings department at The Courtauld. His collection of reproductive material also became a model for the Frick Art Reference Library and Photographic Index. Sir Robert met Helen Frick personally and guided her in the 1920s when establishing this significant research library in New York.[19]

Unlike Courtauld's appreciation and collecting of art, which was strongly guided by aesthetic qualities, Witt's interest in collecting works on paper – a form of collecting he considered "at once the most civilized and least spectacular form of collecting"[20] – was predominantly scholarly. He aimed to put together "a corpus of original works which could help the student to identify the characteristics of a large range of artists"[21] (fig. 4). A successful lawyer, and Samuel Courtauld's neighbour in Portman Square, Witt was in a comfortable position financially,

FIG. 4 David Muirhead Bone, *Sir Robert Witt in his library*, 1919
Graphite, 302 × 472 mm
D.1952.RW.723

FIG. 5 Juan de Juanes (Vicente Juan Macip), Two studies for *Saint Stephen taken to his martyrdom*, 1556
Pen and brown ink, grey wash, 217 × 315 mm
D.1963.WF.4730

but prices for drawings of the great masters, particularly those of the Renaissance, had risen considerably after World War I, when he began to collect. This situation was noted by many contemporaries, including Joseph Meder, an eminent connoisseur and the author of the standard reference *Die Handzeichnung* (1919; translated into English as *The Mastery of Drawings*), who lamented:

> The number of universal drawing experts and passionate drawing lovers is fairly stable; the old class of canny collectors is almost gone, and a revival is hardly to be hoped for, in view of the rarity and costliness of the really great drawings. Merely plutocratic buyers, primarily investors, will lay down their cash only for that well-guaranteed object which will cut a figure as a wall decoration.[22]

Having a clear understanding of these circumstances and given his self-professed "modest means",[23] Witt avoided the famous names and instead sought works by lesser-known artists or those whose works were not highly valued, often acquiring numerous drawings at the same

time. Today, many of these artists count among the most important draughtsmen of their periods and schools. Eleven of the fifty-nine works in our selection have a Witt provenance. In a 1950 lecture on the art of collecting Witt noted: "Just as Homer sometimes nods and as the great Master may throw off careless or inferior work, so the less famous may, and often do, achieve minor masterpieces".[24]

Particularly notable is Witt's collection of Italian Baroque drawings, including a stunning group of more than thirty works by Guercino (cat. no. 22), as well as his Flemish and Dutch drawings of the later sixteenth and seventeenth centuries (cat. nos. 17, 18, 20, 27, 28). He bought fine British and French drawings of the eighteenth century (cat. nos. 33, 40, 41, 48), and his acquisition of significant parts of the Stirling Maxwell collection of Spanish drawings was entirely characteristic of his approach. [25]

Many more examples from the Witt collection and also from the group of eighty-five works bought with the Witt Fund – left by Sir Robert to expand the collection after his death[26] – could have been selected here. Witt Fund acquisitions included works by Renaissance

artists such as Maso Finiguerra (D.1957.WF.4658), Francesco Squarcione (D.1958.WF.4670) and Juan de Juanes (fig. 5) as well as drawings by prominent later artists such as François Boucher (D.1961.WF.4706), Guercino (D.1953.WF.4593) and Hans Rottenhammer (fig. 6). In 1967 the Gallery moved to its new home in Woburn Square, enabling these and other works from the growing collection to be presented regularly to the public through a series of small exhibitions and accompanying catalogues (fig. 7).

Count Antoine Seilern's collection of more than 350 drawings, bequeathed to The Courtauld in 1978, brought many of the greatest masterpieces into the collection. Known as the Princes Gate bequest, and consisting of paintings as well as drawings, this was at the time described as the greatest single bequest to any British gallery in the twentieth century. Seilern (1901–1978) began collecting in the late 1920s – thus somewhat later than Courtauld and Witt.[27]

His first acquisition of a drawing was of a market scene by Pissarro (D.1978.PG.236), purchased about 1928–29. Much like Courtauld, Count Seilern searched for the inherent beauty of an artwork, and his lifelong collecting was motivated by a declared "love and reverence for the highest products of the human genius".[28] He found this expression of outstanding creativity in all media and collected not only paintings and drawings but also prints of superb quality – notably by Dürer[29] – illuminated manuscripts, sculptures, and Greek and Chinese antiquities. Born in England, the son of an Austrian father, Seilern was educated in Vienna, where he first studied business and engineering. After inheriting a fortune in 1931, he intensified his collecting and in 1933 enrolled to read art history at the University of Vienna, concluding his studies in 1939 with a dissertation on the Venetian sources of Rubens's ceiling paintings before emigrating to London in August of that year.[30] His scholarly interests firmly characterized his subsequent collecting. Rubens was the one artist in whom he remained most deeply interested throughout his life, acquiring twenty-three drawings and thirty-two paintings then attributed to him. Seilern evolved to become the archetypal scholar collector, generating a vast and detailed correspondence with curators and academic art historians and travelling extensively to study works at first hand in museums and print rooms across Europe. His research resulted in a series of scrupulous catalogues of his holdings, published according to national schools in seven volumes between 1955 and 1971.

FIG. 8 Count Antoine Seilern and
Johannes Wilde in conversation
in Vienna in the 1930s

Seilern's lifelong respect for and friendship with scholars had
its source in the pre-war years in Vienna (fig. 8), where he first
met Johannes Wilde, then curator of Italian paintings at the Kunst-
historisches Museum. Wilde also emigrated to London and would
become deputy director of The Courtauld Institute of Art. Seilern later
said that it was "a great honour and luck to consider Dr. Wilde my
friend"[31] and that he discussed not only all his catalogue entries with
Wilde but "also relied with the utmost faith – always rewarded – on
his guidance in the formation"[32] of his collection.

In the foreword to his final catalogue, Seilern stated that the purpose
of an art collection was to "induce in the visitor an intense concentration
and absorption in the world of the artist, as revealed in one of his masterpieces".[33] Favouring the intimate and serious discussion of drawings, he
was deeply rooted in a humanist tradition of art collecting established
during the Renaissance. The extraordinary acquisition of Michelangelo's
The Dream (cat. no. 12) in 1952 thus seems particularly meaningful,
as the master's presentation drawings were created as finished works
of art intended to be intimately studied by knowledgeable collectors.

By the time he left Vienna in August 1939, Seilern had already
assembled a very important collection, including some drawings of
the highest quality: in 1934 he had acquired the outstanding portrait
of Rubens's young wife, Helena Fourment (cat. no. 24), which, like

Michelangelo's *The Dream*, celebrates beauty and the art of draughts-manship. He acquired Canaletto's highly finished *View from Somerset Gardens* (cat. no. 38) in 1935, and Bruegel's *Storm in the River Schelde with a view of Antwerp* (cat. no. 16) and Dürer's *Wise Virgin* (cat. no. 7) joined the collection in 1936. A particular focus of Seilern's early collecting was the French eighteenth century, and he purchased drawings by Watteau (cat. nos. 31, 32) and Hubert Robert (cat. no. 34) in 1935 and, in 1936, Fragonard's *Young girl seated* (cat. no. 35). In 1941, during World War II, he bought Picasso's *Female nude* (cat. no. 58) and Cézanne's large pencil drawing *Hortense Fiquet (Madame Cézanne) sewing* (cat. no. 52). Later in life, the focus of his collecting changed, a process upon which he reflected:

> I have lost interest in much of the art of the French eighteenth century – Watteau excepted – and even to some extent in the now so fashionable French nineteenth century – Cézanne excepted. It seems to me now that these certainly very beautiful works of art are concerned primarily with problems of decoration, representation and pure form. They are without doubt most appealing to the eye, and to the mind in so far as it delights in contemplating the development of new representational methods .... Only in the work of Cézanne do I still find the solution of these problems exciting.[34]

At the same time Seilern regretted, "Only fairly recently, and alas too late, have I come to appreciate the art of Rembrandt". Seilern bought his first Rembrandt drawing in 1937[35] and would assemble altogether thirty sheets then attributed to the master; today's scholarship assigns about half of them to Rembrandt's hand, including two in this selection (cat. nos. 25, 26).

Seilern's most significant purchase of a large group of drawings was more than 1,200 sheets of the collection of Thomas Fitzroy Fenwick (1856–1938), which comprised all major schools. It is little known that he donated most of these drawings anonymously to the British Museum in 1946.[36] The twenty-four works he kept for himself included some of the finest Italian Renaissance drawings in the present selection – the sheets by Leonardo (cat. no. 2), Carpaccio (cat. no. 6), Pontormo (cat. no. 11), and Veronese (cat. no. 13). Another major acquisition in this area was made in 1957, when Seilern bought nine sheets of the so-called Gabburri album, with landscape drawings by Fra Bartolommeo (cat. no. 9) and a remarkable collection of about twenty sheets by Parmigianino, the first of which he acquired in 1953 (cat. no. 10). Claude Lorrain was another focus of Seilern's late collecting, by which time the prices for Old Master drawings had risen. Introducing a series of his most recent acquisitions in 1971 he bewailed "the end of the age of the private collector". He wrote, "Works of art are becoming more and more scarce; in other words, beyond the reach of the normal collector trying to be guided solely by his own taste".[37]

Seilern's approach to drawings was in tune with practices of professional museum curators. Like Witt[38] he kept the works in boxes, thus protecting them from excessive exposure to light. His research interests were guided by questions of attribution and dating, the identification of subject-matter, and the discussion of the role of a drawing in the artist's working process or its place in an oeuvre. Seilern was also especially interested in oil sketches, as he must have felt their particular power to give insight into the artist's creative imagination, a quality they share with drawings. For Seilern, an iconographic approach detracted from the appreciation of an art work as a material object. In a letter to Pamela Askew dated 19 October 1964, he expressed this view clearly, referring to Erwin Panofsky:

> I am little bit worried about your new areas of study: theatre, philosophy and theology. Is this not the road to iconol[o]gy and away from history of art? Well, please do not think that I do not consider these subjects important for explanation of works of art, but the danger of the school and teachings of Pan[o]fsky is that these aspects become more important than the aspect of art.[39]

Seilern considered bequeathing his collection to The Courtauld as early as the late 1940s, when Anthony Blunt (1907–1983) began his long directorship (until 1974). Blunt himself was a collector of drawings (fig. 9), and left his collection to The Courtauld on his death in 1983. Bernini's *Design for the Louvre, east façade* (cat. no. 30) is one of the most important of his Renaissance and Baroque drawings, which are primarily related to architectural, sculptural and decorative works. Roger Fry's large collection of drawings from the Omega workshops given to The Courtauld in 1958 by his daughter Pamela Diamand also offers a rich resource in this respect, as it comprises designs for domestic objects, including rugs, screens and pottery (fig. 10).[40]

Finally, there is The Courtauld Gallery's significant group of about 2,500 British drawings. Of these Sir Robert Witt acquired about 1,300, among them fine landscapes by Thomas Gainsborough (cat. no. 40).

FIG. 9 The hall of Sir Anthony Blunt's flat in Home House with a display of drawings, including Perino del Vaga's *Design for a triumphal arch for the entry of Charles V into Genoa* (D.1984.AB.21) at top left

His son, Sir John Witt (1907–1982), added to this part of the collection. The strength of The Courtauld Gallery's English watercolours was substantially enhanced in 1967[41] when the Yorkshire industrialist William Wycliffe Spooner (1882–1967) and his wife bequeathed their fine collection to the Gallery. With the Spooner bequest, the great names of British watercolour entered the collection, here represented by works by John Robert Cozens (cat. no. 39), Francis Towne (cat. no. 42) and John Constable (cat. no. 43). In 1974 thirteen watercolours by J.M.W. Turner were presented in memory of Sir Stephen Courtauld (1883–1967), Samuel Courtauld's younger brother (cat. nos. 44, 45).

As this short and necessarily incomplete narrative has illustrated, the collections of works on paper at The Courtauld are largely the result of a series of important individual gifts and bequests. This tradition of philanthropy has continued to unfold in more recent decades. Most notably, Dorothy Scharf's outstanding collection of more than fifty British watercolours arrived at the Gallery in 2007 (fig. 11). It included nine sheets by Turner, bringing the holdings by that artist to a total of thirty. Her generous bequest serves to signal the continued growth of the collection at the highest level of ambition and quality.

FIG. 10 Attributed to Roger Fry, *Design with confronted peacocks*, 1913–14 Gouache and pencil, 344 × 508 mm D.1958.PD.14

FIG. 11 Richard Parkes Bonington, *Fishing boats moored in an estuary*, c. 1825 Watercolour and gouache over pencil, 174 × 241 mm D.2007.DS.4

The Notion of the 'Master Drawing'

THE BROAD VARIETY of approaches to collecting exemplified by the benefactors who shaped The Courtauld's drawings collection parallels the wide range of ideas about how to define the nature of mastery in drawings. Referring to a sheet as a 'master drawing' evokes, rather than clearly defines, the work's particular meaning and status. It implies that the drawing is a rare work of the highest quality, lending it a unique aura and suggesting that it is from the hand of a 'master'. The notion of what constitutes such a master drawing needs to be examined within the historical framework in which each sheet was created.

In his treatise for painters written about 1400, Cennino Cennini advises young artists to "take pains and pleasure in constantly copying the best things which you can find done by the hand of great masters."[42] He would have hardly accepted the exercises of pupils as master drawings because they were produced in order to help achieve mastery rather than to demonstrate it. For Cennini, a copy of a work of art was only the first step on the long road to mastery; the final aim was the artful interpretation of nature, both in drawings and paintings.

Bearing Cennini in mind, the copy after Hugo van der Goes (cat. no. 4) cannot readily be called a master drawing, as it is clearly based on a mechanical tracing and thus lacks a free hand. Yet, we do not know how the artist's contemporaries in Flanders about 1475–85 – the time the drawing was produced – judged such an exquisitely executed copy. The sheet's brilliant state of conservation speaks for the careful preservation, and hence great appreciation, of the drawing since the time of its production – due, perhaps, to the recognition of its astonishing technical execution, as well as the fame of the figure of the female saint, which is one of the most repeated motifs in early Netherlandish art. Since it is one of very few drawings of its kind, its rarity alone now arguably lends it the rank of a master drawing.

Cennini's understanding of the drawing of a master differed from Giorgio Vasari's Renaissance idea of the internal *disegno,* a concept that laid the grounds for the theoretical opposition of colour and line, painting and drawing, in the following centuries. The author defines this idea as "a certain conception and judgment, so that there is formed in the mind that something which afterwards, when expressed by the hands, is called design; we may conclude that design is not other than a visible expression and declaration of our inner conception and of that which others have imagined and given form to in their idea".[43]

The question of what constitutes a master drawing is a vast topic subject to many perspectives and definitions, but in the preparation of this catalogue the question of mastery was a fundamental challenge governing the process of selecting, researching and discussing the drawings eventually chosen. Some entries address this issue explicitly while others focus on the historical and theoretical context in which a drawing was produced and appreciated. Thus the notion of mastery is addressed in the case of each work rather than taken for granted as a categorical *fait accompli.*

> Why does a beautiful sketch accord greater pleasure than a
> beautiful painting? Because it has more life and fewer forms ....
> Perhaps we find sketches so attractive only because, being somewhat
> indeterminate, they allow more liberty to our imagination, which
> sees in them whatever it likes.[44]

1 The drawings at The Courtauld Gallery are available online; see www.artandarchitecture.org.uk

2 For surveys of the art of drawing, see Meder 1923; Meder (Ames) 1978; Koschatzky 1977; Rosand 2002; and Petherbridge 2010.

3 The earliest paper mills in Europe were in Spain (in Xativa in 1150) and Italy (in Fabriano in 1276). The first paper mill in Northern Europe, the Gleismühle near Nuremberg, was founded in 1390; see Hunter 1978, pp. 475–73.

4 On albums, see Dethloff 1996; Griffith 1997; and Baker et al. 2003.

5 Max Klinger in Harrison et al. 1998, p. 1053.

6 Rosand 2002, p. 2. The definition of drawing has been discussed and broadened in recent years; see Lamert et al. 2007; and New York 2010.

7 Sixteen works in the present selection were inscribed by the artists, twelve with their names (cat. nos. 17, 18, 26, 28, 29, 33, 39, 41, 50, 56, 58, 59).

8 On Dürer as a collector, see Smith 2011; on Vasari, see Monbeig Goguel 1998, pp. 112–13.

9 See also cat. nos. 10, 14, 17, and 35.

10 L. 2228b; see www.marquesdecollections.fr/detail.cfm/marque/9136/total/1.

11 For an introduction to the history of the Courtauld collections, see Murdoch in London 1998a, pp. 6–24.

12 The Fitzwilliam Museum has its roots in the collection of Richard, 7th Viscount Fitzwilliam (d. 1816), who bequeathed his substantial holdings of prints and drawings to the university; the Ashmolean received the Douce Bequest in 1834 and the Lawrence collection in 1842; see Parker 1972, pp. XI–XX. The Fogg Art Museum received its founding bequest of one hundred paintings in 1831; see Brush 2003, pp. 14–43.

13 Brush 2003, p. 185.

14 London 1958b, p. V.

15 For Samuel Coutauld as a collector of Impressionist and Post-Impressionist art, see London 1994.

16 See Wright in London 2008, p. 14. The other two watercolours are A shed and Montagne Saint-Victoire, and Courtauld also owned Cézanne's self-portrait lithograph (London 2008, nos. 12, 14, 20).

17 London 1934a, p. 27.

18 See Ernst Vegelin van Claerbergen in Findhorn 2010, p. 13.

19 Brush 2003, p. 192.

20 Witt 1950, p. 13.

21 London 1953b, p. 4.

22 Meder 1978, p. 6.

23 Witt 1950, p. 14.

24 Ibid., p. 15.

25 For the collection of Spanish drawings see Véliz 2011.

26 The Witt Fund of £5000 was spent between 1953 and 1965; for a complete list, see London 1965a, pp. 19–21.

27 For the history of the Princes Gate collection see Braham in London 1981, pp. VII–XIV.

28 Seilern 1955, Foreword.

29 Most of Seilern's superb Dürer prints – including an impression of Melencolia I in the rarest state, 1a – were sold at auction in 1998; see sale catalogue 'Albrecht Dürer: Prints from the Collection of the Late Count Antoine Seilern', Christie's, London, 8 July 1998.

30 For a full list of Count Seilern's publications, see London 1981, p. XV.

31 Reference letter written by Seilern in Wilde's support in 1947; Courtauld Gallery archives.

32 Seilern 1955, Foreword.

33 Seilern 1971, p. 9.

34 Seilern 1961, Foreword.

35 Ibid., no. 197. The attribution of the Man with a long coat to Rembrandt is now doubted.

36 The mark L.924b was made by the British Museum for the Fenwick drawings; see www.marquesdecollections.fr/detail.cfm/marque/9845. Of the twelve drawings by the Rembrandt school in the Fenwick collection given to the British Museum, The Death of Adonis (1946,0713.168), today attributed to Ferdinand Bol, was then considered to be by Rembrandt himself.

37 Seilern 1971, p. 9.

38 Witt 1950, p. 14: "On the other hand, drawings are small in size, and therefore easy to transport, to house and to show. A single room will comfortably contain hundreds of drawings, kept in convenient solander cases, but easily turned over in them for enjoyment. While, when mounted on the same sized mounts and fitting into the same sized frames, and these provided with movable backs, they can be displayed round the walls, and changed in half an hour, from week to week, and again and again, for friends to see."

39 Letter in The Courtauld Gallery archives. I thank Helen Braham for bringing this letter to my attention.

40 London 1999; and London 2009.

41 London and elsewhere 2005.

42 Cennini (Thompson) 1960, p. 15.

43 Vasari (Maclehose) 1960, p. 206 (§75).

44 Diderot (Goodman) 1995, vol. 2, pp. 212–13.

Catalogue

Measurements are given height before width;
if they differ by more than one millimetre, variant
dimensions are given left/right and top/bottom.

ANDREA MANTEGNA

Isola di Carturo, near Padua *c.* 1431–1506 Mantua

1 Studies for *Christ at the Column*, early to mid 1460s

Verso: Studies for *Christ at the Column*

Pen and brown ink, on laid paper; traces of a later framing line in
pen and black ink at upper left and right corners and lower left;
overall slight undulation and discolouration with localised stain;
several creases; minor losses along upper left edge
237/235 × 145 mm

Samuel Courtauld Trust, D.1978.PG.345

Mantegna's meticulously realised paintings and prints
could only have resulted from extensive preparatory
studies, but only the recto and verso of *Christ at the Column*
indicate how Mantegna began to explore his subjects.[1]
The related engraving of *The Flagellation with a paved floor*
(fig. 12) suggests the way Mantegna transformed his
initial thoughts into dramatic narratives.[2]

The style of *Christ at the Column* places it in the early
to mid 1460s.[3] The lost design for the engraving probably
dates to then as well. As Piero della Francesca and Andrea
del Castagno had done before him, Mantegna transformed
the traditional iconic depiction of the Flagellation into a
fully realised narrative following Leon Battista Alberti's
principles of composition. Giorgio Vasari's description of
Castagno's lost fresco of the Flagellation emphasises the
Albertian characteristics that are shared by Mantegna's
print, among them fidelity to literary sources, a classical
setting, and convincing perspective.[4] Castagno's depiction
of Christ, which revealed "the suffering of the flesh
and the divinity hidden in the body",[5] is also akin to
Mantegna's heroic portrayals of the Saviour on the recto
of the Courtauld drawing. Both artists' ability to capture

FIG. 12 *The Flagellation with a paved floor, c.* 1465–70
Engraving, 442 × 343 mm
London, The Courtauld Gallery, G.1978.PG.6

PROVENANCE
Unknown Italian collector (L. 2798); John Skippe
(1741-1812), by 14 October 1812; Martin family,
by descent; A.C. Rayner Wood, by descent before
1930 until at least 1953; Edward Holland-Martin
(1900-1981), by descent until November 1958;
Count Antoine Seilern (1901–1978), acquired by
Colnaghi for Seilern at Skippe collection sale,
Christie's, London, 20-21 November 1958,
lot 36; Princes Gate Bequest, 1978

SELECTED LITERATURE
Farr (ed.) 1987, p. 118 (as Mantegna); Goldner
1993, p. 174; Lincoln 1993, pp. 45ff.; Christiansen
2009, pp. 18–26

SELECTED EXHIBITIONS
London 1930, no. 708 (recto, as Bellini); London
1931, no. 763 (recto, as Bellini or Mantegna);
London 1953, no. 17 (recto, as Bellini); London
1981, no. 170 (recto and verso, as Mantegna);
London 1983, no. 6; London and New York 1992,
no. 35 (London only); Paris 2008, no. 42

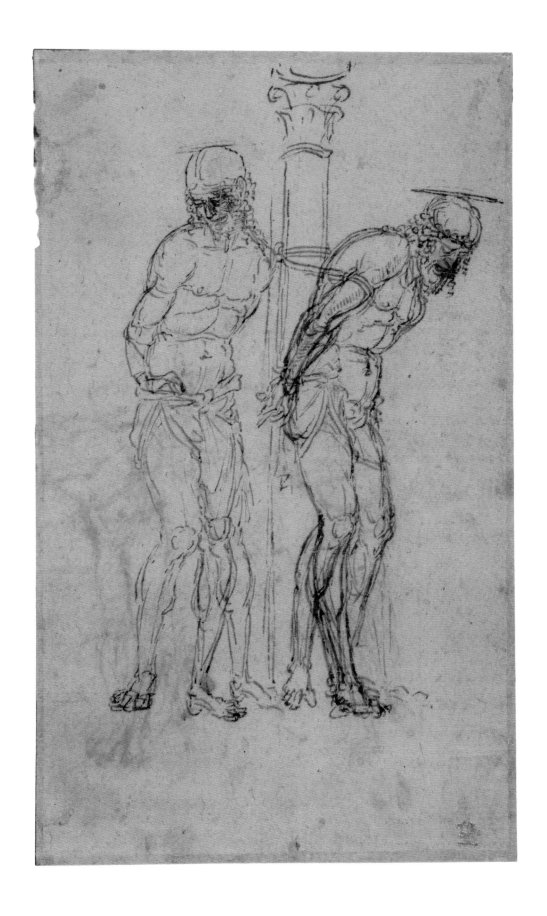

Christ's physical and psychological state through the rendering of pose and expression relate to Alberti's dictum that the motions of the mind should be conveyed through the movements of the body.[6]

Mantegna drew first on the verso of the Courtauld sheet, confronting the most brutal aspects of Christ's scourging.[7] He showed Christ twice as a bound, frail nude, beaten by a single gigantic tormentor. This slumped Christ, broken by suffering, is utterly unlike the terse Gospel accounts or anything in the pictorial tradition. The figures are not life studies but, instead, are exercises of the imagination.[8] Mantegna's conception probably was inspired by contemporary devotional practices – exemplified by Thomas à Kempis's *Meditations on the Life of Christ* – that encouraged the faithful to relive Christ's Passion through imaginative visualisation.[9] Thomas's description of Christ and his tormentors emphasises the vulnerability so graphically rendered by Mantegna: "What hearts of stone had the smiters, who feared not to scourge Thee . . . they stood as giants against Thee, and spared Thee not".[10]

On the recto of the Courtauld drawing Mantegna shifted his focus from the Flagellation's physical brutality to its redemptive purpose. Both versions of Christ are muscular and idealised; their haloes symbolise his divinity. The depictions preserve "the certain splendor of nobility" that Vasari praised in Castagno's Christ.[11] Mantegna redrew the legs and feet so that the figures stand despite the beating. At right, Christ slumps against his bonds, but less so than in the earlier drawing; instead his exhaustion is conveyed by his downturned head, closed eyes and open mouth. At left, he stands upright, clenching his muscles and shutting his eyes and mouth against the pain. Both figures remain within the tradition of depicting Christ at the Column, for they exemplify the belief that the Saviour's acceptance of suffering was required for human salvation.[12]

In the *Flagellation with a paved floor* Mantegna rethought his drawn studies to create a dramatically charged narrative that closely follows the Gospel accounts. The crown of thorns, which Christ received only after he had been scourged, is eliminated. The Flagellation occurs in a loggia, evoking the place of judgement where Pilate condemned him. Christ's hunched pose is based on its counterpart from the recto of the Courtauld sheet, and both figures are of similar dimensions.[13] But the moment shown in the engraving is different, unprecedented, and shocking. In the drawing Christ endures his physical agony. In the print he strains to avoid his tormentors' first blows. Christ's wide eyes and open mouth express fear and the very human anguish of anticipation. The horror of this moment is compounded by the viewer's foreknowledge. By forcing a visceral reaction and an imaginative response, Mantegna makes the viewer empathetically participate in the drama – achieving the goals of Thomas à Kempis's devotional exercises and of Albertian narrative. DA

NOTES

1　See Mazzotta in Paris 2008, p. 141; Ekserdjian in London and New York 1992, p. 193; and Hourihane in Farr (ed.), 1987, p. 118, with references to earlier sources.

2　On the print, see, most recently, de Bosio 2008, no. 8; Paris 2008, p. 141; Landau in London and New York 1992, p. 195.

3　To the late 1450s, Mazzotta in Paris 2008, p. 141; to the early 1460s, Ekserdjian in London and New York 1992, p. 193, and Hourihane in Farr (ed.) 1987, p. 118; to the mid 1460s, Goldner 1993, p. 174.

4　For Castagno's lost fresco in the cloister of the Servi in Florence, see Mack 2005, p. 97; Vasari 1568, vol. 3, pp. 355–56, cited from Mack, p. 97.

5　Vasari 1568, p. 356, cited from Mack 2005, p. 97.

6　Alberti (Sinisgalli) 2011, p. 61.

7　Scholars agree that Mantegna drew the verso of the sheet first.

8　For Mantegna's drawing process, see Lincoln 2000, pp. 34–37; Wiemers 1996, pp. 167–71; Ames-Lewis 1981, p. 111.

9　This method of interpretation follows Christiansen 2009, pp. 18–26, and Mack 2005, pp. 96–98.

10　Thomas à Kempis 1892, p. 105.

11　Vasari 1568, p. 356, cited from Mack 2005, p. 97.

12　Thomas à Kempis 1892, p. 105.

13　See Mazzotta in Paris 2008, p. 141, with reference to earlier sources.

CAT. NO. 1 VERSO

LEONARDO DA VINCI
Anchiano, near Vinci 1452–1519 Cloux, near Amboise

2 Studies for *Saint Mary Magdalene*, c. 1480–82

Pen and brown ink, on laid paper; later framing line in graphite, partially trimmed;[1]
slight undulation and discolouration, light stain at bottom right corner
138 × 80 mm

Samuel Courtauld Trust, D.1978.PG.80

Mary Magdalene, the patron saint of penitents, was
identified as a sinner (*peccatrix*) in the Gospels. Repenting
her worldly life, she humbled herself before Christ,
bathing his feet with perfumed oil and drying them with
her hair. By forgiving her sins, Christ revealed his divine
power to save souls (Luke 7: 36–50). Beloved by Christ
in life, the Magdalene was the first to see him after his
Resurrection (John 20: 1–18).

When Leonardo made these drawings, the depiction
of the Magdalene had already been long established.[2] Yet
independent devotional paintings of her were unknown.
The swift movements of Leonardo's pen captured the
process of creating a novel religious image that elicits the
viewer's imaginative response.[3] Examination of the paper
and the inked, overlapping framing lines has convinced
scholars that Leonardo began by sketching the larger
version of the Magdalene and then rapidly followed it with
the smaller, more summary sketch below, in which he first
drew the saint looking down at the oil jar and then rotated
her gaze straight towards the viewer.[4] Leonardo implied
a narrative by rendering the saint pausing as she opens
the oil jar, halted by something that causes her to turn her

FIG. 13 Bernardino Luini, *The Magdalene*, c. 1525
Oil on panel, 58.8 × 47.8 cm
Washington, National Gallery of Art,
Samuel H. Kress Collection, inv. no. 1961.9.56

PROVENANCE
Sir Thomas Lawrence (1769–1830; L. 2445); Sir
Thomas Phillipps (1792–1872), acquired at
Lawrence-Woodburn sale, Christie's, London,
4ff June 1860, lot 1501; Thomas Fitzroy Fenwick,
by descent by 1946; Count Antoine Seilern
(1901–1978), acquired with the Fenwick
collection, 1946; Princes Gate Bequest, 1978

SELECTED LITERATURE
Pedretti 1973, pp. 104, 184; Ingenhoff-Danhäuser
1984, pp. 17, 103 n. 18; Trutty-Coohill 1988,
pp. 28, 30; Pardo 1989, pp. 80ff.; Jones 1990,
pp. 69ff.; Martin Kemp in New York 2003,
p. 142; Kemp and Barone 2010, no. 27

SELECTED EXHIBITIONS
London 1952, no. 4; London 1981, no. 169; London
1983, no. 5; London 1991, no. 45; London 2011, no. 3

head around to look. Luke Syson has suggested that Leonardo has shown the moment the Magdalene encounters the risen Christ at the tomb. In the larger drawing, she first glimpses him; in the final, smaller version, she gazes directly at him and recognises his divinity.[5]

The spiritual dimension of seeing lay at the heart of Leonardo's rethinking of the Magdalene subject. From the sermons of Gregory the Great onwards, the sense of sight was understood to represent the Magdalene's most elevated love of Christ.[6] After the risen Christ had forbidden her to touch him, the Magdalene announced that she had "seen him" (John 20: 17–18). Her testimony established an example of spiritual love, promising believers that they too could touch Christ as she had done, "with the hand of faith" and "with the mind's eye".[7] The events of the Magdalene's life were given salvational purpose in sermons, in the ritual of her liturgy, and in the devotional suffrages of Books of Hours. Like them, Leonardo's portrayals transcend a particular narrative moment to encompass a deeper religious meaning. The Magdalene's turning towards Christ is a metaphor for her conversion to God.[8] The loosened tendrils of her hair recall her act of repentance.[9] She carries the open oil jar, wrapped in cloth like a sacred vessel, evoking the perfumed scent of anointing. Most of all, Leonardo's rendering of the Magdalene gazing straight at the viewer reveals the beauty of a soul transfigured by Christ's love.

The Courtauld drawing has been dated to various periods in Leonardo's career, from his Florentine debut about 1480 to as late as 1509.[10] It most closely relates to Leonardo's earliest Florentine period, when the young master executed small-scale, framed, pen-and-ink compositional ideas for paintings like *The Madonna of the Cat* and *The Lady with the Unicorn*.[11] These early drawings also exhibit graphic traits in common with the Courtauld sheet – changes to the orientation of the head, using axes for the placement of eyes, abbreviated mitten-like hands, and figures overlaid with vigorous parallel hatching.[12] Like the Courtauld drawing, none of these Florentine sketches was ever realised in paint, and all of them inform later finished works. The first, larger version of the Madgalene served as the basis for Leonardo's portrait of Cecilia Gallerani (*c.* 1490).[13] In the early sixteenth century Leonardo's Milanese followers, such as Bernardino Luini, popularised devotional paintings of the saint (fig. 13) that derived from their master's ideas.[14]

In the fifteenth century the Magdalene's cult thrived in Florence, where she was identified with the city's patron, John the Baptist.[15] Leonardo's portrayal, in which youthful beauty is emphasised and penitence is only evoked, counterbalanced the Florentine tradition represented by Donatello's harrowing sculpture of the penitential Magdalene in the Baptistery. A new type of Magdalene whose beauty inspires love is consonant with the Neoplatonic connection between ideal beauty and spiritual love fostered at Lorenzo the Magnificent's court.[16] Leonardo's Magdalene would have made a devotional image suitable for Lorenzo's daughter, Maria Maddalena (1473–1528). In 1488, using a phrase reminiscent of her namesake, Lorenzo described Maddelena as one so beloved by her mother that she was "her mind's eye".[17] D A

NOTES

1 A cutting, probably from the lower right edge of a larger sheet; Braham in London 1991, p. 98; Syson in London 2011b, pp. 108–09 n. 3.

2 For the medieval and Renaissance cult of the Magdalene and its related images, see Jansen 1999.

3 Syson in London 2011b, pp. 108–09; Pardo 1989, pp. 80–81; Trutty-Coohill 1988, pp. 28–29.

4 See, most recently, Syson in London 2011b, pp. 108–09; Kemp and Barone 2010, pp. 73–74; Braham in London 1991, p. 98.

5 Syson in London 2011b, p. 108.

6 Shuger 1994, p. 186.

7 Bernard of Clairvaux, sermon on the *Song of Songs*, cited *ibidem*, p. 173, also p. 253 n. 29.

8 Pardo 1989, pp. 80–81.

9 Syson in London 2011b, p. 108.

10 For a dating of 1486–87, see Syson in London 2011b, pp. 108–09, with reference to earlier sources. For a dating of 1509, see Pedretti 1973, p. 103.

11 Kemp and Barone 2010, pp. 73–74; Braham in London 1991, p. 98.

12 For these characteristics of Leonardo's early drawing style, see New York 2003, pp. 36–37, 293–99, 302, 307–08.

13 See, most recently, Syson in London 2011b, pp. 101–13.

14 Jones 1990.

15 Jansen 1999, pp. 134–35, 321; Wilk 1985, pp. 685–98.

16 Ingenhoff-Danhäuser 1984, pp. 35–37.

17 Reumont 1876, vol. 2, p. 286: "*l'occhio del capo suo*".

PINTURICCHIO (BERNARDINO DI BETTO)
Perugia, *c.* 1454–1513 Siena

3   Study of *A flying angel*, *c.* 1481–85

Verso: Workshop of Pinturicchio, *A man seen from behind*, *c.* 1481–85

Recto and verso: Metalpoint (silverpoint?), pen and brush and brown ink with white bodycolour, on grey prepared laid paper; slight discolouration and surface abrasion towards the edges

Recto: diagonal crease across bottom right corner, some minor creases with retouching
218 × 139 mm

Samuel Courtauld Trust, D.1978.PG.81

The Umbrian painter Pinturicchio operated one of the most efficacious and historically underrated of the large painting workshops that were active in central Italy in the late fifteenth and early sixteenth centuries. Like his master Perugino's, Pinturicchio's reputation suffered from the emasculation and faint praise of Giorgio Vasari, whose book *The Lives of the Artists* for the first time systematically provided artists' biographies in a historical framework. Vasari applauded Pinturicchio's efficiency and his ability to profit from the greater talents of his pupils and his assistants, including the young Raphael, but remarked that he owed his fame to the vagaries of fortune,[1] and that his contemporary success was due to his "barbarous" habit of decorating his pictures with gilt ornament that pleased the ignorant.[2]

As Vasari noted, Pinturicchio was adept in profitting from others, but this was common practice in the fifteenth and early sixteenth centuries, when painters learnt their trade by imitating the work of their master, and in their turn benefitted from their assistants' ideas when they themselves were in charge of a workshop. The ability to reproduce a composition or a motif was at the heart of this system, and this sheet, because it has been worked on both sides by two different hands,[3] provokes discussion of this issue. The study on the verso fits more easily into the modern conception of copying. It is a drawing after a figure in Byzantine dress seen from behind in Perugino's *Baptism of Christ* (1481–82) in the Sistine Chapel. The manner, technique and media are almost identical to those of the *Flying Angel* on the recto, but the style is more decorative, and the artist has not understood certain elements of his source, such as the right-hand sleeve and shoulder. But at this date copying did not necessarily imply a lack of skill. Rather, it denoted respect and a belief in the prestige of the inventor. A copy was not inherently of lesser importance than its original, as examination of the *Flying Angel* demonstrates.

The *Flying Angel*, looking downwards and inclined gracefully towards the left, can be attributed firmly to Pinturicchio.[4] The figure was not Pinturicchio's own invention, however. It is a type of angel found regularly in the production of Perugino and his associates,[5] and it probably derives from Perugino's *Assumption of the Virgin* for the altar wall of the Sistine Chapel, destroyed in 1535–36 when Michelangelo painted his *Last Judgement*. Perugino's composition is recorded in a competent but unexciting

PROVENANCE
Sir Thomas Lawrence (1769–1830; L. 2445); William Mayor (d. 1874; L. 2799); John Postle Heseltine (b. 1843; L. 1507); Henry Oppenheimer (1859–1932), sold Christie's, London, 10ff. July 1936, lot 169; Count Antoine Seilern (1901–1978), acquired from Colnaghi, May 1953; Princes Gate Bequest, 1978

SELECTED LITERATURE
A Brief Chronological Description 1871, no. 18; Ricci 1912, p. 264; Heseltine 1913, nos. 30, 31; Crowe and Calvacaselle 1914, vol. 5, p. 405 n. 6; Fischel 1917, p. 260, no. 209; Bombe 1933, p. 65; Seilern 1959, no. 81; La Malfa in Perugia 2008, pp. 352, 353–56, 362, 367–68; La Malfa 2009, pp. 59–60

SELECTED EXHIBITIONS
London 1981, no. 176; London 1983, no. 7; Perugia 2008, no. 3

workshop drawing of the early sixteenth century (fig. 14).[6] The angel in the Courtauld drawing appears in the sky at the top right, outside the aureole of the Virgin Mary ascending to heaven. The existence of this high-quality drawing has led to the suggestion that Pinturicchio himself played a major role in the evolution and execution of Perugino's now destroyed *Assumption*. However, both the remarkably good state of preservation and the high degree of finish and elaboration of the *Flying Angel* suggest a different interpretation.

Drawings made in preparation for paintings usually show some signs of this activity, such as pouncing, squaring, or incised lines around the outlines: none of these can be seen on the Courtauld sheet. Moreover, the execution of the *Flying Angel* is unusually complex for a drawing of this kind. The basic contours of the figure were laid in using a medium which may have been black chalk. The angel was worked up further with quick, confident lines of metalpoint, in all probability silverpoint. Then, ink, bodycolour and bodycolour were added, to build up the sense of three-dimensionality in the drapery and clothing of the angel. Very different lines, in white bodycolour applied with a very delicate and thin brush, were used for the exquisite face and gently tumbling tresses of the figure's hair (fig. 15). The intricate folds of the drapery twisting around the angel's feet were also much worked,

CAT. NO. 2 VERSO

45

FIG. 15 Detail of cat. no. 3 (the angel's face) under magnification and in raking light

FIG. 14 Workshop of Perugino, *The Assumption of the Virgin* (after Perugino's fresco in the Sistine Chapel), *c.* 1500
Metalpoint, pen and brown wash, with white heightening on prepared buff paper, 272 × 210 mm
Vienna, Graphische Sammlungen Albertina, inv. no. 4861

in ink and bodycolour.[7] Changes were made at every stage of execution, including one as major as the shift upwards of the angel's proper right foot.

We can explain the exquisite finesse of the *Flying Angel* by recognising that Pinturicchio did not invent the motif it represents, but made his copy with a precision that was intended to add to Perugino's model. The style is identifiably that of Pinturicchio. Thus, this drawing represents more than emulation. It demonstrates Pinturicchio's desire to appear as Perugino's pupil, but also, in his mastery of his materials and the high technical quality of his draughtsmanship, the *Flying Angel* stands as an example of his abilities as a mature artist to make works of equal value and worth to those of his master. CC

NOTES
1 Vasari 1966–87, vol. 3 (1971), p. 572.
2 *Ibidem*, p. 574.
3 Most pertinently, Seilern 1959, pp. 24–26; La Malfa in Perugia 2008, no. 3.
4 For the most recent full discussion, see Perugia 2008, no. 3. The attribution has been contested by Fischel (see Selected Literature) and Francis Russell (unpublished communication to Count Antoine Seilern, 1976).
5 In particular, Pinturicchio's *Glory of Saint Bernardino* (1484, Rome, Santa Maria in Aracoeli, Chapel of San Bernardino).
6 Perugia 2008, pp. 374–75, no. 16.
7 My thanks to Stephanie Buck, Kate Edmondson and Brian Clarke for examining the drawing with me.

WORKSHOP OF HUGO VAN DER GOES
c. 1440?–1485 Rhode Klooster, near Brussels

4   *A seated female saint, c.* 1475–85

Pen, point of the brush and grey ink, heightened with white bodycolour over preliminary black-chalk
underdrawing, on green prepared laid paper, laid down; slight overall undulation and localised staining;
numerous creases across sheet; several small pinholes at lower right and upper right corners; traces of later
framing line in graphite, trimmed; inscribed at lower right corner in pen and brown ink *787* (?), trimmed

Verso: inscribed in pen and brown ink at top centre in an Italian 18th-century (?) hand
Sandro scrive che sicuro fia, and below in a 19th-century hand in pen and brown ink *Petro Perugino*;[1]
in graphite in later hands, *14* and *4*
230 × 189 mm

WATERMARK
Lily

Samuel Courtauld Trust, D.1978.PG.314

Autograph drawings by Hugo van der Goes are rare, but
his influence is evident in a large number of works by
anonymous followers active until well into the sixteenth
century. Based on foundations developed by Dieric Bouts,[3]
Van der Goes established a new chiaroscuro technique,
evident in the *Jacob and Rachel at the Fountain* in Christchurch, Oxford.[4] Clear outlines are paired with parallel
hatchings, which vary greatly in length and may be layered
to form cross-hatching. The prepared slate-coloured
ground provides a mid-tone. Complementing the strictly
linear graphic structure is a loose brush drawing employed
for the landscape and the modelling of figures. Finally, the
artist heightened the figures with white bodycolour, the
strokes often melting into patches in a painterly manner.

The Courtauld drawing of a female saint, dressed in
the outmoded *robe royale*,[5] shares many characteristics
with Hugo's autograph work. Since Max J. Friedländer's
publication in 1935, it has rightly been discussed as one
of an extraordinarily rare group of three chiaroscuro
drawings that are either by the master himself[6] or by
an artist who trained in his manner. The figure type and
chiaroscuro technique on a prepared ground are clearly

FIG. 16 Master of 1499, *The Virgin among Virgins*
Oil on panel, 99 × 59 cm
Richmond, VA, Virginia Museum of Fine Arts,
A. and M. Glasgow Fund

PROVENANCE
Private collection, France;[2] Ludwig Rosenthal
(later known as Lewis V. Randall; 1893–1972),
Berne, then Montreal, by 1935; Count Antoine
Seilern (1901–1978), acquired at Randall sale,
Sotheby's, London, 10 May 1961, lot 4; Princes
Gate Bequest, 1978

SELECTED LITERATURE
Friedländer 1935, pp. 98, 100; Panofsky 1953,
p. 500; Winkler 1964, pp. 165–66, 172–80, 267;
Friedländer 1969, vol. 4, supp. 111, pl. 45; Seilern
1971, no. 314; Byam Shaw 1976, p. 320; Reynolds
1981, p. 563, fig. 73; Campbell 1985, pp. 49–50;
Farr (ed.) 1987, p. 122; Martens 1997, p. 39,
fig. 5; Dhanens 1998, p. 105; Buck 2001, pp. 144
and 170, fig. 49; Antwerp 2002, p. 124, fig. 5;

Martens 2002, pp. 116–18, fig. 8; Buck 2003,
pp. 229–35, fig. 2

SELECTED EXHIBITIONS
Paris 1935, no. 196; Cambridge, MA, 1949, no. 16;
London 1981, no. 167; London 1981a, no. 197;
London 1991, no. 37; Los Angeles and London
2003, no. 30 (London only)

related to Hugo. The Courtauld drawing cannot, however, be attributed to Van der Goes. The white is applied in a more gentle, meticulous manner than his, and the figure's contours lack his characteristic freedom. Instead, the drawing is based on an underlying black chalk tracing – clearly visible in infrared light and under high magnification[7] – that guided the ink lines (see figs. 17 and 18). This working method is typical of a copyist. In addition, the draughtsman misunderstood the saint's meaningful gesture. Van der Goes conceived of the figure as a Saint Catherine. Lost in thought, she touches with the thumb and index finger of her left hand the ring on her right, given to her by the Christ Child to seal their betrothal. This ring is missing in the drawing, so the innovative psychological essence of the figure is lost.

As discussed in the literature, Van der Goes's invention was exceptionally successful: the figure served as a model for more than twenty panel paintings and thirteen miniatures during Hugo's lifetime,[8] the earliest dating about 1480,[9] the latest towards the end of the sixteenth century. In these works the saint's gesture was usually modified to show the Virgin holding a book in her lap, demonstrating that the figure was adaptable to different iconographic requirements. Adding a tower, for example,

FIG. 17 Detail of cat. no. 4 (the right hand) under magnification, showing black chalk underdrawing at the outline

would make her Saint Barbara, whereas a wheel and sword would convert her to Saint Catherine. Only a few painters seem to have understood the meaning of the original gesture, among them Gerard David in his miniature in the Mayer van den Bergh Breviary (c. 1500; Antwerp, Museum Mayer van den Bergh).[10] This is also one of the rare examples in which the dress and extensive folds of the drapery correspond closely to the Courtauld drawing, though the headdress is modified. Only two examples show outlines identical to those of the present sheet, a miniature in the Emerson-White Hours (c. 1480; Cambridge, MA, Houghton Library) by an anonymous artist of the so-called Ghent Associates,[11] and the panel painting *The Virgin among Virgins* (fig. 16) by the Master of 1499. However, neither of these artists is the draughtsman of the Courtauld sheet, and no other drawing by the same hand is known.[12] Although the miniaturist probably trained with Hugo (the chiaroscuro technique was taken up mainly by book illuminators of the Ghent-Bruges school), his modelling lacks the complexity and subtlety of the master's drawing technique, whilst the panel painter's figure seems flatter and stiffer, particularly in the torso and head.

The fragmentary inscription on the verso proves an Italian ownership in the eighteenth century. The attribution to Pietro Perugino by a nineteenth-century scribe was not altogether uninformed, since Perugino executed chiaroscuro drawings, and his female saints display similar devotion.[13] It also points to the roots of the chiaroscuro technique in Italian art.

The elaborate technique and the unusually pristine condition of the Courtauld drawing speak against its having been used as a model drawing in a workshop. Instead, it might have been a presentation sheet, exquisitely finished in the most fashionable Northern style and technique, to please an Italian collector. The fact that a tracing was used for its production proves that other drawings existed – probably executed in a less elaborate pen-and-ink technique – that served as models for workshops well into the sixteenth century.[14] S B

NOTES

1 Thanks are due to Antonella Ghignoli for
helping transcribe and date the inscriptions.

2 According to Friedländer 1935.

3 Antwerp 2002, p. 123.

4 *Ibidem*, pp. 130–35, no. 30.

5 Campbell in Farr (ed.) 1987, p. 122.

6 Besides the Christchurch sheet, only *Christ
on the Cross* (Windsor, Royal Library,
RL 12951) is autograph; Antwerp 2002,
pp. 136–39, no. 31.

7 Infrared reflectography was carried out by
Rachel Billinge, Research Associate in the
Conservation Department at the National
Gallery, London, using the digital infrared
scanning camera OSIRIS, which contains an
indium gallium arsenide (InGaAs) sensor.
For further details about the camera see
www.opusinstruments.com/index.php

8 Kren in Los Angeles and London 2003,
p. 165. Martens 2002 illustrates twenty-
three panels, some of which include free
adaptations of the original figure.

9 See note 10 below.

10 Inv. no. 946, fol. 611v; Dekeyzer in Los
Angeles and London 2003, p. 326, no. 92,
fig. 92b.

11 Typ. 443-443.1, fol. 112v; Los Angeles and
London 2003, no. 32, and p. 165, fig. 57.

12 My thanks to Fritz Koreny for discussing
the attribution with me.

13 For Perugino, see Ferino Pagden 1987,
pp. 77–102; and Venturini in Perugia 2004,
pp. 331–35 and following section.

14 For a drawn copy formerly in Dresden,
Kupferstichkabinett, see Friedländer 1969,
vol. 4, p. 75, no. 38D, pl. 45; Kren in
Los Angeles and London 2003, p. 165.

ATTRIBUTED TO GIOVANNI BELLINI (?)
Venice, active by *c.* 1459–1516 Venice

5 *The Nativity, c.* 1480

Pen and brush and brown ink, on laid paper; upper corners cut away; some off-set of
green pigment in centre and centre left; minor losses and tears at bottom right corner,
lower left edge; inscribed in dark grey ink at lower right *L*

Verso: brown stain at upper right; inscribed in brown ink at lower left *1743* and
along left edge *BAC no 17*

211 × 164 / 211 mm

WATERMARK
Fragment of triple mount with double line

Samuel Courtauld Trust, D.1978.PG.79

This highly accomplished drawing is both unusual in iconographic terms and problematic to attribute. The scene represented is the Adoration of the Christ Child by Mary and Joseph. They are accompanied by an obediently kneeling ass and ox. A dog behind these animals forms a visual link to the shepherds, who approach the Holy Family from a distance through a gate in the wattle fence. Neither the fence nor the kneeling animals, which derive from the *Meditations on the Life of Christ* traditionally ascribed to Saint Bonaventure, are uncommon in such Nativity scenes. One feature of the drawing, however, is unparalleled: Christ, wrapped in the folds of Mary's robes, is supported against his mother's feet.

This drawing is executed in pen and ink, and its technique ranges from the precise hatching seen on the figures of Joseph and Mary to the free drawing of the shepherds. The fall of light and shadow is conveyed emphatically by the heavy working of some areas, such as Joseph's left shoulder, and the use of almost completely unworked paper in others, including the lower section of his left

sleeve. As Marzia Faietti has suggested, the sheet is a compendium of the different ways it is possible to work with pen on paper.[1]

The drawing has been worked with great confidence: there is no underdrawing or preliminary marking in charcoal or chalk. Alterations to the drawing are apparent, however: the ox's tail, for instance, was drawn over the dog. The artist seems to have worked from left to right, deciding the placement of the main figures as he went, starting with the shepherds. Some areas, such as the wattle fence, were re-inked and partially reworked later. Some late changes to the composition were also made, notably to the barn gate and its main timbers. The figures of Mary and Joseph in the right foreground were revised extensively.

Since its rediscovery at auction in 1955, this drawing has been attributed to Giovanni Bellini. This ascription should not be accepted uncritically. All attributions to Giovanni are based on connoisseurial judgement, and the small corpus of his supposed drawings is varied in detail and function.[2]

PROVENANCE
Sir Peter Lely (1618–1680; L. 2092); George Le Hunte, Ireland, by 1842; Misses M.H.L.E. and M.D. Le Hunte, by descent; Count Antoine Seilern (1901–1978), acquired at Le Hunte sale, Sotheby's, London, 9 June 1955, lot 43; Princes Gate Bequest, 1978

SELECTED LITERATURE
Seilern 1959, no. 79; Robertson 1968, pp. 72–73; Goldner 2004, pp. 238–42; Chapman in London and Florence 2010, p. 18

SELECTED EXHIBITIONS
London 1981, no. 125; London 1983, no. 1; London 1991, no. 7

53

The Nativity – if it is by Bellini – is supposed to be the first compositional study by him that we have. Its intimate and naturalistic qualities have been connected with the small painting of the same subject on the predella of Bellini's *Coronation of the Virgin* altarpiece, of the mid 1470s.[3] It can also be linked to some of the highly elaborate compositions of the Nativity, Adoration of the Shepherds and Adoration of the Magi found in the two drawing books by Giovanni's father, Jacopo, and his workshop, now in the British Museum and the Louvre (for example, fig. 19).[4] The Courtauld drawing reflects the practice of composition displayed in Jacopo's drawing books. Like these, it is a complete expression of a visual idea that exists in its own right, but that could also have been used, perhaps, to inspire another composition at a later date.

Stylistically, the closest parallel with the Courtauld drawing is provided by a drawing now in Berlin (fig. 20) of Saint Mark healing Ananias. The Berlin sheet, which can also be connected to Tullio Lombardo's reliefs for the new façade of the Scuola di San Marco, started between 1485 and 1489, has generally been ascribed to Giovanni Bellini.[5] While some of its details, such as the depiction of the shoemaker's tools in the top left corner and the figures in the bottom right, recall respectively the watching shepherds and Mary and Joseph in adoration in the Courtauld sheet, the Berlin drawing is much more freely executed and with monumentally conceived figures. It is also a working drawing, where the artist has not attempted to hide changes to the composition.

One of the central problems with ascribing the Courtauld drawing to Giovanni Bellini is that its spatial organisation contrasts with that found in many of his securely attributable paintings. Most significantly, the disjunction between the foreground and background is absent from other works of the late 1470s, such as the Frick *Saint Francis* or the Naples *Transfiguration*. It is even

missing from earlier pictures with significant landscape elements, such as the Barber Institute's *Saint Jerome*. These are notable for the harmony between the figurative and landscape elements.

Chris Fischer and Marzia Faietti have both drawn attention in conversation to the peculiarly crooked lines in the Courtauld drawing.[6] Parallels seem to exist with the group of artists associated with the decoration of the Palazzo Schifanoia – Francesco del Cossa, Cosmè Tura, and Ercole de' Roberti.[7] Another artist whose work seems akin to the Courtauld *Nativity* is Carlo Crivelli, notably with such small-scale paintings as the predella panels of the National Gallery, London's *Madonna delle Rondine* – although no drawings by Crivelli are known. In short, the attribution of this highly accomplished drawing remains in question and should be debated further. But it seems that we should seek its author in Ferrara or the Marches rather than necessarily in Venice. CC

FIG. 19 Jacopo Bellini,
The Nativity, c. 1430–55
Pen and brown ink on vellum,
380 × 260 mm
Paris, Musée du Louvre,
Département des Arts Graphiques,
RF 1501-38-fol. 33

FIG. 20 Attributed to
Giovanni Bellini, *Saint Mark healing Ananias*, c. 1490
Pen and brown ink on paper,
184 × 172 mm
Berlin, SMPK, Kupferstich-kabinett, KdZ 1357r

NOTES

1 Verbal communication, 2 July 2010.

2 Goldner 2004.

3 Reproduced in Rome 2008, p. 198.

4 Eisler 1989, pls. 170 (Louvre book, fol. 37), 171 (Louvre book, fol. 34), 177 (British Museum book, fol. 79).

5 Schulze Altcappenberg 1995, pp. 66–68. Thanks are due to Dagmar Korbacher and Georg Josef Dietz for examining the drawing in detail with Stephanie Buck and me.

6 Verbal communication, 2 July 2010 and September 2011.

7 For example, see Schulze Altcappenberg 1995, pp. 84–86, 88–90.

VITTORE CARPACCIO
Venice 1460/66–1525/26 Venice

6 *The Virgin reading to the Infant Christ*, late 1480s–early 1490s
Verso: *The Virgin adoring the Infant Christ with Saint John*

Recto and verso: Pen and dark brown ink over red chalk, on laid paper
Two brown stains at lower right; inscribed *3-* (overpainted with white bodycolour)
at lower left, ...*ozzo* (partially scraped out) over indecipherable inscription

Verso: narrow strip of paper adhered to right edge; brown adhesive stains at
upper right and left (with minor skinning); indecipherable inscription at lower centre
128/131 × 92/94 mm

Samuel Courtauld Trust, D.1978.PG.82

Carpaccio's drawings survive in greater number than those
of any other late fifteenth-century Venetian draughtsman.
They include complex compositions that can be related to
the narrative paintings for which he is most renowned;
quick notational sketches made to develop ideas; studies
from life; and detailed drawings, particularly of costume,
for the background figures in his pictures.

These charming drawings on two sides of the same
sheet are inventive mixes of standard prototypes for the
depiction of the Virgin and Child – a stock-in-trade of
every artist's production at this date – and studies perhaps
taken from life. What could be more natural or well
observed than a child flicking desultorily through the
pages of a book (as can be seen on the verso)? Moreover,
the costume of the mother suggests that she was from the
prosperous class of citizens to which Carpaccio, the son of
a furrier, himself belonged. The particular identity of the
figures, however, is suggested by the crown held by the
child and the halo encircling his mother's head.

The architectural setting (the column in the portico
is probably borrowed from the Netherlandish painters
Jan van Eyck or Hans Memling, whose work was greatly
admired in Venice)[1] alludes to the Virgin's honourable

CAT. NO. 6 VERSO

PROVENANCE
Sir Thomas Lawrence (1769–1830; L. 2445);
Samuel Woodburn (1786–1853); Sir Thomas
Phillipps (1792–1872), acquired at Lawrence-
Woodburn sale, Christie's, London, 4ff. June
1860, lot 2; Thomas Fitzroy Fenwick (1856–
1938), by descent; Count Antoine Seilern
(1901–1978), acquired with the Fenwick
collection, 1946; Princes Gate Bequest, 1978

SELECTED LITERATURE
Colvin 1897, p. 201; Popham 1935a, pp. 4–5,
no. 2, pl. V; Tietze and Tietze-Conrat 1944,
pp. 59–60, no. 249, pl. XIII; Popham 1947,
p. 229; Popham 1956, p. 225, no. 1; Fiocco 1958,
p. 229, pls. 265 and 266; Seilern 1959, no. 82;
Lauts 1962, pp. 27, 273, 242, 253, no. 33, pls. 46
and 47; Muraro 1977, pp. 64–65, pls. 20 and 21;
Fletcher 2001, pp. 71–74; Echols in Boskovits
and Brown 2003, pp. 190–91

SELECTED EXHIBITIONS
London 1981, no. 131; London 1981a, no. 119;
London 1991, no. 20

position as Queen of Heaven. Any sense of gravity, however, is banished by the informality of Carpaccio's image, which is concerned to lessen the traditional sense of division between the viewer and the sacred space of the Virgin and Child, particularly in the drawing on the recto. Mary perches on the parapet that often acts as the boundary between these two worlds, while Christ, a toddler about two or three years old, leans into the corner of the window.

Here Carpaccio presents two ideas for a sort of devotional painting that was novel in the late 1480s or early 1490s, the probable date of these studies. The original sheet of paper has probably been cut down and now holds just these two drawings. Perhaps this was done to make them more saleable. As Count Seilern pointed out, they are the ancestors of a novel iconographic type in Venice, the Virgin Reading. This subject became closely associated with the new manner of painting in Venice devised by Giorgione and Titian in the first decade of the sixteenth century.

The drawings must be of the same date, as they seem to depict the same model for the Virgin, and the two studies of the infant Christ (although only fragmentarily shown on the verso) also appear to have been based on one figure. Remarkably, however, they seem to be connected with paintings executed perhaps fifteen years apart. The drawing on the back of the sheet, representing the Virgin and Child with the Infant Saint John, is Carpaccio's first idea for a signed painting now in the Städelmuseum, Frankfurt, of about 1490 (fig. 21). There are close parallels between the two works, and Carpaccio transferred some features directly from this first notational sketch to the finished composition, such as the Virgin's enormous hands, which are quite out of scale to her body. Certain discrepancies are explained by the differences of function

FIG. 21 Vittore Carpaccio, *The Virgin and Child with Saint John the Baptist*, c. 1490 Oil on panel, 69 × 54 cm Frankfurt, Städelmuseum

between a compositional drawing and a highly worked and detailed painting. A marble window frame, entirely absent in the drawing, has been added to the painted image, and the figures are dressed in rich clothing, so that they appear to be in the Court of Heaven.

The sketch on the other side is one of the most intimate drawings to survive from fifteenth-century Italy. The mood is domestic and almost impromptu, as if the figures have been captured unawares. It is connected to *The Virgin Reading* in Washington, DC (which has been considerably cut down), dated about 1505 (fig. 22). The figure of the reading Virgin was also adopted for a bystander on a parapet in Carpaccio's *Birth of the Virgin*, now in the Accademia Carrara, Bergamo. The reworking of the window suggests that this may have been the first of these two studies, and that Carpaccio was not altogether satisfied with the result. Certainly, as Jennifer Fletcher has observed,[1] he excised this element from the later painted compositions that draw on the legacy of this study.

Carpaccio used red chalk to lay in the main rudiments of his compositions, before employing pen and ink. The chalk, however, was not redundant or irrelevant in producing the final result: on the recto, the red-chalk outlines of the Virgin's neck can be observed under her headdress, adding to its sense of three-dimensionality. This combination of materials, often with a broken, fragmentary pen line (as can be seen in Christ's legs on the recto and the verso), is extremely typical of Carpaccio's more exploratory drawings. It is a technique shared by his teacher, Gentile Bellini, which means that it can sometimes be difficult to distinguish between their works. Curiously, this is a manner of working that Canaletto also used, leading the great Austro-Hungarian scholar Johannes Wilde (Count Seilern's close friend) to hypothesise that it was a peculiarly Venetian combination of media. CC

FIG. 22 Vittore Carpaccio,
The Virgin reading, c. 1505
Oil on panel transferred to canvas,
78 × 51 cm
Washington, DC,
National Gallery of Art

NOTE
1 Nuttall 2004, p. 3 n. 19, and in particular
   pl. 152.

ALBRECHT DÜRER
Nuremberg 1471–1528 Nuremberg

7 *A Wise Virgin*, 1493

Verso: Study of a left leg from two viewpoints

Pen and brown ink, on laid paper; slight overall discolouration; minor localised staining; small hole at centre left; later marks in dark brown ink at upper edge centre and inscription in a later (16th century?) hand, *1508 Ad*

Verso: inscribed by the artist in pen and brown ink at upper centre, *1493*

291 × 202 mm

WATERMARK
Three lilies, above crown and leaf, beneath letter

Samuel Courtauld Trust, D.1978.PG.251

CAT. NO. 7 VERSO

Upon completion of his training in the Nuremberg workshop of Michael Wolgemut in 1490, Dürer left his hometown to work as a journeyman. He travelled to the Upper Rhine, where he hoped to meet the eminent painter and engraver Martin Schongauer in Colmar, who, however, had died before Dürer arrived. During this period the young artist produced some of his most ambitious early figurative pen-and-ink drawings, including this work.

Here, Dürer used both sides of the large sheet, probably starting with the elaborate figure of a virgin before flipping the paper, turning it 180 degrees, and sketching his own left leg. He then reoriented the sheet in the direction of the main figure to date it 1493. This deliberate placement of the date demonstrates that recto and verso are conceived as a single artistic unit.

The virgin holds a burning oil-lamp and wears a garland of fresh leaves atop her abundant curls, her eyes modestly lowered. She graciously bends to her right, her arm outstretched in a salutatory gesture. These attributes

PROVENANCE
Sir Thomas Lawrence (1769–1830; L. 2445); Ernst Rietschel (1804–1861), acquired at sale, Dresden, 17ff. March 1862, lot 621; Sir Charles Murray (1806–1895); C.W. Murray, acquired at sale, Sotheby's, London, 27 April 1927, lot 89; Henry Oppenheimer (1859–1932); Count Antoine Seilern (1901–1978), acquired at Oppenheimer sale, Christie's, London, 10–14 July 1936, lot 365; Princes Gate Bequest, 1978

SELECTED LITERATURE
Dresden 1862, no. 621; Friedländer 1896, p. 19; Liverpool 1910, p. 9; Winkler 1927, p. 16; Lippmann 1927, vol. 6, nos. 610, 611; Tietze and Tietze-Conrat 1928–38, vol. 1, pp. 7, 148, 286, nos. 28, 29; Flechsig 1928–31, vol. 2, pp. 69, 396–97; Biermann 1928, p. 129; Weinberger 1929, pp. 142, 145–46; Gebarowicz and Tietze 1929, pp. 11–12; Meder 1932, pp. 19–20; Schilling 1934, p. 10, no. 15; Winkler 1936–39, vol. 1, p. 20, nos. 31, 33; Oppenheimer 1936, p. 176, no. 365, fig. 81; Panofsky 1943, vol. 1, pp. 24, 163, vol. 2, p. 1219, no. 645; Winkler 1949, pp. 10 and 27, no. 5; Tietze 1951, pp. 35, 59, no. 7; Musper 1953, pp. 20 and 341, fig. 8; Winkler 1957, pp. 34 nn. 2 and 37; Seilern 1961, no. 251; Talbot 1971, p. 27 n. 2 and 28 n. 2; London 1971, p. 4; von Borries 1972, pp. 25–31, nos. 16 and 18; Strauss 1974, vol. 1, pp. 136–37, no. 1493/1, vol. 6, p. 3280, no. 1493/1; Strieder 1981, fig. 97, pp. 87–88; Koerner 2006, pp. 27–29, figs. 13, 14

SELECTED EXHIBITIONS
Nuremberg 1928, p. 110, no. 240; London 1981, no. 161; London 1983, no. 3; London 1991, no. 31; London 2002, no. 30

FIG. 23 Martin Schongauer,
A Foolish Virgin
Engraving, 145 × 109 mm,
Bartsch VI.156.87
London, British Museum,
inv. no. 1845,0809.292

identify her as one of the five Wise Virgins from the Gospel of Saint Matthew (25: 1–13). Ten virgins were asked to expect the arrival of the bridegroom in order to attend his marriage: five were wise enough to keep their oil-lamps filled and therefore could join the bridegroom at midnight; the foolish five, whose lamps were empty, could not.

Although the subject-matter was not uncommon in Franconian art,[1] some of the most powerful examples were found in the Upper Rhine, where sculptures of the Virgins adorn the portals of the cathedrals of Freiburg, Basel and Strasbourg. Schongauer followed this tradition and produced in addition to a much-copied series of ten small engravings that depict the Virgins full length (Bartsch VI.153.77–86) one engraving of a half-length Foolish Virgin (see fig. 23). It has been suggested that this print was part of a series and that Dürer based his drawing on one of Schongauer's designs for a Wise Virgin now lost, which he might have studied when staying with Schongauer's brothers in Colmar.[2] Yet Dürer's drawing is twice the size of Schongauer's print and frames the figure differently, expanding the lower body with added volume. By showing a more dynamic twist of the upper body, Dürer had to foreshorten the arm holding the lamp. The resulting complex posture is not convincingly captured, and the

anatomy is contorted (see the placement of the virgin's left breast). These difficulties arise from the great ambitions of the young artist, who wished to surpass, rather than imitate, Schongauer. Schongauer's *Foolish Virgin* addresses the viewer directly. She presents her empty lamp as an attribute of her failure, underscoring the moral of the parable. Dürer, by contrast, presented the biblical narrative as an immediate encounter, focusing on the moment the virgin greets the groom. His presence is evoked through gesture alone.

Dürer sketched the figure directly with slight pen-lines with no preliminary outline in charcoal or chalk – media that allow for corrections. Changes remain visible – at the virgin's right hand, for instance – revealing the artist at work. Dürer modelled the figure with interwoven hatching and dashes of varying lengths. This elaborate cross-hatching reveals him as Schongauer's pupil. The intensity of this shading is guided by the fall of light from the left. The virgin's costume, a classical peplos, belted at the waist with overhanging material, falls in a complex arrangement of drapery that at right accentuates the opposing motion of upper and lower body. The composition follows classical principles of a contrapposto figure revived in Italian Renaissance art and possibly known to Dürer before his trip to Italy through the so-called 'Mantegna' *Tarocchi*.[3]

FIG. 24 Albrecht Dürer,
Self-portrait, 1493
Oil on canvas, 57 × 45 cm
Paris, Musée du Louvre

Dürer not only challenged artistic traditions but also recognised the need to work from the live model. The young artist must have realised his lack of skill in rendering anatomy and foreshortening, since he studied his own left leg from two viewpoints on the verso of the present drawing. Such studies are known in the North.[4] Schongauer's astute observation of the body, manifest in his prints, must have been based on drawings from nature, now lost. Dürer's persistent study of his own body was, however, unprecedented. It is telling that the virgin's face shares features with Dürer's own, as seen in his famous *Self-portrait* (fig. 24) – full lips; broad, strong nose; and pronounced chin unusual for a female and distinctly different from Schongauer's model.[5]

Without interpreting the Wise Virgin as a self-portrait, it seems clear that Dürer's studies of his own body became the basis for his invented figures. Later, he would articulate this process: "For in truth, art lies hidden within nature; he who can wrest it from her, has it".[6] SB

NOTES

1 Franconian, *A Foolish Virgin*, c. 1480, Stadt-museum Bautzen, L.237; see Dresden 2002, p. 178.

2 Braham in London 1991, p. 70.

3 For Dürer's copies of the 'Mantegna' *Tarocchi*, see Winkler 1936–39, vol. 1, pp. 90–93, nos. 122–41; Wood 2008, pp. 92–95.

4 Master of the Drapery Studies, *Study of a foot, traces of a second foot and a leg*, black chalk and pen and ink, 256 × 202 mm, inv. no. 1863.389, verso, Oxford, Ashmolean Museum; Parker 1938, pp. 109–10, no. 257.

5 Also noted by von Borries 1972, p. 25.

6 *Die Lehre von menschlicher Proportion* (1528), in Rupprich 1969, p. 295: "*Denn wahrhaftig steckt die Kunst in der Natur, wer sie heraus kann reißen, der hat sie*".

ALBRECHT DÜRER
Nuremberg 1471–1528 Nuremberg

8 *The Emperors Charlemagne and Sigismund, c. 1507–10*

Pen and brown ink and watercolour, on laid paper; inscribed by the artist in shields for
coats of arms in pen and brown ink *hongern* (initial capitalised in darker brown ink) *beheim*
(initial capitalised in darker brown ink) *daltz* (crossed out and changed to *Dalmatien* in darker brown ink)
crobatz (crossed out and changed to *Croatien* in darker brown ink); overall sight undulation and foxing;
vertical centre fold flattened; vertical crease at centre right and horizontal crease across lower centre
178 × 205 mm

WATERMARK
Two crossed arrows[1]

Samuel Courtauld Trust, D.1978.PG.253

This freshly preserved design for a diptych unites
two rulers of the Holy Roman Empire – its founder,
Charlemagne (r. 800–814), on the heraldically more
important left side, and Sigismund of Luxembourg
(r. 1410–37). Both hold the regal sceptre and globe, but
whilst Charlemagne wears a double-arched crown
Sigismund is crowned with a wreath of roses. The chain
with a pendant cross and ring-shaped dragon must be
the Order of the Dragon, which Sigismund introduced in
1408.[3] The rulers are additionally identified by the coats
of arms – the imperial eagle for both,[4] with a fleur-de-lys
above Charlemagne and four shields for Sigismund's
territories.

Since the drawing is highly finished, including even the
diptych's hinges, it must have functioned as a *modello* for
a panel painting. This is generally identified with Dürer's
two emperor portraits of 1511–13 (fig. 25), which are related
to Nuremberg's most important treasure, the imperial
regalia. On 29 September 1423 Sigismund had granted the
city the privilege to keep them permanently,[5] to be moved
only at the coronation of a new emperor.[6] Shown to the

FIG. 25 Albrecht Dürer, *Charlemagne* and
Emperor Sigismund, 1511–13
Oil on panel. 188 × 88 cm (each panel)
Nuremberg, Germanisches Nationalmuseum

PROVENANCE
Willibald Imhoff collection, by 1588 (?); possibly
Albertina, Vienna, by end of 18th century (?);
lost in Napoleonic Wars (?); art market (?);[2]
Prince Heinrich (Henryk) Lubomirski (1777–
1850), by 1834 (?); Lubomirski collection,
Ossolinski Institute, Lwów, after 1868;
nationalised by the Soviet Union, September
1939; confiscated by German occupation forces,
28 June 1941; United States Army, May 1945;

Prince Georg (Jerzy Rafal) Lubomirski (1887–
1978), 26 May 1950; Colnaghi, by 20 February
1953; Count Antoine Seilern (1901–1978),
2 December 1954; Princes Gate Bequest, 1978

SELECTED LITERATURE
Heller 1827, no. 96 (?); Reitlinger 1927, p. 159,
no. 8298; Winkler 1927, p. 17; Gebarowicz and
Tietze 1929, pp. 19–20, no. 15, fig. 17; Wilde

1930, p. 216 n. 7; Flechsig 1928–31, vol. 2, p. 580,
no. 766; Winkler 1936–39, vol. 2, pp. 151–52,
no. 503; Tietze and Tietze-Conrat 1928–38,
vol. 2, part 1, p. 60, no. 435; Panofsky 1943,
vol. 1, pp. 132–33, 163, vol. 2, no. 1008, fig. 176;
Tietze 1951, pp. 23, 44, 60, fig. 40; Musper 1953,
p. 258; Winkler 1957, p. 211; Stange 1957,
pp. 12–14 and 18, fig. 5; Seilern 1961, p. 128,
no. 253, pl. LXXIX; Kuhrmann 1964, pp. 73–86;

Della Chiesa 1968, p. 109; Musper 1969,
pp. 12–13, 16, 30–32, fig. 13; Rosenthal 1971,
pp. 33–40, fig. 24; Koschatzky and Strobl 1971,
p. 274; Anzelewsky 1971, pp. 48, 91, 233; Kéry
1972, pp. 144–45, fig. 108; Strauss 1974, vol. 3,
pp. 1212–13, no. 1510/5, and vol. 6, p. 3282;
Strieder 1981, pp. 67–71, fig. 73; Löcher in
Nuremberg and New York 1986, p. 306, fig. 130;
Nuremberg 1997, p. 206; Saurma-Jeltsch
2002–03, pp. 446–48, fig. 9; Doosry 2003,
p. 36; Juzwenko 2004, pp. 27, 31, 38 and 150,
no. 5; Papa 2007, pp. 26 and 30

SELECTED EXHIBITIONS
London 1981, no. 163; London 1983, no. 2;
London 2002, no. 111

people of Nuremberg every second Friday after Easter, they were kept the night before in the Heiltumskammer of the Schopperhaus at the Markt. Dürer's paintings functioned as the doors of a cupboard or a niche in which the regalia were stored.[7]

The prestigious commission of these panels is documented in payments to Dürer – he received a first remuneration between 19 and 21 July 1511 and a final payment on 16 February 1513[8] – as well as in coloured pen-and-ink drawings of the regalia dated 1510, designs that Dürer followed for Charlemagne's crown, sword, glove, globe and gown in the Nuremberg panels.[9] The Courtauld drawing must have been executed before these studies of 1510, since Charlemagne's costume differs from the actual regalia. Here, Dürer had not yet seen the regalia with his own eyes but followed a local Franconian iconography known from the Deocarus Altarpiece (c. 1430; Nuremberg, St Lorenz),[10] which shows the emperor with a lily crown, brocade dalmatic and ermine collar.

The relationship between the panels and the Courtauld drawing remains far from clear, as it depicts a diptych, which would be unsuitable for functioning doors of a cupboard or a niche. Also, the initial instructions given to Dürer when he executed the Courtauld drawing must haven been rather vague, as he was even uncertain about Sigismund's coats of arms. He labelled them in the drawing Hungary, Bohemia, Dalmatia and Croatia – following inscriptions on seals used by Sigismund[11] – whilst in the final panel they became the coats of arms of Old and New Hungary, Bohemia and, Sigismund's homeland, Luxembourg.

Walter Strauss pointed out that the sheet is on paper with a watermark of crossed arrows, which Dürer mainly used in Venice (1505–07). The general consensus is that Dürer did not take any paper back to Germany,[12] and it is thus likely that he made the Courtauld drawing in Italy. The swift execution speaks for a sketch of an initial idea and the technique does not rule out a date of about 1507 on stylistic grounds.

In the intervening three years – before Dürer executed studies of the regalia in 1510 – the plan for the portraits of the two emperors must have changed, possibly because of a change in the general political situation. In 1507, while Dürer was in Italy, Maximilian I was ruling as emperor but had not yet been crowned by the pope. Negotiations were under way to allow Maximilian to pass through the territory of the Republic of Venice. This right was refused, and Maximilian instead was declared *Imperator Romanorum Electus* on 4 February 1508 in Trent.[13] The physiognomies of both Charlemagne and Sigismund in the Courtauld drawing resemble Maximilian's sharp-nosed profile, suggesting his legitimacy as successor of the emperors.

The work that occupied Dürer most during his stay in Venice was his celebrated *Feast of the Rose Garlands* (fig. 26), showing Maximilian crowned with a rose garland – strikingly similar to the one Sigismund wears in the Courtauld drawing – rather than an imperial crown. Since the garland is a detail unknown in other portraits of Sigismund,[14] the choice was deliberate. The preaching of Alanus de Rupe began the restoration of the devotion of the rosary only in 1460, so Sigismund cannot be seen as a devotee of the rosary. However, when Dürer drew the Courtauld sheet, he might have given Sigismund the Marian symbol of the rose garland instead of the imperial crown to underscore the parallels between Sigismund's and Maximilian's reigns: in 1423, the year the regalia were given to Nuremberg, Sigismund had also not yet been crowned.[15]

Therefore, the Courtauld drawing may relate to an undocumented commission from the city of Nuremberg, connected to the planned coronation of Maximilian. When this project failed to materialise, such a commission would have had to have been adapted. Thus, the doors for the cupboard or niche in the Heiltumskammer may have been planned instead, the final portrait showing Sigismund as crowned emperor with the insignia of the double-arched lily crown that Charlemagne wears in the Courtauld sheet. S B

FIG. 26 Albrecht Dürer, *The Feast of the Rose Garlands* (detail), 1506
Oil on panel, 62 × 194.5 cm
Prague, Nationalgalerie

NOTES

1 The two arrows are relatively rare but similar to Piccard online nos. 123340–41 (Ravenna 1480), 123353 (Venice, 1457), 123358 and 123342 (Brixen, 1458); http://www.piccard-online.de/struktur.php?klassi =009.002.007&anzeigeKlassi=009.002.007. 002&Id=100486&sprache=en&weitere= struktur. The arrows on documents dated after 1500 (e.g., no. 123366, Innsbruck, 1506) are considerably larger.

2 The preceding provenance is based on the identification of our drawing with the sheet mentioned in Willibald Imhoff's catalogue of 1588 and published by Heller 1827, no. 96 as "*Ein römischer Kaiser und König abgerissen*".

3 Rosenthal 1971, p. 34.

4 Kéry 1972, p. 129, figs. 97–98.

5 *Ibid*., p. 144, quotes the *Regesta Imperii* XI (182), no. 5619.

6 Härter 2006, p. 182.

7 Strieder 1973, p. 156.

8 Kuhrmann 1964, p. 134 n. 135.

9 Winkler 1936–39, vol. 2, pp. 152–54, nos. 504–07.

10 See Saurma-Jeltsch 2002–03, p. 447; Kéry 1972, fig. 85.

11 See Budapest and Luxembourg 2006, pp. 189–90, nos. 3.20–3.23.

12 Koreny in Venice 1999, p. 246; H. Widauer in Vienna 2003, p. 358.

13 See Schmid 2006, p. 124.

14 For the portrait iconography of Sigismund, see Jenni 2006. Wilde 1930, p. 216 n. 7, fig. 234, points out the portrait of *Ladislaus Posthumus*, Vienna, Kunsthistorisches Museum; Saurma-Jeltsch 2002–03, pp. 447–48, portraits of Matthias Corvinus.

15 The coronation took place on 31 May 1433 in Rome; see Budapest and Luxembourg 2006, p. 47.

FRA BARTOLOMMEO (BARTOLOMMEO DELLA PORTA)
Florence 1472–1517 Florence

9 *The sweep of a river with fishermen and a town in the background,*
c. 1495–1509

Pen and brown ink, on laid paper; overall undulation; losses at upper left and top left corner,
repaired paper fold near lower left edge; sheet inset in a leaf from Gabburri's album (see provenance),
inscribed in pencil at bottom right corner 5
211 × 290 mm

Samuel Courtauld Trust, D.1978.PG.88

This delightful view is typical of Fra Bartolommeo, by whom about fifty drawings of landscapes and trees are known. It was included in an album of forty-one sheets that had been assembled by Cavaliere Gabburri about 1730 and were forgotten until they appeared at a sale in 1957, where they were sold separately.

As is to be expected in the case of a High Renaissance artist, the bulk of Fra Bartolommeo's almost 1,500 preserved drawings are figure studies preparatory for his many monumental altarpieces. The large number of landscape drawings, however, shows that he also paid much attention to this subject. They are in fact the largest group of drawn landscape views by any Italian Renaissance artist, comparable, for their date, only to the drawings and watercolours of Albrecht Dürer. Similar landscape views by other artists in the fifteenth and early sixteenth centuries probably existed, as indicated by the somewhat later group of small red=chalk drawings by an artist belonging to the circle of Andrea del Sarto, now scattered between the Uffizi, the Louvre and the British Museum.[2]

Fra Bartolommeo's landscapes are depictions of lonely hermitages or convents, small towns, wooded hillsides, trees and rock formations. To judge from the subjects that have been identified, most of them seem to be topographically precise renderings of particular sites, and a few are rearrangements of such drawings. All the landscape drawings are in pen and ink, and they constitute a uniform group datable within the period 1495–1508.[3]

The rapidity of line in the present drawing points to a spontaneity reflecting reaction to a living image. In 1986 I suggested that it was a view of Florence seen from the Valle del Mugnone, which runs north beyond Fiesole, a place Fra Bartolommeo knew well since he often spent time at the convent of Santa Maria Maddalena some five miles up the valley.[4]

As opposed to the studies of figures, heads, draperies and other details, which were all preparatory for finished works, only three of his known landscape drawings recur in Fra Bartolommeo's paintings, and, as observed by Helen Braham in 1991, the present drawing is one of them.[5] We recognise parts of it in the landscape seen through a doorway in the Carondelet *Madonna*, the masterpiece painted in 1511–12 (fig. 27).[6] Behind the naked men placed in the paved foreground, we find the curved embankment

PROVENANCE
? Fra Paolino da Pistoia (1488–1547), bequeathed by the artist; ? Suor Plautilla Nelli (1523–1588), bequeathed by Fra Paolino; ? convent of Santa Caterina da Siena in Piazza San Marco, Florence; Cavaliere Francesco Maria Niccolò Gabburri (1676–1742); William Kent (known 1742–61), acquired from Gabburri's heirs and sold at auction, London, 1760–61;[1] private collection, Ireland; Count Antoine Seilern

(1901–1978), acquired by Colnaghi for Seilern at Sotheby's, London, 20 November 1957, lot 36; Princes Gate Bequest, 1978

SELECTED LITERATURE
Gronau 1957, lot 36, repr.; *Illustrated London News*, 2 November 1957, p. 742; Seilern 1959, no. 88; Manning and Byam Shaw 1960, pl. 61; Härth 1960, p. 129; Berenson 1961, vol. 2,

no. 433F, p. 73, fol. 36; Florence 1986, p. 53,. under no. 17; Farr (ed.) 1987, p. 126; Rotterdam 1990, pp. 377, 399 n. 17

SELECTED EXHIBITIONS
London 1981, no. 124; London 1983, no. 13; London 1991, no. 5

and cluster of trees seen in this drawing, but the building to the left has been replaced by a group of farmhouses of a Northern character. In addition, the city in the distance has become in the painting a fortified town with a gateway, which is apparently based on the motif of a castle in Dürer's engraving *Hercules at the Crossroads*, which Fra Bartolommeo had derived from a drawing in the Louvre and inserted in one of a view of a hill town now at the Metropolitan Museum of Art, New York.[7] Like the landscape of the Carondelet *Madonna*, the imaginary New York drawing was also based on a realistic view of a Tuscan hill town, a drawing now in the Musée du Louvre,[8] and there are other examples of similar composite views in which Fra Bartolommeo combined the visionary and realistic.[9] It thus seems that he did not make his landscape drawings for pleasure alone, as hitherto presumed,[10] but that he intended to use them in invented compositions in much the same way as his figure studies were made from live models later to be inserted in paintings. This inclination was not unique at the time. Giovanni Bellini, whose paintings Fra Bartolommeo must have seen during his sojourn in Venice in 1508, produced similarly composite landscapes. An example is the background of the somewhat later Doná delle Rose *Pietà* (Venice, Accademia), where a view of Vicenza was combined with buildings from Ravenna.[11] Accidental subjects like topographically correct landscapes were only of minor interest to the artists of the High Renaissance. Their goal, instead, was to penetrate the chaos of palpable reality and give substance to the abstract eternal order that they believed ruled the universe. C F

FIG. 27 Fra Bartolommeo,
The Carondelet Madonna (detail), 1511–12
Oil on panel, 255 × 229 cm
Besançon, Cathedral

NOTES

1 According to Mariette 1851–60, vol. 2, p. 275. For Kent, see Fleming 1958, p. 227, and Ingamells 1997, pp. 571–72.

2 Florence, Galleria degli Uffizi, inv. nos. 10P and following nos., 814 P, 1313E and following nos., 1357E and following nos., 14546F (Gaetà Bertelá in Florence 1980, p. 66, no. 59, gives them to Francesco Bachiacca); Paris, Musée du Louvre, inv. no. 11038, 11041, and 11043 (Cordellier in Paris 1986, pp. 96–98, nos. 68–70, refrains from any attribution); London, British Museum, inv. no. 1946-7-13-34 (Turner 1986, pp. 103–04,

no. 69, attributes these to Michele di Ridolfo). Silvani 1991–92, p. 133, gives all the drawings to Antonio del Donnino del Mazziere on the basis of the ascription on the drawing in London; cited by Sframelli in Florence 1996, pp. 272–75, nos. 93–93b.

3 Fischer 1989, p. 329.

4 Florence 1986. A second view of Florence also presumably from the Mugnone Valley is seen in a drawing now in Paris, Institut Néerlandais, Fondation Custodia, inv. no. 7088; Byam Shaw 1983, vol. 1, pp. 22–23, no. 16, vol. 3, pl. 24.

5 Braham in London 1991, no. 5.

6 For this painting, see Fischer in Rotterdam 1990, pp. 234–51.

7 Rogers Fund 1957, 57.165.

8 Inv. no. 18645.

9 Fischer 1989, pp. 307–10; Fischer 2007, pp. 59–68.

10 Fischer 1989, p. 334; questioned by Ellis 1990, pp. 6–7.

11 Links 1982, p. 91.

PARMIGIANINO (GIROLAMO FRANCESCO MARIA MAZZOLA)
Parma 1503–1540 Casalmaggiore

10 *Woman seated on the ground, c. 1523–24*

Verso: *Woman holding a distaff* (upside down to recto)

Black chalk and white bodycolour, on light brown tinted laid paper; slight overall undulation, minor foxing and localised staining; horizontal natural paper crease following bottom edge, vertical crease along left edge, vertical cut at centre right edge, repaired, minor loss centre left edge; cluster of small vertical scratches with abrasion at lower left; inscribed on recto and verso in an old hand in pen and brown ink, strengthened in darker ink in bottom right corners *Permegiano*; on recto in pale brown ink *No 29/a* and on verso, in graphite *92*

Verso: black chalk and white bodycolour on untinted laid paper with traces of red chalk

231 × 175 mm

Samuel Courtauld Trust, D.1978.PG.96

Nearly one thousand drawings survive from Parmigianino's brief career, representing Renaissance practice in all its forms and media. For Parmigianino, drawing was a means of invention. *Woman seated on the ground* was made as an experiment in technique and expressive form.

The drawing's unusual combination of white bodycolour, black chalk and buff-coloured paper is associated with the artist's early activity.[1] Yet the distinctive sequence of application in *Woman seated* has not been described. Parmigianino first lightly marked out the draped figure with spidery black-chalk lines. Instead of continuing to model the form in black and using white for highlights, he turned immediately to white bodycolour, touching in the face, hands and turban and cross-hatching the folds of the cloak. By modelling the huddled woman in brilliant white, Parmigianino daringly exploited light's capacity to capture voluminous form as well as exquisite detail. He then used black chalk to define the cloak and to emphasise the hands and facial features. He struggled with the transition from light to dark, correcting some areas, such as the sleeve at upper right, by covering the bodycolour with chalk.[2] These changes probably occurred when Parmigianino enlarged

CAT. NO. 10 VERSO

PROVENANCE
William Coningham (1815–1884; L. 476);
Dr Christian D. Ginsburg (1831–1914; L. 1145),
sold Sotheby's, London, 20–23 July 1915, lot 26;
Henry Scipio Reitlinger (1885–1950), by 1953;
Count Antoine Seilern (1901–1978), acquired at
Reitlinger sale, Sotheby's, London, 9 December
1953, lot 73; Princes Gate Bequest, 1978

SELECTED LITERATURE
Popham 1971, no. 764 and pp. 7, 15, 61, 117, 148;
Emison 1985, pp. 207ff.; Landau and Parshall
1994, p. 267; Ekserdjian 2006, pp. 168, 226ff.;
Gnann 2007, vol. 1, pp. 12, 76, 89, 167, no. 173

SELECTED EXHIBITIONS
London 1981, no. 173; London 1983, no. 33
(verso); London 1987, no. 10; London 1991,
no. 53; London and New York 2000, no. 72
(London only)

the figure. His additions include the broad, jagged edge of the cloak that projects from the woman's shoulder and falls in looping folds under her buttocks and feet. He accentuated the bulky figure's shadowed setting using swift parallel strokes that overlap the drapery. Lastly, he balanced the dark tones with highlights, placing a pool of white on her raised knee and sparkling dashes at her neck. Through rigourous revision, Parmigianino developed a chiaroscuro effect that evokes the figure's meditative mood. The young woman appears enfolded within her thoughts, pensively subsumed in shadow while graced by light.

Parmigianino's interest in chiaroscuro reflects the art of Correggio, the master who most influenced him at the start of his career in Parma and Fontanellato. The figure's monumentality, however, allies it with Parmigianino's emulation of the grand manner of Raphael in Rome.

Parmigianino probably made this drawing between 1523 and 1524, towards the end of his Fontanellato sojourn, when he created the ambitious paintings that he took to Rome as gifts for Pope Clement VII.[3] Among these, *The Holy Family with Angels* (Madrid, Museo Nacional del Prado) is closest to this drawing. In both works large-scale figures, shown from above in three-quarter view, emerge from the confines of a shallow space in a play of light and dark. The Virgin's heart-shaped face with upturned eyes is also similar to the seated woman's. Both represent an ideal female type characteristic of Parmigianino's work at Fontanellato, exemplified by a study of *A female head, a winged lion, and finials* (New York, The Metropolitan Museum of Art, promised gift of David M. Tobey).[4] The use of a formulaic ideal discourages complete acceptance of the suggestion that *Woman seated* is a genre study drawn after a live model.[5] The woman's pose derives

FIG. 28 Ugo da Carpi after Raphael, *Sibyl reading with a child, c.* 1510–30 Chiaroscuro woodcut, 268 × 212 mm London, British Museum, inv. no. 1874,0808.189

Permegiano

73

FIG. 29 Parmigianino, *Woman seated on the ground*
Etching, 129 × 112 mm
London, The Courtauld Gallery,
G.1978 PG.40

instead from female captive figures – common on ancient reliefs and coins – which were frequently reproduced in North Italian drawings.[6] By altering the classical pose to a three-quarter view and animating it through the manipulation of light and dark, Parmigianino reconceived this figure in the mode of a life study.

In Parma and Fontanellato Parmigianino became conversant with Raphael's Roman style through the engravings of his follower, Marcantonio Raimondi.[7] Parmigianino also probably studied prints as sources for drawing techniques. Although his combination of media recalls silverpoint heightened with white and Venetian chalk-and-bodycolour drawings on coloured paper, it is also possible that he was inspired by the new art form of the chiaroscuro print.[8] The colourism of *Woman seated* seems a graphic analogue to the three-toned harmonies of Raphael-school prints, such as *Sybil reading with a child* (fig. 28).[9] The dramatic salience of the areas in white reserve that is characteristic of chiaroscuro prints may even have prompted Parmigianino to begin modelling *Woman seated* in bodycolour. He later used this drawing as a source for one of his first etchings (fig. 29), in which he masterfully translated chiaroscuro effects into a restricted palette of black and white.[10] DA

NOTES

1 Popham 1971, p. 7; Ekserdjian 2006, pp. 168–69. I would like to thank Kate Edmondson for explaining the sequence of application, and Marjorie Shelley.

2 Braham in London 1991, p. 114.

3 Popham 1971, no. 764 and pp. 7, 15; Braham in London 1991, p. 114; and Gnann 2007, vol. 1, p. 377, no. 173, vol. 2, p. 180, date the drawing to the late Fontanellato period. Clayton in London and New York 2000, p. 115, suggests the early Roman period, beginning in 1524. For Parmigianino's gifts

to Clement VII, see Ekserdjian 2006, pp. 70, 73–74, 129–32.

4 See, most recently, Vaccaro in New York 2010, pp. 46–49.

5 Braham in London 1991, p. 114.

6 Emison 1985, pp. 205–06. For ancient and Renaissance examples, see Giuliano in Rome 2007, pp. 38–39, 42.

7 Ekserdjian 2006, pp. 33, 39; Emison 1985, pp. 204–05. For the influence of Raphael-school prints, see Landau and Parshall 1994, pp. 260–61.

8 For connections between Parmigianino's graphic style and prints, see Ekserdjian 2006, pp. 174, 184–85. I would like to thank Aimee Ng for suggesting the relationship between this drawing and chiaroscuro prints.

9 For this and related Raphael drawings and prints, see Landau and Parshall 1994, pp. 252–54; Edinburgh 1994, pp. 84–85, 142; Rossi in Carpi 2009, pp. 127–28.

10 For the iconography, see, most recently, Gnann 2007, vol. 1, pp. 167–68.

PONTORMO (JACOPO CARUCCI)
Pontormo 1494–1557 Florence

11 *Seated youth*, c. 1520

Verso: Study for *Saint Jerome*

Black chalk, on laid paper; main contours incised; overall undulation and foxing with slight discolouration; extensive splashes of grey-black ink (all retouched with lead white now darkened); extensive creases and some natural paper folds; several tears and losses, repaired; later framing lines in pen and black ink partially trimmed; inscribed in graphite at top right 21/10

Verso: red chalk; inscribed in red chalk at lower right *Pont...* (original?); in graphite, at lower right corner *10*; lower left corner *1414*
405/401 × 274/280 mm

Samuel Courtauld Trust, D.1978.PG.92

Of more than four hundred surviving drawings by Jacopo Pontormo, the great majority are nude figure studies. Amongst this number, however, is a small group that features apprentices (*garzoni*) from Pontormo's workshop, dressed in artisan's clothing and posed both singly and in groups.[1] Made between 1517 and 1523, they cannot be directly connected to any of Pontormo's finished works.[2] The Courtauld study provides a superb example of this rare variant of traditional Florentine workshop drawings.[3]

Seated youth shows a *garzone* crouched on stone steps in a spiral posture. His left hand curled into a fist in front of his mouth and his hunched shoulders suggest an attitude of fear and worry. His outsize hands and oval eye sockets, framed by sharply angled eyebrows, amplify the psychological charge. The unhesitating quality of the line, as well as the change of contour in the right arm, hints at a rapid execution.

A red-chalk study on the verso depicts the standing, praying figure of Saint Jerome, commonly dated to 1520–25. This drawing is problematic in that parts of the figure and drapery seem to have been reworked in a hand other than Pontormo's.[4] The heavy staining of the sheet

CAT. NO. 11 VERSO

PROVENANCE
Sir Thomas Lawrence (1769–1830; L. 2445); Samuel Woodburn (1786–1853); Sir Thomas Phillipps (1792–1872), acquired at Lawrence-Woodburn sale, Christie's, London, 4ff. June 1860, lot 21; Thomas Fitzroy Fenwick, by descent; Count Antoine Seilern (1901–1978), acquired with the Fenwick collection, 1946; Princes Gate Bequest, 1978

SELECTED LITERATURE
Vasari Society, vol. 12 (1921–22), no. 8; Popham 1935a, p. 83; Berenson 1938, no. 1957A; Florence 1956, p. 27; Seilern 1959, no. 92, pl. 49; Cox-Rearick 1964, no. 254, fig. 243 and pp. 10 n. 26, 248, 255; Seilern 1971, no. 92; Cox-Rearick 1981, no. 254, fig. 243 and pp. 10 n. 26, 248, 255; Shearman 1972, p. 211; Scrase 1983, p. 308; Farr (ed.) 1987, p. 134; Costamagna 2005, pp. 286–87

SELECTED EXHIBITIONS
London 1983, no. 34; London 1991, no. 57

and the reworking of the verso suggest this was a workshop drawing and lend weight to the theory that these drawings were casual sketches related to the daily practice required to train the hand.[5]

It is clear, based on the visual evidence of Pontormo's drawings and paintings from 1513 onwards, that he made at least one trip to Rome, where he encountered the work of Raphael and Michelangelo.[6] Pontormo's *garzone*, dressed in apron and stockings, closely resembles Raphael's slouching figure of Heraclitus/Michelangelo in the centre foreground of *The School of Athens* in the Stanza della Segnatura (fig. 30).[7] In quoting Raphael's figure, Pontormo also emulated his practice, in that Raphael openly re-used and thus re-invented the canonical images of other masters.[8] In this instance, Raphael's Heraclitus/Michelangelo was inspired by Michelangelo's *ignudi* on the Sistine Ceiling. Michelangelo's source for the *ignudi* had been sculptural, the ancient fragment known as the Belvedere *Torso*, by Apollonius.[9]

Pontormo deftly quotes Raphael's invention while also acknowledging its prior sources in Michelangelo and antiquity. The two-dimensional, highly inflected and reinforced outline of the drawing contrasts with the sense of a sculpted figure existing in a cube of space. Pontormo is known to have modelled figures in clay for use in his studio, and the planes of relief, made with broad, parallel strokes of black chalk, and the compact way in which the figure hugs the stairs point to a sensibility that bows to the physical limitations of a block of stone.[10]

Pontormo brings movement and a sense of drama to the figure despite the inherently static position. The youth's engagement with the viewer, directed by his gaze, and the expression of an emotion introduce a notion of performance replete with an implied narrative and audience. Pontormo's deliberate transcription of the theatricality of the pose excavates the layers of identity presented. The *garzone* becomes an actor, and Pontormo delineates both the boy and his performance of fear.

FIG. 30 Raphael, *The School of Athens* (detail), *c.* 1510–12
Fresco
Vatican City, Vatican, Stanza della Segnatura

The narrative and visual aspects of this study link it to another *garzone* drawing in Florence that can be convincingly dated to 1519–21 (fig. 31).[11] Pontormo employed the same boy, costume and setting in this more finished drawing, and once again, the subject is the expression of fear. The Uffizi *garzone* recoils as if from a shocking presence. His hand shields his face, seemingly displaying the raised second and fifth fingers of the *mano cornuta* (horns of the bull), a gesture meant to ward off evil that enters through the eyes.[12] This use of hands to indicate character and mood is deeply indebted to Raphael, and the pose recalls the figure of the apostle Peter in Raphael's *Transfiguration* of 1517–20 as well as Raphael's 1501–02 silverpoint study in Oxford for one of Pilate's guards in *The Resurrection of Christ*, which clearly depicts the *mano cornuta* in the fallen soldier's upraised hand.[13] These scenes, narrated in the Gospels, describe the figures' "amazement and fright at the sight of the risen and transcendent Christ".[14]

In Pontormo's Uffizi drawing, the *garzone*'s position is rotated so that his facial features, distorted with emotion, are visible to the viewer. Together, the Courtauld and Uffizi sheets permit us to observe Pontormo's exploration and development of the depiction of fear. MC

FIG. 31 Pontormo, *Seated youth with raised arm*, c. 1519–21
Red chalk over faint black chalk,
395 × 284 mm
Florence, Galleria degli Uffizi,
inv. no. 6632Fr

NOTES
1 Chapman and Faietti 2010, pp. 236–37.
2 See Cox-Rearick 1964, p. 247, for a dating to *c.* 1525.
3 Others include Florence, Uffizi, 6530Fr, 6632Fr, 6632Fv, 6741Fr; *Four singers*, Budapest, Szépművészeti Múzeum; *Two boys reading a book*, Rotterdam, Museum Boijmans Van Beuningen, I.117.
4 Florence 2010, pp. 68–69. The composition appears, with modifications, in the Uffizi panel *Madonna and Child between Saint Jerome and Saint Francis of Assisi*. Current scholarship tentatively attributes this painting to Mirabello Cavalori (Florence 1535–1572 Florence) and dates it 1550–70. See Florence 2010, pp. 68–69.
5 Petherbridge 2010, pp. 212, 290.
6 Costamagna 1994, pp. 18–19. See also Cox-Rearick 1964, p. 38.
7 Nesselrath 1997, vol. 1, pp. 20–21, 97–98.
8 Joannides 1983, pp. 92–93.
9 Summers 1977. p. 336.
10 Vasari (Bettarini) 1984, vol. 5, p. 333.
11 Costamagna 1994, p. 185; Berenson 1938, no. 2018; and Clapp 1914, p. 122.
12 Lykiardopoulos 1981, p. 227, and Wainwright 1961, pp. 492–95.
13 Raphael (1483–1520), *Studies for a Guard in a Resurrection and of an Angel*, Oxford, Ashmolean Museum, WA1846.150.
14 London 2004, p. 108. See also Matthew 28:3–8 and 17:6–7.

MICHELANGELO BUONARROTI
Caprese 1475–1564 Rome

12 *The Dream (Il Sogno), c.* 1533

Black chalk, on laid paper; overall slight discolouration and foxing; slight overall undulation;
minor edge tears and losses; two old restorations on the right thigh and right calf of the main figure

Verso: four circular skinned areas along the top edge; red offset marks in centre (possibly red chalk);
inscribed in graphite in upper left corner *94*; in graphite at lower centre *126. Michelangelo*;
in purple crayon at lower centre *Der Traum*
398 × 281/278 mm

Samuel Courtauld Trust, D.1978.PG.424

Meticulously modelled with black chalk to a high degree of finish, Michelangelo's *Dream* was made as an independent artwork. The enigmatic composition shows an idealised male nude resting on a sphere set on an open box filled with masks; above, a winged figure descends, sounding a trumpet. The youth seems unaware of the figures surrounding him: some greedily prepare food and drink, others make love; a disembodied hand holds a large phallus,[1] and another clasps a purse. These motifs, smaller and more sketchily executed than the two main figures, are traditionally linked with gluttony, lust, avarice, wrath and sloth. Emerging from clouds, they occupy a different level of reality. The viewer is left in a state of doubt about the exact nature of the depiction, much as in a dream; in 1568 Giorgio Vasari entitled the drawing *Il Sogno*.[2]

Regarding its meaning, most scholars have adopted Erwin Panofsky's Neoplatonic interpretation as a starting point – the youth embodies the human mind awakened from evil dreams[3] – even though this reading does not take the figure's physicality sufficiently into account. Christian iconography provides a useful context, and corresponds with the interpretation of a maiolica painter who, as early as 1545, copied *The Dream* on a dish (The Detroit Institute of Arts) and identified the subject as the Old Testament Prophet Daniel haunted in a nightmare by the seven deadly sins.[4] Henry Thode, recognising the youth as a paraphrasing both of Adam in Michelangelo's *Creation of Man* in the Sistine Ceiling and of Lazarus in his design for Sebastiano del Piombo's *Raising of Lazarus* (London, National Gallery),[5] explained the protagonist as the

PROVENANCE
? Casa Buonarroti; ? J.B.J. Wicar (1762–1834); W.J. Ottley (1771–1836), sold in 1814; Sir Thomas Lawrence (1769–1830; L. 2445), probably acquired in 1814; Samuel Woodburn (1786–1853), acquired in 1834; William II, King of Holland (1792–1849), acquired in 1838; Samuel Woodburn (1786–1853), acquired at William II sale, The Hague, 1850; Alexander August Johann, Grand Duke of Sachsen-Weimar-Eisenach (1818–1901), by 1875; Grand Duke Karl August of Sachsen-Weimar-Eisenach (1757–1828), by descent; Count Antoine Seilern (1901–1978), acquired from Colnaghi, 25 September 1952; Princes Gate Bequest, 1978 (accepted in lieu of tax by HM Government and presented to the Home House Society [now the Samuel Courtauld Trust], 1981)

SELECTED LITERATURE
Ottley 1823, p. 33; Woodburn 1836, p. 25, no. 77; Gotti 1875, vol. 2, pp. 210, 234–35; Thode 1908–13, vol. 2, pp. 375–82; Justi 1909, pp. 345–48; Frey 1909–11, vol. 3, pp. 76–77; Thode 1912, pp. 671–73; Brinckmann 1925, pp. 47–48, no. 59; Panofsky 1939, pp. 223–25; Goldscheider 1951, pp. 18, 49–50, no. 93; Wilde 1953, p. 95; Marabottini 1956, vol. 1, pp. 349–58; Dussler 1959, pp. 268–69, no. 589; Tolnay 1960, pp. 181–82, no. 169, fig. 131; Hartt 1971, p. 251, no. 359; Tolnay 1975, vol. 2, pp. 102–03, no. 333; Wilde 1978, pp. 153–56, no. 148; Testa 1979, pp. 45–58, esp. 52–56, fig. 4; Zehnpfennig 1979, pp. 31–74; Summers 1981, p. 215; Saslow 1986, pp. 34, 45–47, 58, fig. 1.14; Farr (ed.) 1987, p. 132; Perrig 1991, pp. 33, 43, 122 n. 35, 126 n. 74; Paoletti 1992, pp. 428–29, no. 13; Winner 1992, pp. 227–42; Washington and elsewhere 1996, pp. 54–55, 60, 65; Morganti 1997, pp. 2–6; Leuschner 1997, pp. 201–04, 523, fig. 93; Gombrich 2000, pp. 130–32; Peck 2003, pp. 32–36, fig. 3; Ruvoldt 2003, pp. 86–113; Hall 2005, pp. 192–98, 218, 235, fig. 25; Schumacher 2007, pp. 35, 58, 60–61, 73–74, 171, 272, fig. 21; Zöllner *et al.* 2007, pp. 596 and 586–89, no. 194; van den Doel 2008, pp. 179–220, 396–97, fig. 56; Sickel 2008, pp. 170, 174, 196 n. 26 and 142, fig. 10; Frankfurt am Main 2009, pp. 126–27, fig. 33; Robertson 2010, pp. 339–40; Petherbridge 2010, p. 260, pl. 183

SELECTED EXHIBITIONS
London 1975, no. 128; London 1981, no. 139; London 1983, no. 30; London 1991, no. 50; London 2010, no. 1, pp. 100–09

FIG. 32 Ulm artist, *Ars moriendi*, *c*. 1470, woodcut
Wolfenbüttel, Herzog August Bibliothek, i. 7 Xylogr.

FIG. 33 Albrecht Dürer, *The Opening of the
Seventh Seal*, *c*. 1498
Woodcut, 394 × 285 mm (Bartsch VII.128.68)
London, British Museum, 1895,0122.565

embodiment of mankind created and maintained by the divine, called to abandon vice and aspire to a virtuous life.

The trumpet is directed at the youth's forehead. According to Renaissance medical tradition this is, as Maria Ruvoldt has explained, the location of the imagination and the spot identified by Leonardo da Vinci as the *imprensiva*, "the part of the brain that receives and processes visual impressions".[6] Like the youth, the viewer is asked to awaken, stimulated by the virtuosity and beauty of the drawing, created by an artist who is the embodiment of divine artistic powers.

It is undocumented whether Michelangelo made *The Dream* for a particular recipient. It is, however, closely related to several drawings of about 1533 that, according to Vasari, Michelangelo presented to the beautiful young Roman nobleman Tommaso de' Cavalieri - *Ganymede* (preserved only in copies), *Tityus*, *Phaeton* and *Bacchanal* (all Windsor, Royal Library).[7] Extant letters record that Tommaso studied the drawings carefully,[8] and they were greatly admired by sophisticated connoisseurs, including the pope. Even if *The Dream* was not made for Tommaso, the drawings that were - which circulated widely through printed copies - establish a framework for understanding it as an intimate conversation both between artist and individual and between artist and public.

Whereas the Cavalieri drawings are based on classical subjects, *The Dream* does not illustrate a specific source. Addressing one of the most essential human questions - how to overcome temptation and achieve a virtuous life - its theme is universal and lends itself to a variety of interpretations. The question is also at the heart of medieval moralistic literature, including the popular *Ars moriendi*, which Michelangelo probably knew, since Savonarola dedicated a sermon to it in Florence in 1496.[9] It introduces the importance of the soul over the body, presenting five temptations. Demons and angels fight, whilst Christ and his saints provide consolation. In the end, an angel receives the victorious soul. The numerous editions of the text are accompanied by illustrations that derive from a fifteenth-century German block book and include compositions remarkably similar to *The Dream* (fig. 32).[10]

The Apocalypse, Saint John's revelation of the end of the world, also resonates with the themes of *The Dream*. Illustrated throughout the Middle Ages, it was interpreted most powerfully by Albrecht Dürer, whose fifteen woodcuts of 1497–98 seem to have inspired Michelangelo, who is known to have studied Dürer's prints.[11] Michelangelo's use of bands of clouds to separate and unite seemingly disparate motifs follows the same compositional strategy as found in Dürer's woodcuts and there are also trumpets sounded by angels, the rear view of a plunging bird, and a pair of hands reaching from the clouds (fig. 33).[12] However, neither the *Ars moriendi* nor the Apocalypse displays an eroticism comparable to that in *The Dream*. For this, Guillaume de Lorris and Jean de Meun's popular medieval romance *Roman de la rose* provided a tradition that fused dreams with the desire for carnal love.[13]

The meanings of *The Dream* unfold on multiple levels when it is understood as an object of contemplation: the enjoyment of the beautiful figures equals the admiration for the outstanding artistry of the draughtsman. Reflections about the nature of the world, of man, and of the possibilities of his rising to a new life are revealed subtly, with love for beauty as a catalyst. As such the drawing was certainly meant for detailed discussion in a learned environment. S B

NOTES

1 The partially erased phallus is clearly visible in printed copies after *The Dream*; see London 2010, pp. 167–70, no. 14.

2 Vasari 1966–87, vol. 5 (1984), pp. 19–20; Vasari 1996, p. 94.

3 See Buck in London 2010, pp. 100–09, no. 1.

4 Peck 2003, pp. 32–36.

5 Thode 1908–13, vol. 2, pp. 375–82.

6 Ruvoldt 2003, p. 89.

7 London 2010, pp. 110–45, nos. 2–8.

8 See Tommaso's letter to Michelangelo of 1 January 1533, *Carteggio* 1965–83, vol. 3, pp. 445–46, DCCCXCVIII.

9 For the sermon, see Sander 1969, vol. 3, pp. 1180–81, nos. 6812–17, and vol. 6, fig. N. 5171–72; Burke 2004, pp. 183–87.

10 See Cust 1898; Weil 1922; Sander 1969, vol. 1, pp. 109–11, nos. 627–37, and vol. 6, figs. N. 571–74; Cologne 2002, pp. 546–57, no. 34. For an edition published in Florence about 1510–13, see Mortimer 1974, p. 44, no. 31.

11 See Hall 2005, pp. 174–77; Echinger-Maurach 2009; London 2010, pp. 155–56. See Robertson (forthcoming) on the role of Northern prints as a visual source for Michelangelo's highly finished drawings.

I thank the author for sharing his forthcoming publication, *The Filthiest Pictures: Michelangelo and Tommaso dei Cavalieri; A Career Strategy*.

12 Even the back view of a nude man stepping out of a bed in *The Dream* appears in Dürer's Apocalypse illustration of the Opening of the Fifth Seal with the dressing of the martyrs, *Illustrated Bartsch* 10 (Strauss) 1980–81, VII.128, 65.

13 Dahlberg (ed.) 1971; König 1992.

PAOLO VERONESE
Verona 1528–1588 Venice

13   Studies for *Christ carrying the Cross, c.* 1571

Pen and grey-brown ink and wash, on laid paper, laid down;
overall slight discolouration with localised staining and minor foxing;
rust stain at upper right corner; horizontal and three vertical folds,
flattened, tears along folds and small hole in centre, repaired
202 × 297 mm

Samuel Courtauld Trust, D.1978.PG.102

Veronese made this drawing in preparation for an important commission in about 1572 – a set of four enormous canvases for the palace of the Cuccina family on Venice's Grand Canal. The pictures are all now in the Gemäldegalerie in Dresden. They represent the Adoration of the Magi, the Nativity, Christ carrying the Cross (fig. 34) and that peculiarly Venetian subject of the presentation of the patron and his family to the Virgin.[1] The Cuccina were not patricians but immensely wealthy merchants, originally from Bergamo, who were relatively recent immigrants to the city.[2] They were naturalised members of the *cittadino* class, the middle level of Venice's tripartite social hierarchy. With these pictures, which are packed with portraits of family members, they further proclaimed their Venetian identity. Like many of Veronese's grand religious dramas, such as the celebrated *Wedding at Cana* (Paris, Musée du Louvre), the canvases he made for the Cuccina are both sacred and secular.

FIG. 34 Paolo Veronese,
Christ carrying the Cross, 1571
Oil on canvas, 166 × 414 cm
Dresden, Staatliche
Kunstsammlungen.
Gemäldegalerie Alte Meister

PROVENANCE
Sir Joshua Reynolds (1723-1792; L. 2364); Sir Thomas Lawrence (1769-1830; L. 2445); Samuel Woodburn (1786-1853), by 1860; Sir Thomas Phillipps (1792-1872), acquired at Lawrence-Woodburn sale, Christie's, London, 4ff. June 1860, lot 1023; Thomas Fitzroy Fenwick (1856-1938), by descent; Count Antoine Seilern (1901-1978), acquired with the Fenwick collection, 1946; Princes Gate Bequest, 1978

SELECTED LITERATURE
Popham 1935a, no. 1; Tietze and Tietze-Conrat 1944, no. 2057; Seilern 1959, no. 102; Pignatti 1976, p. 134; Cocke 1984, no. 59, Rearick in Washington 1988, p. 114

SELECTED EXHIBITION
London 1991, no. 76

Veronese drew prolifically: more than 150 sheets survive, which probably represent only a small fragment of his work as a draughtsman.[3] A large number of his surviving drawings can be categorised as exploratory and imaginative studies of the possibilities afforded by a particular subject. The Courtauld sheet is one of his most exciting essays in this genre and, typically, is executed in pen and ink with wash. It contains Veronese's only studies for the painting *Christ carrying the Cross* for the Cuccina palace and includes drawings of specific motifs as well as more general explorations of the structure of this composition. This picture was always intended to be long and narrow, like its counterpart, Veronese's *Presentation of the Cuccina Family to the Virgin*, which was probably made for the opposite side of the same room.

The middle part of the sheet is dominated by his various explorations of the central group of the Way to Calvary, with particular concentration on the figure of Christ with the cross and the two men who bully him and urge him on. The horsemen who appear at the left and right edges of the Cuccina painting can just be discerned on the far sides of this group. Veronese experimented with the length and angle of Christ's cross and also the figure who holds the rope around Christ. Veronese's first drawing for this group has this individual flanking Christ on the other side of the cross, but shown from behind. In the second study, above, this man is rotated 180 degrees, so that he looks at Christ. The painted composition amalgamates these two ideas, and the executioner's back is turned to the viewer while he gazes at Christ.

In the bottom third of the drawing, and in particular in the right-hand corner, Veronese has tried out various positions for another important section of his composition, the swooning Virgin Mary, supported balletically by a male figure as she watches her son go to his death. In the picture, their positions have been reversed. The Virgin is seen from behind, while her companion – traditionally John the Evangelist, the disciple whom Jesus loved – stares out of the canvas. His sixteenth-century costume, strongly individualised features and direct gaze at the viewer suggest that this figure is a portrait of a member of the Cuccina family, possibly Antonio, the youngest of the three Cuccina brothers, who died in 1573.[4]

Following these figure studies, Veronese made several sketches of the drapery of the Virgin's falling form, which he went over in wash. Despite the multiple studies of the Virgin, she is not the most prominent female figure in the finished painting. This is Saint Veronica, who stands immediately before Christ, holding out her veil. Again, Veronese rehearsed this moment several times, at the top right and in even more notational form below, beside a further extremely cursory study of Christ and the cross.

The drawings on this sheet seem to have been made quickly, even breathlessly. Figures and compositions almost merge into each other. The rocky forms of the landscape, crudely hatched and blocked-in in the uppermost compositional sketch for Christ carrying the cross among his tormentors, have been drawn over the smaller study of this grouping. Roughly drawn lines attempt to separate these two entwined compositions and also impose some sense of the spatial dimensions of the rectangular canvas that Veronese and his patrons had in mind for the painting of Christ carrying the Cross. The sheet still conveys a sense of the excitement with which it was made. One feels the artist's ideas tumbling over each other in his desire to express them in some form and, also, the way these ideas evolved as part of the process of putting pen to paper. CC

NOTES

1 Pignatti 1976, pp. 133–34, nos. 167–70.

2 De Maria 2010, p. 20.

3 Cocke 1984, p. 15.

4 For this identification, see De Maria 2010, pp. 154–55.

JACOPO TINTORETTO
Venice 1518–1594 Venice

14 Study of *A male figure bending forward*, c. 1575–85

Black chalk, and traces of white chalk, on blue laid paper, laid down;
slight undulation and overall discolouration with numerous small losses,
repaired and retouched; numerous creases; inscribed in pen and brown ink
at bottom left *Tintoretto* and, on verso, in pen and brown ink *18*
251 × 201 mm

WATERMARK
Circle

Samuel Courtauld Trust, D.1978.PG.370

Jacopo Robusti, known as Tintoretto, the 'little dyer', was the most explosive talent of sixteenth-century Venice. His dynamic pictorial compositions, such as *The Miracle of the Slave* (1548; Venice, Accademia), the first work that brought him public acclaim, seem to have an electric charge. In comparison, the painted works of his contemporary and rival Paolo Veronese appear more restrained, classical and composed.

Tintoretto's manner as a draughtsman as well as a painter is immediately recognisable, but it can be difficult to ascribe authorship to drawings in his style, since it was much admired and copied by his children and workshop assistants as well as by other Venetian artists well into the seventeenth century. This inventive life study, which has never been exhibited, has a very good likelihood of being by Tintoretto. At the very least, it is in his manner of the late 1570s and 1580s. It is a fabulously exuberant and quick drawing of a model holding a pose that would be impossible to maintain for long.

This drawing may have been made as part of a project for a painting commission, such as *The Victory at Argenta* in the Ducal Palace (fig. 35), where there are two or three not dissimilar figures.[1] But, more importantly, it demonstrates how Venetian painters and draughtsmen were capable of creating idealised visions of the human body based on life studies, something that the Tuscan

artist and historian Giorgio Vasari said they never did. In his *Life* of Titian, Vasari successfully propagated the misleading myth that Venetian artists preferred not to draw and were not accustomed to compile a repertory of studies made from life.[2] The surviving evidence completely destroys this argument: both Veronese and Tintoretto made life drawings, as did Titian.[3]

In the cases of Veronese and Tintoretto, a corpus survives sufficient to enable us to begin to understand these artists' use of works on paper, something more difficult for Giovanni Bellini (see cat. no. 5). Tintoretto, like Carpaccio (cat. no. 6) and Veronese, developed a successful formula for his drawings. While Veronese preferred to make rapid, notational pen-and-ink sketches for compositions (such as cat. no. 13), Tintoretto's practice as a draughtsman was dominated by work in chalk and charcoal (sometimes with the addition of white highlights), both from sculpture and from models. These drawings are almost exclusively on coloured paper. Tintoretto seems to have preferred to work with a rather rough support, in which the fibres of the cloth from which the paper was made are still evident.

Carlo Ridolfi, whose biography of Tintoretto (first published in 1642) remains the essential source for the artist's life, commented on the significance that Tintoretto attached to drawing from life, setting himself "to draw

PROVENANCE
Bank Julius Bär & Co., Zurich; Count Antoine
Seilern (1901–1978), acquired from Arthur
Goldschmidt, Paris, 1959; Princes Gate
Bequest, 1978

SELECTED LITERATURE
Seilern 1969, p. 74, no. 14

FIG. 35 Jacopo Tintoretto,
The Victory of Argenta of 1482
(detail), *c.* 1579–82
Oil on canvas, 424 × 568 cm
Venice, Palazzo Ducale,
Sala del Gran Consiglio

from the live model in all sorts of poses, endowing them with grace in their movements, drawing from them endless kinds of foreshortenings".[4] As Ridolfi noted, Tintoretto specialised in placing his models in the most contorted positions. These were derived from his study of sculpture, and in particular sculptural models, of which he owned a considerable collection, notably of works after Michelangelo.[5]

This drawing is one such sheet, a life drawing inspired by Tintoretto's admiration for this three-dimensional art form. Here, the model clasps a stick in his left hand, which enables him to hold the complicated pose of balancing on one leg while holding the other up, and looking downwards. It is probable that the man's floating knee was supported by a stool, an ancillary element which the artist chose not to include in his drawing.[6] The subject was probably a workshop apprentice, but he wears the very rudimentary clothing seen in a number of Venetian life drawings of the sixteenth and seventeenth centuries, so he may have been

a professional model. We know that Tintoretto used life models, as his expenses related to painting *The Battle of Lepanto* (1572; Venice, Doge's Palace, destroyed by fire in 1577) include the costs of hiring men who posed for him.[7]

The peculiar muscle tone shown in many of Tintoretto's life drawings is also highly sculptural and, in this case, as in many of Tintoretto's drawings of male figures either from a sculpture or from life, a sequence of curved lines denotes the contours of the body. Tintoretto used his study of sculpture to supplement what nature lacked; without this, the bodies of his sitters "would never have been brought to such beauty".[8] His ability to synthesise his thinking about the ideals of male beauty within the forms of particular models enables studies from life made by him or in his workshop, such as this sheet, to be at once spontaneous drawings of an individual at a certain moment and expressions of his more conceptual thinking about the representation of the human body. CC

NOTES

1 See Seilern 1969, p. 74, who rightly drew connections both with *The Victory of Argenta of 1482* and with *The Brazen Serpent* (1576; Venice, Scuola di San Rocco).

2 Vasari 1966–87, vol. 6 (1987), 'Descrizione dell'opere di Tiziano da Cador', pp. 155–56.

3 Whistler 2004, pp. 374–76.

4 Ridolfi (Hadeln) 1965, vol. 2, p. 15.

5 Nichols 1999, p. 54.

6 Catherine Whistler, comment, 23 July 2010; see object record file for D.1978.PG.370 held at The Courtauld Gallery.

7 Hadeln 1921, p. 88 n. 1.

8 Ridolfi (Hadeln) 1965, vol. 2, p. 18.

PIETER BRUEGEL THE ELDER
Breda (?) *c*.1525–1569 Brussels

15 *Kermis at Hoboken*, 1559

Pen and brown ink, on laid paper; outlines incised for transfer with traces of charcoal (over ink); extensive localised staining; vertical crease down the centre, some retouching; inscribed with pen and brown ink by the artist at lower left *1559/ BRVEGEL*; on the banner at left *Gilde* [?]/ . . ./*hoboken*/ . . ./ . . .

Verso: remnants of charcoal

265 × 394 mm

WATERMARK
Two crossed arrows

Samuel Courtauld Trust, D.1947.LF.45

The banderole at the top of the banner at left proclaims the setting for Bruegel's scene of a church festival (*kermis*) as the village of Hoboken, a few miles south of the city of Antwerp. The banner's motif of crossed arrows, in juxtaposition with the group of archers standing just below, identifies the *kermis* with the festival of the Longbowmen (*Handboog schutters*), held the day after Pentecost, typically in the month of May.[1] The shooting contest, depicted as improbably taking place in the middle of a crowded village square, was the centrepiece of the celebration. The elevated perspective and high horizon line allow the viewer to wander spectatorially through a variety of activities – a church procession, figures dancing in the round, crowds enjoying a play or local rhetorician (*rederijker*) performance, amorous couples embracing.

Festivals like the *kermis* were popular entertainments. As early as 1531 Charles V had tried to impose limits on their number and duration. Visitors from Antwerp descended on villages like Hoboken for rural entertainment, and wealthy merchants bought up country estates nearby. Ludovico Guicciardini, an Italian merchant famous for his description of the Low Countries, owned

a home near Hoboken.[2] The publisher Tylman Susato included a festive dance from the village in one of his popular Dutch songbooks.[3] Contemporary inventories attest to the popularity of painted and printed scenes of the peasant *kermis*.

Scholars are divided on how the viewer was meant to interpret Bruegel's picture of festivity. An engraving after the drawing, published by Bartholomaeus de Mompere, is inscribed: "The peasants delight in such festivals: to dance, jump, and drink themselves as drunk as beasts. They insist on holding their *kermisses*, even though they have to fast and die of the cold."[4] This text paraphrases the inscription on another print of a peasant festival published by de Mompere, designed by Pieter van der Borcht (fig. 36).[5] Van der Borcht's print clearly depicts those drinking to excess, brawling and vomiting, leading some to read Bruegel's drawing as conveying a similar moralizing and satiric viewpoint.[6]

Yet while several couples embrace and a number of festival goers have lowered their trousers (most notably the squatting figure positioned for comic effect directly next to the archer's target), Bruegel's image is devoid of

PROVENANCE
Gairloch collection; Sir Kenneth Mackenzie, acquired at Gairloch sale, Sotheby's, London, 15–16 February 1921, lot 216; Henry Oppenheimer (1859–1932), by 1936; Matthiesen Gallery, acquired at Oppenheimer sale, Christie's, London, 10–14 July 1936, lot 223; Matthiesen; Lord Lee of Fareham (1868–1947), acquired from Slatter Gallery, 1944; Lee Bequest, 1947

SELECTED LITERATURE
Vasari Society 1916–35, vol. 2 (1921), no. 12; Tolnai 1925, p. 73; Tolnay 1935, no. 36; Glück 1937, p. 88; Lebeer 1949, pp. 99–103; Tolnay 1952, no. A20 (as after Bruegel); Münz 1961, no. 141; Lebeer 1969, no. 30; Marlier 1969, pp. 213–17; Monballieu 1974; Riggs 1977, pp. 167, 172; Miedema 1981, p. 199; Raupp 1986, p. 226; Monballieu 1987; Marijnissen 1988, pp. 115–16; Mielke 1996, no. 44; Kavaler 1999, pp. 186–89;

New York 2001, pp. 198–99; Gibson 2006, pp. 80–86; Sellink 2007, no. 74; Sullivan 2010, pp. 54–56

SELECTED EXHIBITIONS
London 1927, no. 526; Manchester 1965, no. 280; Berlin 1975, no. 68; Brussels 1980, no. 36; London 1983, no. 19; New York and London 1986, no. 7; Washington and New York 1986, no. 28; Tokyo 1995, no. B5

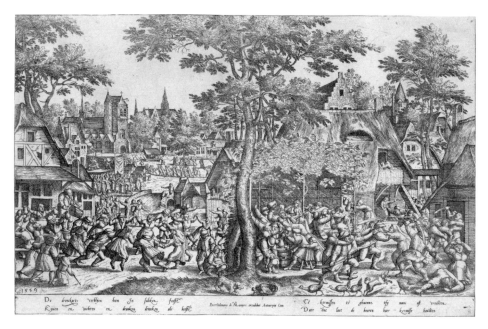

FIG. 36 Pieter van der Borcht, *Peasant fair*, 1559
Etching and engraving,
298 × 477 mm
New York, The Metropolitan
Museum of Art, inv. no. 2000.437

fighting and excessive drinking. The inscription on another *kermis* print designed by Bruegel, *Kermis of Saint George* (fig. 37), bears a more ambiguous inscription: "Let the peasants hold their *kermis*".[7] Published around the same time as the *Kermis at Hoboken* by Bruegel's usual publisher, Hieronymus Cock, the inscription on *Kermis of Saint George* signals the possiblity of a more positive interpretation of the scene.

The year Bruegel drew *Kermis at Hoboken*, 1559, marked a change in Hoboken's ownership: William of Orange sold the manor to Melchior Schetz, who passed the title to his brother Balthazar. The same year Philip II, ruler of the Low Countries, reissued his father's decrees limiting festivals. Since Hoboken was known for celebrating three major feast-days, the inscription on Bruegel's *Kermis of Saint George* has been seen as an appeal to the new lord of Hoboken to maintain the *status quo* despite the renewed limitations on feast days.[8] However, the precise relation-ship between Bruegel's two designs is not clear – which

print was designed first, why the artist published similar designs with two different publishers in a short space of time (Bruegel only worked with de Mompere in this single instance), and if the two prints were meant to be seen as a pair.[9] The compositional similarities between the two designs are striking, as both include games in the lower left corners, a strong diagonal with a wagon at centre, and a fool with children in the foreground.

While visiting such feast days and buying images of peasant festivity were popular activities among the middle class, Bruegel includes no one with whom the viewer easily can identify. The figures positioned either side of the artist's signature seem to indicate both a visual invitation and a warning. While the figure to the left faces the scene, his hand extending towards the artist's name, the pair of figures to the right, one man seated next to a jug, the other man apparently admonishing him, offer a warning – a *kermis* may be diverting but should not tempt overenthusiastic participation. SCP

FIG. 37 Johannes and Lucas van
Doetecum after Pieter Bruegel,
Kermis of Saint George, c. 1553–56
Etching and engraving,
332 × 523 mm
London, British Museum,
inv. no. 1870,0625.650

NOTES

1 Monballieu 1987, pp. 193–94.

2 Gibson 2006, p. 82.

3 See Porras 2011, pp. 3–6; Riemsdijk 1888.

4 Gibson has suggested the final word of this
   inscription (*kauwen*) could mean 'chewing',
   creating a more comic tone. See Gibson
   2006, p. 81.

5 *New Hollstein* 2004 (Mielke, vol. 12), no. 170;
   Raupp 1986, van der Borcht no. 4.

6 For example, see Raupp 1986, pp. 245–47;
   Sullivan 2010, pp. 56–58. Nadine Orenstein

has suggested that the prints be viewed as a
pair, with their difference in tone and style
reflecting de Mompere's ambition to appeal
to a wide market: see New York 2001, p. 198.
At the time of the print's publication, de
Mompere was the manager of Antwerp's
Schilderspand (dedicated art market) and
must have been savvy about consumer
demand. See Vermeylen 2003, pp. 54–61.

7 New York 2001, no. 79; *New Hollstein* 2006
   (Orenstein, vol. 15), no. 42.

8 Monballieu 1974; Monballieu 1987.

9 Orenstein (in New York 2001) has suggested
   that the current sheet postdates the *Kermis
   of Saint George*, as Bruegel would have first
   worked with his regular publisher, Cock,
   before turning to his rival de Mompere.

PIETER BRUEGEL THE ELDER
Breda (?) c.1525–1569 Brussels

16 *A storm in the River Schelde with a view of Antwerp, c. 1559*

Pen and brown ink, reworked in areas in darker ink, and traces of graphite (over ink),
on laid paper, laid down; traces of later framing line in pen and brown ink, trimmed; overall slight
undulation and discolouration; pinholes at centre top edge, repaired, loss at bottom left corner
and upper left, repaired and retouched; inscribed in a later hand in pen and dark brown ink
at lower left within an oval outline *Breughel*
202 × 299 mm

Samuel Courtauld Trust, D.1978.PG.11

This exquisite and understudied drawing of a stormy marine view is unique in Bruegel's oeuvre. Nearly two-thirds of the sheet is devoted to the study of rows of waves receding into the background. Leonardo da Vinci's water studies from the early sixteenth century are the only precedents for such a vivid transcription of wave motion.

Bruegel's treatment of the waves here is similar to that in the design for the engraving *Spes* (fig. 38), signed and dated 1559 by the artist, leading most scholars to date this sheet to around that year. In both drawings Bruegel used a graphic system of short strokes – dashes, hooks, dots and squiggles – to depict the water's surface. In contrast, at upper right he used long, straight lines of varying density to convey the drama of a strong downpour punctured by a shaft of sunlight.

The limited scholarship on the drawing has focused on the juxtaposition at upper left of the small island with gallows and a city skyline reminiscent of sixteenth-century Antwerp. The large tower at the centre is similar in outline and relative scale to the city's Onze-Lieve-Vrouwekerk. However, the scale of the river and the silhouette of other spires at upper right seem antithetical to this identification,

leading some to conclude the scene depicts a generic or unknown view. The difficulty in reading the drawing's topographic accuracy may be due to the traditional under standing of the sheet's viewpoint as being across a river. If, however, we think of the view as being onboard a vessel heading upriver, approaching the port of Antwerp from the North Sea, these topographic inconsistencies are resolved.

If Bruegel meant to depict Antwerp, the gallows island in the middle of the river is certainly the work of fantasy. According to several mid-century maps of the city, including one published by Hieronymus Cock in 1557 (fig. 39), the wheel and gallows were placed outside the city walls across the river.[1] Thus Bruegel's artistic invention may have had particular local resonance, as the riverside was the site for executions. The island, with its symbols of death and municipal justice, is tiny among the waves, underscoring man's fragile hold on life and fortune. This was a timely message, as there were a number of prominent deaths in the years around 1559 (including those of Charles V, former ruler of the Low Countries; Queen Mary of England; Christian II and III of Denmark; and Pope Paul IV).

PROVENANCE
Sir Bruce Stirling Ingram (1877–1963); Count Antoine Seilern (1901–1978), acquired from Alfred Scharf (1900–1965), 1935; Princes Gate Bequest, 1978 (accepted in lieu of tax by HM Government and presented to the Home House Society [now the Samuel Courtauld Trust], 1981)

SELECTED LITERATURE
Popham 1935, no. 36; Tolnay 1952, no. 1; Seilern 1955, no. 11; Münz 1961, no. 50; Marijnissen 1988, p. 158; Mielke 1996, no. 52; Roberts-Jones 2002, p. 286; Sellink 2007, no. 79

SELECTED EXHIBITIONS
London 1981, no. 127; London 1983, no. 22

The depiction of a stormy sea would also have had particular poignancy for the inhabitants of Antwerp, one of the North Sea's premier merchant ports. Bruegel's fellow Antwerp residents would recognise the large three-masted ship at upper centre heading towards the squall as a reminder of the dangers of the sea trade. Lodovico Guicciardini, describing Antwerp in 1567, wrote: "At one glance one can take in a great sweep of river with the perpetual ebb and flow of the sea … observe so many different kinds of ships … so that every hour there is something new".[2] Reflecting the importance of the marine economy to the city, Bruegel probably began his numerous designs for ship engravings around the time of this sheet's execution.[3]

The drawing's most striking feature, however, is the waves themselves. The water's visual dominance under-scores the power of the natural world, dwarfing the architecture of the skyline and the modern technical prowess of the sailing vessels. Pushed to the top third of the sheet, man's place in the world is rendered as limited. Hans Mielke suggested that the drawing was an allegory of man's struggle against the dangers of the world; more recently, Manfred Sellink posited reading the gallows as a symbol of transgression and the strong beam of light at upper right as a sign of hope.[4]

Yet the composition of the sheet with its high horizon also directly parallels the elevated viewpoints of Bruegel's earlier series of prints, the *Large Landscapes*.[5] The sense of

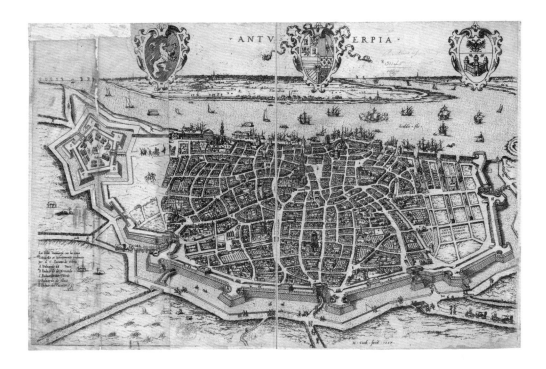

FIG. 38 Pieter Bruegel
the Elder, *Spes*, 1559
Pen and dark brown ink,
224 × 295 mm
Berlin, Staatliche Museen zu
Berlin, Kupferstichkabinett,
Kdz 715

FIG. 39 Hieronymus Cock,
View of Antwerp, 1557
Engraving, 365 × 445 mm
London, British Library,
Cartographic items, maps,
*31145.(3)

NOTES
1 *New Hollstein* 2006 (Orenstein, vol. 15), no. 4.
2 Guicciardini 1567, p. 107.
3 New York 2001, nos. 89–94; *New Hollstein*
  2006 (Orenstein, vol. 15), nos. 62–71.
4 Mielke 1996, p. 61; Sellink 2007, p. 133.
5 New York 2001, nos. 24–35; *New Hollstein*
  2006 (Orenstein, vol. 15), nos. 49–60.
6 Müller-Hofstede 1979; Koerner 2004,
  pp. 221–22.

physical distance in these designs has been compellingly related to the contemporary interest among Antwerp humanists in neo-Stoic philosophy.[6] The early modern Christian neo-Stoic sought to detach himself from the world, not in the model of an ascetic, but to gain philosophical perspective on his surroundings.

A Latin proverb, published in emblem form in Jacob Cats's 1627 *Sinne- en minne-beelden* but probably known earlier, encapsulates this Stoic perspective: "*Tangor, non frangor, ab undis*" (I am touched but not broken by the waves). From 1559 onwards, there was an atmosphere of increasing religious and political tension in the Low Countries, as Philip II imposed a new system of bishoprics alongside tougher heresy laws, upsetting the local nobility and those sympathetic to the new Reformist religion. The appeal of neo-Stoic detachment, therefore, was not just a philosophical fashion but an increasingly useful tactic for negotiating the fractious politics of the region.

In such an environment, Bruegel's drawing could have functioned as an autonomous work, intended to generate discussion among erudite collectors who appreciated both the artist's skill and the network of potential interpretations and references (historic, literary, contemporary) the sheet generated. SCP

MAERTEN VAN HEEMSKERCK
Heemskerck 1498–1574 Haarlem

17 *The Colossus of Rhodes*, 1570

Pen and brown ink, contours incised for transfer with traces of black chalk, on laid paper;
inscribed by the artist in pen and brown ink at bottom left *Martijn van Heemskerck/inventor*;
numbered at bottom centre right *5*; bottom right *1570*; inscribed by another contemporary hand
in pen and brown-grey ink at top left *5. Colossus Solis*; overall slight discolouration and minor foxing;
a light brown stain at lower left; one vertical and two horizontal paper folds; later framing line
in pen and brown ink
205 × 263 mm (sheet unevenly trimmed on all sides)

WATERMARK
Scroll with letters *N…FBE* (?)

Samuel Courtauld Trust, D.1952.RW.648

Heemskerck drew this fanciful depiction of the Colossus of Rhodes in 1570. It and seven other sheets by the artist constitute the *Octo Mundi Miracula* (Eight Wonders of the World), engraved by Philip Galle (1537–1612) in 1572 and published by his grandson Johannes.[1] The brawny sun-god Helios stands with staff and weaponry, his haloed head and blazing torch illuminating the fervent worshippers below. Classical buildings encircle Mandraki Harbour, which teems with craft. In the foreground, dramatically juxtaposed to the main scene, lie portions of the statue attended by muscular workmen and a wreathed figure consulting a sketch.

This clever aside complementing the central feature probably depicts the Colossus's creation – between about 294 and 282 BC – under the watchful eye of its architect, Chares of Lindos. The craftsmen, who have been described previously as polishing or gilding the statue with gold from the sea, are probably sculpting a clay model.[2] Using a scraper-like tool, an artisan works a malleable material to fashion the lower face. The appearance of the tool and the medium's pliable nature suggests he is shaping clay, a substance more likely to be mined from the shoreline than

gold. It is reasonable to assume, too, that the garlanded architect would consult the design during the modelling stage instead of when finishing the bronze surface.[3] The remnants may likewise reference the statue's demise following an earthquake in about 226 BC.[4] Left lying for centuries, the artefacts were reportedly conveyed eventually to Syria.[5] Ancillary scenes like this and the drawing's prominent cross-hatching typify Heemskerck's mature drawing style.

Although inscribed *5*, the *Colossus* appeared fourth in the printed series. Besides this sheet, three of the eight drawings remain. *The Temple of Diana at Ephesus* is also in The Courtauld's collection, while *The Walls of Babylon* and the *Amphitheatrum* are owned by the Louvre.[6] In his career Heemskerck produced nearly six hundred drawings from which engravings were made. The artist also collaborated with the humanist Hadrianus Junius (1511–1575), who supplied historical information and composed Latin verses to identify Heemskerck's pictures, as in Galle's impression (fig. 40).[7]

The Courtauld drawing unquestionably served as the design for the print, but, on comparing the two, subtle

PROVENANCE
Jan Pietersz. Zoomer (1641-1724); A. G. B. Russell (b. 1879); F. R. Meatyard (a. 1912–c.1964); Sir Robert Witt (1872–1952; L. 2228b), acquired from E. Parson & Son, London, before 1935; Robert Witt Bequest, 1952

SELECTED LITERATURE
Kerrich 1829, no. 5; Brett 1949, pp. 339–59; Courtauld Institute of Art 1956, no. 648; Kramer 1966, pp. 25–29, fig. 2; Duclaux 1981, p. 378, fig. 7; *Illustrated Bartsch* 56 (Dolders) 1987, no. 101:4; *New Hollstein* 1 (Veldman) 1994, no. 516

SELECTED EXHIBITIONS
Oxford 1929, no. 7; Auckland 1960, no. 60; Manchester 1962, no. 25; Manchester 1965, p. 95, no. 318; London 1983, no. 25; New York and London 1986, no. 43

COLOSSVS SOLIS.

SEPTINOS DECIESQ CVBITOS ÆQVARE, COLOSSVS ÆRE CAVO FACTVS, SAXORVM VASTA CAVERNA
DICTVS, PAR TVRRI MOLE SVB NOMINE SOLIS INTVS, APVD RHODIOS SACROS ACCEPIT HONORES.

FIG. 40 Philips Galle after
Maerten van Heemskerck,
The Colossus of Rhodes, 1572
Engraving, 213 × 260 mm
Amsterdam, Rijksprentenkabinet,
RP-P-1926-416

differences emerge. Galle's composition is reversed – owing
to the engraving process – and it translated Heemskerck's
delicate strokes into bolder, more rigid forms. Galle
eliminates some elements (the Colossus's nimbus) and
enhances others (the distant mountains). A recent examination of the sheet under magnification reveals how Galle
utilised Heemskerck's design. Incised lines reinforced
with black chalk follow the primary contours but are not
visible in the cross-hatching. Conversely, incised marks
diverging from Heemskerck's ink outlines are apparent
in the Colossus's face, arms and legs, delineating the
features and musculature.[8] Galle duplicated the essential
compositional components of Heemskerck's drawing
yet devised minor adjustments.

In both drawing and print, the titanic sentry straddles
the harbour. Representations like the woodcut by Jean
Cousin the Younger published in André Thevet's popular
Cosmographie de Levant (Lyons, 1554 and 1556; fig. 41) may
have influenced Heemskerck's conception.[9] As in Cousin's
image, Heemskerck's Colossus – said to measure a lofty

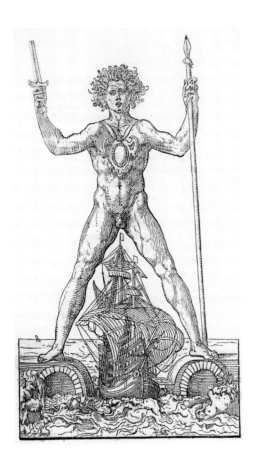

FIG. 41 Jean Cousin the Younger
The Colossus of Rhodes, woodcut
published in André Thevet's
Cosmographie de Levant
(Lyons, 1556)
London, Middle Temple Library

seventy cubits (about 33 metres or 110 feet in height)[10] – bestrides the port's entrance as vessels pass between his imposing limbs. Modern scholars contend that this stance would not have supported the weight of the massive torso.[11] Nor, probably, did the statue stand at the harbour entrance, as it was traditionally described as doing.[12]

Heemskerck first rendered the ancient wonders in the painting *The Abduction of Helen* (1536).[13] Here mythological characters navigate a landscape studded with classical edifices and other ancient marvels. Among these is a diminutive but recognisable Colossus. The whimsical painting celebrates the artist's training in Italy during the 1530s, when he produced myriad copies after Roman monuments and sculptural remnants.[14] These *ricordi* were undoubtedly valuable references when creating the *Octo Mundi Miracula* series.

In his encomium to Chares's fallen masterpiece, Pliny writes, "That which is by far the most worthy of our admiration … [is] the colossal statue of the Sun, which stood formerly at Rhodes … but, even as it lies, it excites our wonder and imagination".[15] Inspiring artists' imaginations centuries after its demise, the bronze giant's legend would endure, as would Heemskerck's lively rendering of it, in the prints and tapestries based on his design.[16] MI

NOTES

1 *New Hollstein* 1994 (Veldman, vol. 1), pp. 192–97; *Colossus* is no. 516.
2 Polishing: London and New York 1986, p. 110, no. 43; gilding: Kramer 1966, p. 25; sculpting, on the assumption that the indirect method of bronze casting – known to the Greeks and in use again by 1570 – was employed to construct the Colossus.
3 I am indebted to my Frick colleagues Joseph Godla, Conservator, and Julia Day, Assistant Objects Conservator, who cleverly identified the modelling process in this image.
4 London and New York 1986, p. 110.
5 Clayton and Price 1988, p. 137.
6 Duclaux 1981.
7 Ilja Veldman examines this collaboration in Veldman 1977, chap. 5.
8 My deepest thanks to Kate Edmondson, Paper Conservator at The Courtauld Gallery, for her assistance in examining the sheet.
9 As noted by Kramer 1966, p. 27.
10 Pliny (Bostock and Riley) 1857, p. 165.
11 Clayton and Price 1988, pp. 127–28.
12 Clayton and Price 1988, pp. 133–34.
13 Baltimore, Walters Art Museum; see Zafran 1988.
14 See Hülsen and Egger 1913 and Preibisz 1911.
15 Pliny (Bostock and Riley) 1857, p. 165.
16 Listed in London and New York 1986, p. 110.

JOHANNES STRADANUS (JAN VAN DER STRAET)
Bruges 1523–1605 Florence

18 *Pearl diving, c. 1596*

Pen and brown ink with wash and white bodycolour, on laid paper; bodycolour partially
turned grey owing to oxidisation, resulting in diminished opacity covering of underlying ink
drawing with various pentimenti; inscribed by the artist at lower right centre: *ioan stradanus*;
two original framing lines, one incised and the second in pen and brown ink; inscribed below
the framing lines at the bottom …*aro Balbi Venetiano in den Reÿse van indie di levanta schet iur*[?]
isole de ormus Nessesense[?]*e de perlen op dese maniere maken op derde tenten…* (further text trimmed);
overall undulation and slight discolouration; pinholes in each corner; upper left corner repaired
195 × 273 mm

WATERMARK
Triple mount in circle consisting of two lines

Samuel Courtauld Trust, D.1952.RW.1633

Stradanus describes this industrious community of pearl
divers with flowing lines and passages of velvety shading.
Shown nude or wearing feathered skirts, the intrepid
hunters navigate the waters in rowing boats, descending
crude tethers weighted with stones to scour the ocean
floor in search of oysters. At day's end, the shellfish are
shucked and evaluated, and an accounting is made.

Born in the Flemish city of Bruges and initially trained
by his father, Jan van der Straet (d. 1535), the junior Jan
moved to Antwerp to study with Pieter Aertsen (1507/08–
1575), becoming a master there in 1545. Following a brief
stay in Lyons, he travelled to Italy, where he spent the
majority of his career rechristened Johannes Stradanus,
Giovanni Stradano or Giovanni della Strada.[1] The Courtauld drawing is a work of his maturity. The elongated
figures indicate a Mannerist influence, evidence of his
long-term residence in Italy, while the copious details
confirm his Northern roots.

Pearl diving was composed about 1596 as a design for a
print by the Antwerp engraver Cornelis Galle I (fig. 42). It
appeared as number 93 in the series of 104 hunting images
*Venationes ferarum, avium, piscium. Pugnae bestiarorum:
et mutuae bestiarum*, published in 1600 by Philip Galle.
While the drawing and print have similar compositions
(the print's image is understandably reversed), a comparison reveals significant differences. The engraving's lines
are less fluid, with the drawing's diaphanous waters
becoming successions of regulated, frozen ripples. Figures
are recast: a seated diver sorting oysters in Stradanus's
image is transformed into a stooped fisherman unloading
a satchel of molluscs; the standing child kindling the fire
is re-imagined squatting and fanning the flames with
a blowpipe; an older, kneeling man evaluating shellfish
seems to have aged considerably in the print, the oyster he
has opened now disclosing a pearl. His foot dips into the
drawing's border, a delightful trompe-l'oeil detail missing

PROVENANCE
William Adolf Baillie-Grohman (1851–1921);
Mrs Baillie-Grohman, by descent; Sir Robert
Witt (1872–1952), acquired at Baillie-Grohman
sale, Sotheby's, London, 14 May 1923, lot 162;
Robert Witt Bequest, 1952

SELECTED LITERATURE
Baillie-Grohman 1899, pp. 158–66, fig. 8;
Courtauld Institute of Art 1956, no. 1633;

Bok and van Kammen 1977, pp. 517–18; Achilles
1982, pp. 161–72, fig. 159; Vannucci 1997,
no. 693, fig. 693.93; van Sasse van Ysselt 2002,
pp. 237–42, fig. 3; *New Hollstein* 2008 (Leeflang,
vol. 19), no. 491, fig. 491/1

SELECTED EXHIBITIONS
London 1927, no. 553; London 1977, no. 8;
London 1983, no. 35

Cesar Balbi venetiano in sou Reise den India di Levanta schat jnr isole de ormus Nossenese de perlen op dese manieren mahen op eerde nehmen

FIG. 42 Cornelius Galle I after Johannes Stradanus,
Indians fishing for pearls, 1600
Engraving, 207 × 265 mm
Rotterdam, Museum Boijmans Van Beuningen,
BdH 13203 (PK), Bequest Dr. J.C.J. Bierens de Haan 1951

from the engraving. Perhaps most unfortunate is the elimination of Stradanus's depictions of the lithe divers underwater.[2]

These disparities imply that the Courtauld sheet was not the final design, which is confirmed by the absence of incised lines.[3] Several elements formerly effaced are now discernible,[4] indicating Stradanus was still refining his composition. For example, a previously eliminated figure in the bow of the nearest boat re-emerges where the bodycolour deteriorates. Microscopic analysis of the sheet reveals traces of white bodycolour atop the now visible signature, which was presumably obscured to alter its position. Magnification also shows that the pentimenti were fairly developed when concealed. Such late changes and the sheet's high degree of finish suggest the Courtauld sheet was a rejected design.[5]

A study at the Cooper-Hewitt Museum, New York, anticipates the composition of the Courtauld sheet (fig. 43). Although rapidly executed, the primary elements – boats, campsite and underwater divers – are positioned as in the Courtauld drawing. Another Stradanus study in the Cooper-Hewitt features a feather-skirted man and three oyster shells accompanied by handwritten notes, indicating Stradanus's care in presenting an authentic rendering of the scene's details.[6] While these sketches elucidate the design's development, later modifications made by the artist versus those of the engraver cannot be distinguished since Stradanus's ultimate design for the print is lost.

Fortunately, recent research clarifies the subject, which was previously described as indigenous Americans pearl diving in the Caribbean.[7] Dorine van Sasse van Ysselt

FIG. 43 Johannes Stradanus,
Pearl fishing, c. 1596
Pen and brown ink, brush and
wash on cream laid paper,
105 × 147 mm
New York, Cooper-Hewitt,
National Design Museum,
Smithsonian Institution.
Museum purchase through gift
of various donors, 1901-39-2664

identified the Persian Gulf as the setting, following an inscription that was revealed following treatment in 1983.[8] Stradanus often added descriptions – in commingled Italian and Flemish – for his engravers in Antwerp.[9] Although incomplete, the caption refers to the Venetian Gasparo Balbi's 1580 expedition to Hormuz Island in the Strait of Hormuz. A dealer in precious stones, Balbi valued local pearl-fishing methods. *Viaggio all'Indie Orientali*, published in Venice in 1590, recounts his journey to Persia and India between 1579 and 1588. The Courtauld drawing follows Balbi's commentaries closely, from rudimentary pulley and breathing methods to the "mountains of oysters" in distinct piles.[10] A denizen of Italy when

Balbi's adventures were printed, Stradanus probably knew his chronicle.

The drawing's inscription is replaced by Latin phrases in the print. These correctly reference Balbi's reports of the "Indians" using oil to plug their noses and ears[11] but fail to include the Venetian's name and the location, which occasioned mistaken interpretations. The print's caption also implies a familiarity with Balbi's narrative, possibly deriving from Stradanus's missing script. While the absence of Stradanus's complete text and of his final design is frustrating, the recent discovery of the scene's actual setting adds significantly to our understanding of this remarkable drawing. M I

NOTES

1 Borghini (Ellis) 2007, pp. 177–281.
2 Additional differences are detailed in van Sasse van Ysselt 2002, p. 240.
3 London 1983, no. 35, p. 23; and van Sasse van Ysselt 2002, p. 240.
4 Mentioned in London 1977, p. 3.
5 London 1983, p. 23.
6 Bok-van Kammen 1977, p. 518.
7 Achilles 1982, pp. 164–65. Achilles publishes Galle's print, and this was probably her point of reference, not Stradanus's drawing.

8 Van Sasse van Ysselt 2002, pp. 237–42. The Courtauld treatment report from January 1983 cites removal of a "false margin", which apparently had previously hidden the inscription.
9 Benisovich 1956, p. 249.
10 Pinto 1962, pp. 120–22, reprints Balbi's description of pearl diving in Hormuz. See also van Sasse van Ysselt 2002, pp. 238–40.
11 Bok-van Kammen 1977, p. 517.

JOSEPH HEINTZ
Basel 1564–1609 Prague

19 Studies for *The Flight into Egypt*, c. 1595

Black, red and (traces of) white chalk, on laid paper, laid down twice; overall discolouration and
extensive foxing; water stain at top centre where an old inscription shows through from the verso;
numerous minor creases and a heavy diagonal fold across lower right corner; inscribed in pen
and brown ink at lower right: *Barocci* and stamped *BAR...*
269/267 × 212 mm

Samuel Courtauld Trust, D.1952.RW.2374

When this powerful sheet was exhibited in 2003 with
its traditional attribution to Giovanni Mannozzi, called
Giovanni da San Giovanni, a Florentine artist of the early
1600s, it seemed to fit well with the artist's style and could
be linked to other works.[1] But when one makes a wrong
attribution, as has been said, there are two artists one does
not understand, and this was the case: I owe both Giovanni
da San Giovanni and Joseph Heintz an apology.[2] The
polished sheen of the drapery, the facial type of Joseph,
and the button-nosed Virgin with high forehead are more
characteristic of Heintz than of Mannozzi, but one may
also note the old inscription demonstrating that someone
once thought it was by Federico Barocci.[3] The sheet is
Italianate in many ways: the mix of chalks is characteristic
of Florentine and Roman artists of the late 1500s and early
1600s, and the fleeting, soft outlines could easily derive
from an artist such as Taddeo Zuccaro or Francesco Vanni.
This particular composition of the Flight into Egypt,
with the figures tumbling forward, is strongly Venetian,
influenced by Jacopo Tintoretto's famous treatment of
1583–87 in the Scuola di San Rocco.[4]

It is thus no surprise to learn that Heintz spent many
years studying in Italy, principally Rome and Venice, in the
late 1580s and early 1590s (including time in Venice just
after Tintoretto had completed his work at the Scuola di
San Rocco).[5] Many of his copies still survive.[6] From which
artist Heintz adopted the Italianate mix of red and black

chalks is not clear, but this technique was widely used by
the peripatetic and influential Federico Zuccaro by the
1570s and was adopted by many followers.[7] By 1587, when
Heintz combined red and black chalks to draw a portrait
of Giambologna in Florence, this technique was on the
rise in his own practice.[8] Although it is difficult to date
the drawings from the main period of Heintz's production,
between 1590 and 1609, since his style did not evolve much
then, the present drawing probably dates from around –
or shortly after – the mid 1590s, to judge by other similarly
treated drawings.[9] An involuntary counterproof of part of
it appears on the back of a Heintz drawing mount in the
Metropolitan Museum of Art, New York.[10]

Since the sheet is clearly preparatory, it makes sense
to look for a related finished work of this scene. The only
recorded treatment of this subject by Heintz is an *"inventio"*
noted in the Grosse Stammbuch (Great Book of Arms) of
Philipp Hainhofer (1578–1647), a famed Augsburg-based
international cloth-merchant and art dealer. Hainhofer
mentioned in a letter to Duke Philipp II of Pommern-
Stettin "Heintz's inventio [in my book,] which depicts the
Flight into Egypt".[11] Although this extraordinary book
surfaced recently at auction, no trace of this finished
composition remains, and it must be assumed that it was
one of a number of pages Hainhofer is known to have
sold or given away before his death.[12] J B

PROVENANCE
Archibald George Blomefield Russell (b. 1879;
L. 2770a); Sir Robert Witt (1872–1952;
L. 2228b), acquired at Russell sale, Sotheby's,
London, 22 May 1928, lot 84; Robert Witt
Bequest, 1952

SELECTED LITERATURE
Zimmer 2007, pp. 80–83, no. 11, repr.;
Alsteens and Spira 2012, pp. 146–47

SELECTED EXHIBITION
Oxford and elsewhere 2003, pp. 116–17,
no. 59 (as Giovanni da San Giovanni)

NOTES

I am extremely grateful to Veronika Mader-Huemer for her help in cataloguing this drawing, and also to Stijn Alsteens.

1   Brooks in Oxford and elsewhere 2003, p. 116. At the opening of the Oxford 2003 exhibition, first Hugo Chapman, then Luca Baroni, Julien Stock and Stephen Ongpin each gently told me that they thought the drawing was by Heintz.
2   This statement, often cited in the world of connoisseurship, derives from Max Friedländer (Friedländer 1942, p. 177). I am grateful to Paul Joannides for pointing this out.
3   Other drawings by Heintz with previous attributions to the Italian school include Zimmer 1988, nos. A31 (Perino del Vaga); A32 (Cesare da Sesto); A50 (Benvenuto Cellini); A58 (Camillo Boccaccino/Camillo Procaccini); A60/61 (Cesare da Sesto); A68 (Anon. Italian 16th century); A71 (Bassano). Röttgen, p. 474, pointed out that a drawing (sold Christie's, London, 2 July 1991, lot 12, as attributed to Francesco Vanni) is by Heintz.
4   Noted also by Zimmer 2007, p. 83.
5   Zimmer 1988, pp. 23, 38–39, reconstructs Heintz's whereabouts – Rome, 1584–87; Venice, December 1587–February 1588; Rome, February 1592, November 1592–February 1594; Rome, March–October 1595.
6   Ibid., p. 60; for example, nos. A18, A19, A24, A31, A32 and A51.
7   Brooks in Oxford and elsewhere 2003, p. 33.
8   Zimmer 1988, p. 77, no. A16, Washington, DC, National Gallery of Art.
9   See, for example, ibid., nos. A63–A66.
10 Alsteens and Spira 2012, pp. 146–47.
11 Zimmer 1988, pp. 288–89, no. C32, and Doering 1896, p. 218, entry for 14 March 1612: "… dieses haintzen inventio [in meinem Buch] die flucht in Aegypten bedeuten soll". Zimmer notes this as a red- and black-chalk drawing, but the link is far from certain, and the book still contains at least one other drawing by Heintz (a portrait of Ferdinand Mattioli in red and black chalks).
12 The book was sold at Christie's, London, 27 June 2006, lot 263. Doering 1896 published letters concerning it, and Doering 1901 attempted a reconstruction, but Hainhofer's letters and the index he sent to Stettin are unclear at best.

113

ABRAHAM BLOEMAERT
Gorinchem 1566–1651 Utrecht

20 *Death and the Lovers, c. 1620–30*

Black chalk, pen and brown ink, brown and red washes, traces of white bodycolour,
on laid paper, laid down; minor foxing; two pinholes at upper left; later framing line
in pen and brown ink

Verso: inscribed in graphite *PNº 42 Death by Ab Bloemaert*
211 × 167/169 mm

Samuel Courtauld Trust, D.1952.RW.3744

Despite the drawing's graceful execution – lyrical figures
(characteristic of Bloemaert's Mannerist works) and the
delicate modulation of washes, this is no chivalric scene of
courtship. Mesmerised by his lover's exposed breasts and
comely face, the soldier is oblivious to the skeletal vestiges
of her legs and the figure of Death with poised arrow. The
mourning skeletons, smoky flames and winged devil add
to the macabre impression of this enigmatic image.[1]

Jaap Bolten entitles this sheet *The Mortal Hazards of
the Battlefield* in his catalogue raisonné of Bloemaert's
drawings.[2] He identifies the woman as *Vita brevis*, though
she lacks the attributes prescribed by Cesare Ripa.[3] The
lute, according to Bolten, represents knowledge, with the
soldier's back to it construed as his "turning away from
Knowledge". While this is an accepted meaning for the
instrument, another interpretation seems more appropriate
here. The lute's waning notes, together with the mirror,
hourglass and smoke, acknowledge the transience of
human life. Complex allegories and *vanitas* pictures are
rare in Bloemaert's oeuvre, though by no means unknown.[4]
Bolten's title emphasises the soldier's occupation even if
he seems more intent on his romantic encounter than
on the battlefield.

The drawing probably derives from an earlier visual
tradition equating illicit love and death. A woodcut by Urs
Graf, for example, shows two soldiers who meet a coquettish,
lavishly dressed woman (fig. 44). Their protuberant, phallic
weaponry reveals their excitement much like the soldier's

FIG. 44 Urs I Graf, *Two mercenaries
and a woman with Death in a tree*, 1524
Woodcut, 204 × 117 mm
The Cleveland Museum of Art,
Dudley P. Allen Fund 1942.118

PROVENANCE
Leonard Gordon Duke (1890–1971), London (?);
unknown collector (E. A. Philips?; L. 1299a);
Sir Robert Witt (1872–1952; L. 2228b), acquired
from Colnaghi; Robert Witt Bequest, 1952

SELECTED LITERATURE
Courtauld Institute of Art 1956, no. 3744;
Bernt 1979, no. 70; Bolten 2007, no. 602

SELECTED EXHIBITIONS
Manchester 1962, no. 17; London 1991, no. 10

FIG. 45 Abraham Bloemaert,
Cupid and the maiden
(The Hazards of Love), c. 1620–30
Pen and brown ink, brown wash
over black chalk, heightened with
white bodycolour on paper,
209 × 164 mm
Hamburg, Hamburger Kunsthalle,
inv. no. 52327

strategically placed sword in the Courtauld drawing. Also excited is Death, who, armed with his ubiquitous ebbing hourglass, is depicted as a provocateur leering at the lovers in both works.

In the Courtauld sheet, the woman's costume and bared breasts suggest she is a courtesan. Soldiers were partnered frequently with prostitutes, probably Bloemaert's reason for attiring the man in such a manner. Notwithstanding the female figure's half-hearted attempt to stop her suitor, she is Death's pawn, luring the soldier to ruin. Death's arrow is a symbol of pestilence and God's wrath and alludes to the man's possible physical disease and certain moral death resulting from his ghoulish tryst.[5] An image denouncing lust – a mortal sin – would be in accordance with Bloemaert's staunch religious beliefs.[6] A devout Catholic, he accepted surreptitious Church commissions despite Utrecht's official denouncement of Catholicism in favour of Reformation doctrines.

Another drawing by Bloemaert likewise admonishes reckless love (fig. 45). Bolten entitled it *The Hazards of Love*.[7] He postulates that the sheet, featuring a female figure lounging against a knoll accompanied by a lute, a

book and a cupid with readied arrow, might be a pendant to the Courtauld work. Bolten again interprets the lute and book as symbols of wisdom, surmising that the young woman is virtuously turning away from love and towards knowledge. She shows little interest in the objects, however. Her ambiguous posture could be read instead as an abandonment of knowledge in favour of love. The lute, which had lascivious connotations from the fifteenth through the seventeenth centuries, is probably a sexual metaphor in both drawings. Julia Craig-McFeeley notes, "The Flemish for lute, *luit*, was also the word for vagina, explaining a host of pictures involving prostitutes".[8] She further notes that Venetian courtesans often played the instrument, making it a recognised "badge of their trade".[9] The woman's dreamy gaze and revealing décolleté suggest she is ripe for the cupid's imminent strike.

When considering whether the drawings are pendants, Bolten cites the complex subjects (noting they "stand alone" among Bloemaert's allegorical drawings),[10] their very close (though not identical) size and like media. The repetition of certain compositional elements – such as the lute and the knoll on which both female figures are

propped – further strengthens his proposal. Moreover, the analogous positioning of the cupid and Devil figures in the Courtauld and Hamburg drawings would be significant if the sheets were intended to be viewed together, since these figures were often conflated.[11] William Bradford cites this merged imagery when identifying the skeleton in the Courtauld picture as "both Death and malign Cupid".[12] Love and Death, inexplicably intertwined companions, employ a common weapon – the arrow – with which they deal their lethal blows.[13] Bolten's proposal requires additional examination but cannot be dismissed. His characterisation of Bloemaert's allegories as "reminders

of the right way to achieve the eternal salvation of the soul" aptly describes the objective of these images.[14] Related thematically, similar in scale, and featuring shared elements, these complex allegorical narratives may have been pendant designs for unrealised prints, warning of the dangers of succumbing to temptation.

For the soldier in the Courtauld drawing, the result of licentious behaviour is catastrophic. Upon consummation, the vulture-like Devil will claim its prey, leaving the weeping mourners to lament the loss of their paradisiacal world and the iniquitous lover's soul. MI

NOTES

1 I thank Allison Deutsch for helping me gather material for this entry.
2 Bolten 2007, pp. 211–12, no. 602.
3 These include a garland, rose-branch, fish and insect of brief life span: Ripa (Buscaroli) 1999, pp. 475–76.
4 Bolten 2007, pp. 209–13; and Röthlisberger 1991, pp. 20–27.
5 Boeckl 2000, pp. 46–48.
6 St Petersburg, FL, 2001, pp. 17 and 26.

7 Bolten 2007, p. 212. The sheet was entitled simply *Amor und das Mädchen* in Hamburg 2011, pp. 112–13.
8 Craig-McFeeley 2002, pp. 300–01.
9 *Ibid.*, p. 300.
10 Bolten 2007, p. 212.
11 Guthke 1999, pp. 106–07.
12 London 1991, p. 28.
13 Ann Arbor 1976, p. 6.
14 Bolten 2007, p. 7.

JUSEPE DE RIBERA
Játiva, *c.* 1590–1652 Naples

21 *Man tied to a tree, and a figure resting, c.* 1630–35

Red chalk, on laid paper; later framing line in dark-brown ink;
horizontal flattened fold at centre; foxing, slight discolouration,
localised staining on all sides and upper edge centre, some abrasion;
inscribed in dark-brown ink at lower left (similar to framing line) *spagnoletto*
241 × 150 mm

Samuel Courtauld Trust, D.1952.RW.2505

Many of Ribera's extant drawings represent male figures in scenes of torture, in physical extremity, or in some way deprived of physical liberty – typically, male saints prepared for martyrdom.[2] *Man tied to a tree*, one of the most gentle in mood of these drawings, has traditionally been interpreted as Saint Bartholomew awaiting his martyrdom:[3] he was flayed alive, an ordeal Ribera represented on various occasions.[4]

It is evident, however, that the bearded old man tied to a tree trunk by lengths of rope, his disproportionately long arm stretched out to the left, lacks the attributes by which he may be so specifically identified. His gesture could be intended to be rhetorical, interpretable as beseeching, reaching out for help. At lower right, his back near the base of the tree, another figure sits, hunched over in a pose that implies a lack of awareness or concern about the restrained man. The absence of narrative detail emphasises the isolation of the figure in the tree, and the projection of the blasted tree's single branch into the space above adds to the complexity of the scene. In his drawings, Ribera's figures often seem remote, in a state of existential suspension that is at once serene and unsettling. This impression is strengthened by Ribera's refined judgment of the negative space defined by his drawn characters. The scale of the figures on the page creates in the viewer an illusion of encountering Ribera's men and women as if

by chance in a vast expanse of emptiness. The relationship between the figures here remains ambiguous: are they part of the same scene? Were they studied from life?

Throughout his career Ribera produced drawings, although these were not primarily connected with painted compositions but, rather, "autonomous and independent".[5] Thematically and conceptually, however, the subjects of his paintings and drawings are related. It is possible to hypothesise various functions for his drawings. Some, such as the Courtauld sheet, may record his reflections on physical suffering and spiritual conflict. Although such sheets may not have been connected with larger-scale commissions, they might yet be seen as preparatory to the artist's interpretation if not necessarily his compositions dealing with physical suffering. Other sheets, such as the signed and dated *Saint Albert* (fig. 46), make a more public statement, weighting the concepts of authorship, chronicity and finish, imparting a sense of being a completed essay in composition, a sense missing in the ambiguous, unsigned sheets.

Ribera employed red chalk on many occasions, varying the handling. Highly finished composition drawings from the 1620s such as the *Saint Albert* of 1626 have a full range of internal shading and are treated in a pictorial way, with the half-tones carefully laid in, the contours and details described, not implied, with chalk. By about 1630 this

PROVENANCE
Possibly sale of vicomte de Castelruiz, Christie's, London, 27 April 1846, lot 97; André de Hevesy (d. 1952), acquired at Sotheby's, London, 20 June 1932;[1] Sir Robert Witt (1872–1952; L. 2228b), received as a gift; Robert Witt Bequest, 1952

SELECTED LITERATURE
Courtauld Institute of Art 1956, p. 162; Mahoney 1965, no. 71 n. 4; Paris 1967a, under no. 20; Brown 1972, p. 5, no. 3; Finaldi 1995, p. 296, no. 69; Véliz 2011, pp. 232–34, no. 79; Payne 2012, *passim*

SELECTED EXHIBITIONS
London 1958a, no. 34; Barnard Castle 1962, no. 98; Adelaide 1968, no. 22; Princeton 1973, no. 18; London 1978, no. 13; Nottingham 1980, no. 26; New York 1992a, p. 435, no. D.24; London 2011a, no. 23

Spagnoletto

119

FIG. 46 José de Ribera, *Saint Albert tied to a tree*, 1626
Red chalk, 232 × 170 mm
London, British Museum, 1850,0713.4

FIG. 47 José de Ribera, *Saint Sebastian*, c. 1630
Red chalk with pen and brown ink, 173 × 124 mm
The Cleveland Museum of Art,
Delia. E. Holden Fund, inv. no. 1997.53

approach gave way to a less rigorous treatment, such as that seen in *Saint Sebastian* (fig. 47). Here the medium is used more freely. The absence of marks seems as expressive as the areas drawn with a light, slightly dematerialised touch, and more open forms are defined by subtle shades of contrast. Yet for all the lack of high finish in sheets like *Saint Sebastian* and the Courtauld *Man tied to a tree*, Ribera nevertheless took great care in balancing the weight of contours and their role in conveying the plasticity of his figures. An example is the careful emphasis given to

passages like the right side of the torso of the figure in the tree, where the artist strengthened the chalk line where the nude body is covered by a loincloth; visually, the line thus weighted counterbalances the long, extended arm. The Courtauld sheet compares closely with the Cleveland *Saint Sebastian* in handling, proportion of the figure and the compositional focus on a single arm and hand reaching into the void – a gesture that seems to signify the extreme vulnerability of these captive men. zv

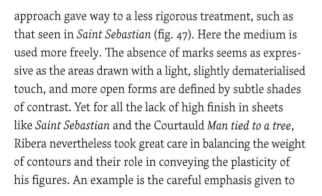

NOTES

1 Most lots in this sale contained multiple drawings, not all described; none of the described sheets represents this subject. Lots 3 and 17 were purchased by Hevesy (also spelled 'Hevesi'), who, according to Witt records, gave this drawing to Sir Robert Witt (Witt card file, The Courtauld Gallery). André de Hevesy was active in Paris as a dealer, writer and collector.

2 See Princeton 1973, nos. 33–37, 39–41, 44–47, 51, 55, 58–59, 62–63.

3 Paris 1967a, pp. 13–14, nos. 20, 21, 23. For a more recent interpretation of the depiction of suffering in the graphic works of Ribera, see Payne 2012, *passim*. This scholar has also proposed in a conference paper ('Drawn to Spain', Courtauld Institute Research Forum, 14 January 2012) that the sitting man is

defecating in a chamber pot – which it is strange he should use outside. It is possible, though, that his activity is furtive.

4 See, for example, Jusepe de Ribera, *The Martyrdom of Saint Bartholomew*, oil on canvas, 145 × 216 cm, Florence, Galleria Palatina, Palazzo Pitti, inv. no. 19.

5 Mena in New York 1992a, p. 196.

GUERCINO (GIOVANNI FRANCESCO BARBIERI)

Cento 1591–1666 Bologna

22 *A child seen from behind, standing between his mother's knees, c. 1625*

Red chalk with stumping, on laid paper; some abrasion resulting from the taking of
a counterproof; several scored marks in drapery along child's body; rope-line along right edge;
inscribed in graphite at bottom left corner *4*
301/305 × 213 /211 mm

Samuel Courtauld Trust, D.1952.RW.1327

Drawn on a rough, fibrous buff-coloured paper, this image encapsulates the magic of fine draughtsmanship, in which a sense of three-dimensional reality can be conjured from a two-dimensional sheet of blank paper. A child stands between his mother's legs, supporting himself with one arm, while she firmly grasps him by the other. The figure of the mother is only briefly sketched in; a few lines depict her upper body and head, and only two strokes outline the pooled drapery on the floor. Such lines were probably the beginning of the entire composition, but to place the child firmly in space the artist created patches of dense darkness for the recess between the knees. Made by repeatedly hatched strokes with the chalk pressed hard, these areas offset the child's body, much of which consists of bright, blank reserves of paper. The slight valley of the spine is conveyed by delicate traces of red chalk spread with a stump (a tightly rolled piece of paper or leather that was tapped on chalk to disperse the particles gently). Use of a stump with red chalk was not recommended by some artists' manuals because it lightened the chalk's colour, making it more orange. Guercino turned this to his advantage by stumping the left side of the child's body, his legs and his left arm, using the warmer, more orange tone for the skin that contrasted well with the cooler, darker, unstumped chalk of the drapery folds around it.

The stump is also used effectively in the child's right leg and left arm to convey subtle effects of reflected light.

Pentimenti around the head of the child introduce an element of motion that is lacking in the lower body, despite the unstable pose. The lost profile of the right cheek encloses an earlier line to the left, suggesting that the head with its tousled hair was originally intended to be tilted further to the left. Movement is also implied by several strokes in the right shoulder and the gripping hand. The sense of realistic spontaneity conveyed by the drawing is entirely convincing, and the scene must have been taken from life, or at least begun from life. So credible is the image that the viewer happily puts aside the innate improbability of capturing such a restless and mobile subject as a small child in such a carefully worked drawing as this.

Although Guercino was renowned for his many sketches of genre scenes, he principally used drawings to make detailed studies of poses, drapery and characters for his oil paintings. The likely purpose of this sheet depends on its relationship to a drawing in Frankfurt, much more briefly sketched, but showing an infant in a similar position between his mother's legs and clearly nursing at her breast (fig. 48).[1] Nicholas Turner and Carol Plazzotta have proposed that the Courtauld and Frankfurt sheets

PROVENANCE
Casa Gennari; John Bouverie (*c.* 1723–1750); Anne Bouverie (d. 1757), by descent; John Hervey (d. 1764), by descent; Christopher Hervey (d. 1786), by descent; Miss Elizabeth Bouverie (d. 1798); Sir Charles Middleton, later 1st Baron Barham (1726–1813), by bequest; Sir Gerard Noel Noel, 2nd Baron Barham (1759–1838), by descent; Sir Charles Noel, 3rd Baron Barham and 1st Earl of Gainsborough (1781–1866), by descent; 3rd Earl of Gainsborough, by descent; Sir Robert Witt (1872–1952; L. 2228b), acquired by F.R. Meatyard at Earl of Gainsborough sale, Christie's, London, 27 July 1922, lot 81; Robert Witt Bequest, 1952

SELECTED LITERATURE
Russell 1923, p. 38, pl. VII; Courtauld Institute of Art 1956, p. 75

SELECTED EXHIBITIONS
London 1937, no. 26; London 1958a, no. 28; Auckland 1960, no. 32; Manchester 1962, no. 81; Bologna 1969, no. 187; London 1977b, no. 43; London 1991, no. 42; London 1991b, no. 44; Los Angeles and London 2006, no. 9

FIG. 48 Guercino,
Child suckled by his mother
Red chalk, 293 × 191 mm
Frankfurt, Städelsches
Kunstinstitut,
inv. no. 448

FIG. 49 Guercino,
The Holy Family
Black, red and brown
chalk, blue pastel, with
grey wash, 356 × 267 mm
New York, Morgan
Library and Museum,
Gift of J.P. Morgan, Jr,
1924, inv. no. I, 99

Whatever the subject, the sheet remains one of the most famous drawings in the Courtauld collection, and it is a highlight among the superb and representative group of drawings by the artist housed there.[5] Nicknamed 'Guercino' (Little squinter) after the squint he apparently acquired in a childhood accident, the artist was a prolific draughtsman, whose drawings are scattered far and wide. During his long and productive career, Guercino ran an effective studio, one that he inherited from his master Benedetto Gennari the Elder (1563–1610) at the age of only nineteen. Although Guercino never married and had no children himself, his sister Lucia married one of Gennari's sons, Ercole, in 1628. Guercino's two nephews, Benedetto the Younger and Cesare, joined his workshop. After his death, the nephews continued to run the studio and published prints of some of their uncle's famous drawings. J B

are closely related and are both preparatory to the same project in the mid 1620s – perhaps early ideas for the *Rest on the Flight into Egypt* frescoed in a lunette in the cupola of Piacenza Cathedral.[2] In that scene Joseph holds the infant Christ, who reaches out to his mother as she prepares to breast-feed him.

Turner and Plazzotta further suggested that both studies may relate instead to a highly finished presentation drawing in the Morgan Library and Museum that features the Christ Child standing at the casually offered breast of his mother, while Joseph looks on (fig. 49).[3] While the link between the Frankfurt and Morgan sheets seems clear, a direct connection with the Courtauld drawing is possible but less certain. The absence of a breast, lack of focus on the spatial relationship between the mother's upper body and the child, and the more awkward stooping pose of the mother perhaps indicate instead that she is simply about to lift him into her lap.[4]

NOTES
1 London 1991b, p. 74, fig. 9.
2 *Ibid.*; Piacenza fresco repr. Salerno 1988, no. 114L.
3 Cambridge, MA, and elsewhere 1991, p. 57, no. 23, pl. 23.
4 Brooks in Los Angeles and London 2006, p. 39. This now seems less certain to me, but the child in the Courtauld drawing is clearly less engaged than those in the Frankfurt or Morgan drawings.
5 Exhibited in Los Angeles and London 2006. For more on Guercino's drawings, see London 1991b, Mahon and Turner 1989, and Brooks in Los Angeles and London 2006.

PETER PAUL RUBENS
Siegen, Westphalia 1577–1640 Antwerp

23 *Head of the Farnese Hercules, c. 1608–10*

Verso: Studies of the head and profile of the Farnese Hercules,
seen from a lower viewpoint

Black chalk, heightened with white chalk, on grey laid paper with red chalk offset at bottom;
slight overall undulation and discolouration; localised light brown stains; vertical crease parallel with
right edge; small loss at top left corner inscribed in pen and brown ink at bottom centre *AVDÿck*

Verso: water stains at upper right and bottom right corner showing through to recto
363/366 × 245 mm

WATERMARK
Monogram JM surmounted by a 4+ within a circle

Samuel Courtauld Trust, D.1978.PG.53

In 1540 excavators in the ancient Baths of Caracalla had
unearthed a huge marble head, which was followed, six
years later, by a muscular torso. These were recognised
as fragments of a Roman copy of a lost Greek masterpiece
and moved to the Palazzo Farnese, the family palace of the
Dukes of Parma that was being magnificently remodelled
by the Farnese pope, Paul III. There the statue was
restored to full height with legs created by Giacomo della
Porta, a protégé of Michelangelo. Michelangelo himself
designed a façade to showcase the work, together with
another monumental marble Hercules.

The statue soon became one of the sights of Rome,
contemplated by visitors, drawn by artists and reproduced
in prints.[1] Its presence helped to generate an international
interest in Hercules as a model of heroic masculinity that
continued into the seventeenth century. Rubens encountered the statue during his stays in Rome between 1601 and
1608, but the position from which the head is observed
on this sheet suggests that the drawing was not made
in situ. The giant statue, set on a plinth, towered above its
beholders, and it seems more likely that the drawings
were made from one of the many heads and busts of the

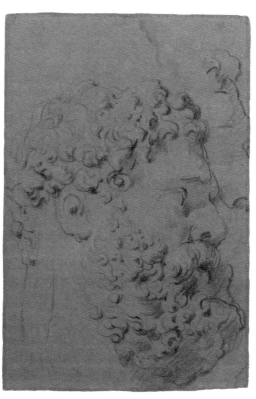

CAT. NO. 23 VERSO

PROVENANCE
Private collection, Ireland; Leo Franklyn,
London; Alfred Scharf (1900–1965), acquired
from Franklyn, 1951; Count Antoine Seilern
(1901–1978), acquired from Scharf, 21 January
1951; Princes Gate Bequest, 1978

SELECTED LITERATURE
Seilern 1955, p. 85, no. 53; Seilern 1971,
pp. 35–36; Muller 1982, p. 236, fig. 2; van der
Meulen 1994, vol. 2, pp. 44–46

SELECTED EXHIBITIONS
London 1989, no. 27; London 1991, no. 61;
London 2005a, no. 28

124

FIG. 50 After Peter Paul Rubens,
*The head of the Farnese Hercules
compared with a bull and a lion*
Pen and brown ink, 210 × 158 mm
London, The Courtauld Gallery,
MS.1978.PG.1, fol. 51

figure that were carved in marble and cast in plaster.[2] The figure was one of the canonical exemplars of an antiquity that Rubens considered, in his fragmentary theoretical text *De imitatione statuarum*, to be more physically perfect and literally larger than contemporary life.[3] It was the prototype for a head and seemingly a statue of the hero that presided over the garden of Rubens's magnificent house in Antwerp, and for the muscular male characters that recur throughout his painted oeuvre.[4]

Rubens drew the *Farnese Hercules* in many different ways. Here the concern is with the head, drawn in profile on the recto and from below on the verso.[5] Like the drawing of Helena Fourment (cat. no. 24), this sheet probably formed part of the artist's archive, from which he developed his paintings. In other studies Rubens considered the statue as a whole or sought out the inherent qualities that, according to classical authorities, gave the figure its strong character.[6] Count Seilern's bequest to The Courtauld included a close copy of Rubens's lost pocketbook, which contains a number of analytical drawings of the sculpture in pen and ink.[7] In one of them (fig. 50), the head is compared

to a bull and a lion, in accordance with ancient – and fashionable – physiognomic principles whereby perceived facial resemblances between human beings and animals indicate similarities in temperament or character.[8] One of the surviving sheets from the original pocketbook proposes the cube, a geometric figure that Plato associated with the element of earth and with stability, as the structuring principle of the head of the *Farnese Hercules* (fig. 51).[9]

Here the subtle use of the chalk medium, shifting from the most delicate traces to dense, firm strokes and smudges, produces a play of light that animates the head. A powerful sense of human presence and nuanced expression is created (especially on the recto) by intense black marks and subtle white heightening that carefully delineate the structure and position of the cheek, brow and facial features. Yet neither the drawing on the recto nor the one on the verso could be mistaken for images from life. The choice of rough, light-grey paper and the open texture of the chalk invoke the visual and tactile proximity of unpolished or weathered stone as much as the softness of skin. The curved chalk marks of different intensity describe the deeply drilled locks, ear, eye socket and nostril of a sculpture even as they imbue them with vitality and sensory cognition. Moreover, the erectness of the neck, which is set against the strong horizontal of the brooding brow, the squared-off beard and the chunky profile seem informed by Rubens's understanding of the head of the *Farnese Hercules* as "the proof of the cube".[10] These same characteristics transform the pensive character of the sculpture into a depiction of immense physical and mental power. JW

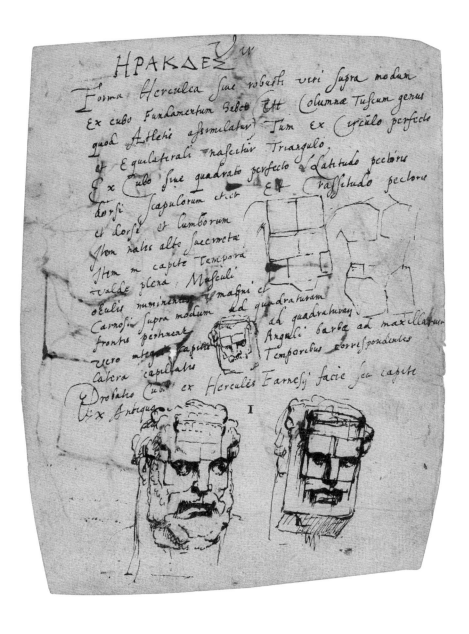

FIG. 51 Peter Paul Rubens,
Studies of the *Farnese Hercules*,
c. 1601–02
Pen and brown ink, 198 × 156 mm
(maximum)
London, The Courtauld Gallery,
D.1978.PG.427

NOTES

1 It was engraved by Jacob Bos for the
Speculum Romanae Magnificentiae, Rome,
Antonio Lafreri, 1562.

2 Count Seilern dated the drawing to *c.* 1606–
08, assuming that it was made in Rome,
but Van der Meulen 1994, vol. 2, p. 45,
states that Rubens was more concerned with
physiognomical studies and comparisons
after his return to Antwerp in 1608. The
closely related head in the right wing of
Rubens's *Raising of the Cross* in Antwerp
Cathedral, 1610–11, suggests that the drawing
could have been made before that date.

3 Muller 1982, pp. 231–32; London 2005a,
p. 92.

4 Muller 1989, pp. 31, 41, 153, 155; Antwerp
2004, p. 199.

5 On the verso what seems to be a second
attempt at the outline of the nose and brow
at the upper right is cut off by the edge of
the page, suggesting that the sheet might
have been reduced in size.

6 Muller 1982, p. 236.

7 On Rubens's pocketbook, see Jaffé with
Bradley in London 2005a, pp. 21–28; Jaffé
2010, pp. 94–98.

8 Compare Giacomo della Porta, *De Humana
Physiognomonia Libri IIII*, first published
1586, with many subsequent editions.

9 Muller 1982, p. 236, citing Plato's *Timaeus*
(Loeb) 1929, p. 135.

10 From Rubens's Latin inscription on fig. 51.
For the full text and English translation,
see Braham in London 1989, pp. 52–53.

PETER PAUL RUBENS
Siegen, Westphalia 1577–1640 Antwerp

24 *Helena Fourment, c. 1630–31*

Black, red and white chalk, on laid paper; retouched with pen and brown ink
in some details of the head and headdress, white bodycolour following the contour
of the figure, now darkened; figure cut out and laid down on coarser laid paper tinted grey;
some foxing; vertical band of light brown staining down the right side of the figure;
numerous small tears and creases repaired
610 × 550 mm

Samuel Courtauld Trust, D.1978.PG.64

The model for this stunning drawing was Helena Fourment, whom the artist married in December 1630, after the death of his first wife, Isabella Brant, in 1626.[1] The drawing establishes an eroticised relationship between the figure and the beholder, who stands in for the artist. The subtlety and variety of the red- and black-chalk marks, with graceful touches of white, create a body that seems to vibrate with delicate energy. Poised between inside and outside, Helena seems about to put on or divest herself of her outer garment. A bare hand reaches up to catch the mantle that would have been suspended from the projection on the cap, enveloping the whole body. The face is thus unveiled as a revelation; its unwavering gaze follows the beholder's every move.

Within the Christian humanist culture to which the artist belonged, the drawing would have been understood to combine a portrayal of the artist's lovely young wife with an evocation of the perfect beauty of Pictura, which all artists desired and worked to attain. Painting's Christian myth of origin, in which Saint Luke depicted his miraculous encounter with the youthful Virgin Mary, was particularly powerful in the Netherlands.[2] For Lucius Annaeus Seneca, the Roman Stoic philosopher whose thought was of great interest to humanists in the early seventeenth century, love was the highest motive for art, encompassing both honour and profit.[3]

For at least a century Netherlandish artists had embodied these ideals in the forms of their wives.[4] Thus Rubens's drawing, although seemingly observed from a lived encounter, was mediated by concepts of an ideal yet natural beauty that was associated with the Virgin Mary. A spherical face with large, widely spaced eyes and a mass of light-coloured hair was a feminine type that Rubens had developed long before his marriage to Fourment, especially in painting the Assumption of the Virgin.[5] The iconography of the drawing is not contingent, either; in 1625–26 Rubens had portrayed his first wife in a very similar way, fingering what seems to be a prayer book and reaching for her veil (fig. 52). In the portrait of Isabella, the devotional context is more explicit; the figure is set against a pillar and a cloth of honour, like a Virgin in a church.

At the same time, the slight déshabillé, proximity and direct look in the Courtauld drawing shift the figure into a more informal space, in which it seems possible not only to worship visually but to touch. This intimacy becomes

PROVENANCE
Prince Charles Alexandre de Lorraine (1712–1780); comte de Cuypers de Rijmenam (1760–1773); Schamp d'Averschoot; Fanu (?), acquired at Averschoot sale, Van Regemorter, Ghent, 14ff. September 1840, lot 192; Robert Stayner Holford (1808–1892); Sir George Lindsay Holford (1860–1926), by descent; Knoedler, acquired at Holford sale, Christie's, London, 17ff. May 1928, lot 3; with E.J. van Wisselingh (b. 1838), Amsterdam, in 1932; Count Antoine Seilern (1901–1978), acquired from Zatzenstein-Matthiesen, London, 1934; Princes Gate Bequest, 1978

SELECTED LITERATURE
Seilern 1955, p. 102, no. 64; Vlieghe 1987, no. 100a and p. 102 under no. 100b; Petherbridge 2010, p. 132, pl. 83

SELECTED EXHIBITION
London 1983, no. 57; London 1989, no. 40

FIG. 52 Peter Paul Rubens,
Isabella Brandt, 1625–26
Oil on panel, 86 × 62 cm
Florence, Galleria degli Uffizi

FIG. 53 Peter Paul Rubens, *Young woman looking down* (*Helena Fourment*), 1628
Black and red chalk heightened with white, retouched with pen and brown ink, 414 × 287 mm
Florence, Galleria degli Uffizi, inv. no. 1043E

more apparent when this sheet is connected with two other exceptionally large drawings of a young woman that correspond closely to it in technique, appearance, and dress. Helen Braham has argued that these works all represent the same woman and relate to the same series of sittings.[6] In the other drawings, which are in the Uffizi in Florence (fig. 53) and the Museum Boijmans Van Beuningen in Rotterdam, attention is concentrated on the exposed flesh rather than the dress, and the cap, mantle, glove, book and pearl necklace are not included. In *Helena Fourment*, tactility is evoked by the way in which the fingers toy with the veil and the book. It is also evident in the mark making. The enticing surfaces of rosy, silky smooth skin are felt, as well as imitated, in fine strokes of red chalk, and black chalk marks ranging from the most delicate touches to bolder thrusts evoke the various fabrics. In this context,

the proper left hand in its outsize glove is imaginable as a surrogate for the hand of the artist himself.[7]

The monumental size and virtuosity of *Helena Fourment* have justified the suggestion that it is an independent work, while others have considered it a preparatory study for a full-length portrait now in the Musée du Louvre, in which the dress and conception of the subject are similar.[8] Perhaps these arguments are not as incompatible as they seem. Rubens's *cantoor*, the private room in his house in which he kept his drawings, oil sketches and other valuable objects, was both a space in which works such as *Helena Fourment* could have been shown to privileged visitors and an archive from which the artist drew to create new work.[9] In this space, *Helena Fourment* lies at the heart not only of a particular portrait but of the kind of beauty that became closely identified with Rubens through the 1630s.[10] J W

NOTES

1 Helena Fourment was the sixteen-year-old daughter of the silk and tapestry merchant Daniel Fourment.

2 Filedt Kok 2006, with extensive bibliography.

3 *On Benefits* (Lodge) 1899, p. 75 (Book 2, chap. 33). For the importance of neo-Stoicism in Rubens's circle, see Morford 1991 and Miller 2000. On the aphorism 'Love produces art' (*'liefde baart kunst'*) in the Netherlands see De Jongh in Haarlem 1986, pp. 57–59.

4 Woodall 2007, pp. 444–54.

5 For example, *The Assumption of the Virgin*, c. 1611–14, Vienna, Kunsthistorisches Museum, and *The Assumption of the Virgin*, c. 1622–25, The Hague, Mauritshuis.

6 London 1989, p. 35. New York 2005, p. 210, connects the Uffizi drawing to an altarpiece dated 1628.

7 Compare the gloved hand of the artist in *Self-portrait*, c. 1635, Vienna, Kunst-historisches Museum, and in *Rubens, Helena Fourment and Clara Johanna Rubens*, New York, The Metropolitan Museum of Art. This idea develops arguments made in

relation to Albrecht Dürer in Koerner 1993, pp. 139–59.

8 Seilern 1955, vol. 1, no. 64; Seilern 1971, no. 64; Vlieghe 1987, p. 102, nos. 100a, 100b.

9 Muller 1989, pp. 21–22.

10 A letter from the Cardinal-Infante Ferdinand to Philip IV, 27 February 1639, identifies Helena Fourment with the Venus in Rubens's *Judgement of Paris*, 1639, Madrid, Museo del Prado: Rooses and Reulens 1887–1909, vol. 6 (1909), p. 228, DCCCVXVI.

REMBRANDT VAN RIJN
Leiden 1606–1669 Amsterdam

25 *Saskia (?) sitting up in bed, holding a child, c. 1635*

Red chalk, on laid paper; later framing line in graphite, partially trimmed;
slight undulation, minor loss at top left corner and lower right edge.

Verso inscribed in graphite at lower left corner *5*

141 × 106 mm

Samuel Courtauld Trust, D.1978.PG.183

The adage *'cherchez la femme'* might, in Rembrandt's
case, be meaningfully changed to *'cherchez sa femme'*, so
regularly has the image of his wife Saskia been sought in
his representations of youngish women, with or without
children, drawn, etched or painted in the 1630s. Here,
a young woman, dressed in a gown tied with a ribbon
around her neck and wearing a frontlet bound around her
forehead supposed to prevent wrinkles after confinement,[1]
looks out from behind the bed curtain; she clasps a baby in
swaddling clothes lovingly and protectingly in both arms.
The drawing might eloquently stand as a universal image
of mother and child.

Working in two stages, Rembrandt laid in the general
composition with red chalk and then, with darker lines,
picked out such details as the headdress and the ribbon
tied around her neck. Red chalk was a medium that the
artist used relatively often in his early years but abandoned
in the early 1640s.

Saskia van Uylenburgh (1612–1642) was the daughter
of a former burgomaster of Leeuwarden in Friesland. In
1632, by that time an orphan, she moved to Amsterdam,
where several members of her family, including her

cousin Hendrick van Uylenburgh, an art dealer, were
living. Saskia must have met the young artist in his house,
where Rembrandt was residing. Their marriage in 1633,
when she was twenty-one, was followed by the early
deaths of their first three children: Rumbartus, baptised
on 15 December 1635, died two months later; the first
Cornelia, baptised 22 July 1638, died three weeks later;
and the second Cornelia, baptised 29 July 1640, died two
weeks later. Only Titus, born in September 1641, lived
beyond infancy.

It is not without reason that the mother in the
Courtauld drawing is generally identified as Saskia. The
documented image of her is the betrothal drawing in
silverpoint, inscribed with her name and the occasion,
that Rembrandt made in 1633.[2] All other supposed identifi-
cations of her are, with varying degrees of conviction,
dependent on this likeness. In the 1630s Rembrandt
produced a number of drawings of a woman lying in
bed, among which the present study, given her general
appearance and the intimacy of the occasion, can probably
be accepted as depicting Saskia. Another very similar
representation, also in red chalk, of her sitting up in bed

PROVENANCE
James Harris, Earl of Malmesbury (?); Viscount
Fitzharris, by descent; Count Antoine Seilern
(1901–1978), acquired by Colnaghi for Seilern at
Fitzharris sale, Christie's, London, 21 April 1950,
lot 95; Princes Gate Bequest, 1978

SELECTED LITERATURE
Benesch 1954–57, vol. 2, no. 280a; Seilern 1961,
no. 183; White 1964, pp. 34–35; Kitson 1969,

pp. 15, 90; Seilern 1971, no. 183; White 1984,
p. 43; Schatborn 1985, p. 28 n. 1 under no. 12;
Slive 2009, p. 85

SELECTED EXHIBITIONS
London 1981, no. 143; London 1983a, no. 8;
London 1991, no. 58; Edinburgh and London
2001, no. 48 (London only)

but without a baby in her arms can be seen in a drawing made about the same time, in the Rijksprentenkabinet, Amsterdam (fig. 54), but since she wears different nightclothes, it cannot have been done on the same occasion.

In view of the dates of birth of the children, only the first, Rumbartus, can be considered as the child represented here. At that time the family was living in a house in the Nieuwe Doelenstraat, near the river Amstel. In 1636 the infant was buried under 'a small stone' between the pillars in the nave of the Zuiderkerk, the nearest large church.[3] Saskia is probably seen again with Rumbartus, touchingly clasping the baby to her cheek, in the drawing *Four heads of Saskia (?) with a child* (fig. 55), in the Museum Boijmans Van Beuningen, Rotterdam.[4] At the time of the Fitzharris sale in 1950, the Courtauld sheet was mounted with another red-chalk drawing, *Two studies of a child asleep*, in a private collection in Basel in 1973, which could also speculatively be said to portray Rumbartus.[5]

In assessing images of an artist's family, a distinction can be made between those clearly intended as portraits for posterity, such as Albrecht Dürer's drawings of his wife or Peter Paul Rubens's images of his first wife, Isabella Brant, and those that may either be portraits or represent the use of the family member as a convenient model, as clearly happened with Rubens's various depictions of his second wife, Helena Fourment (see cat. 24).[6] Although several of Rembrandt's paintings and at least one etching were conceived as portrayals, in the case of his drawings it is probably correct that, with the exception of the betrothal silverpoint, all his supposed studies of Saskia fall into the latter category and were made with his art in mind. An inventory made in 1680 of the estate of the marine painter Jan van de Capelle showed that among at least 350 drawings by Rembrandt he owned was included "A [portfolio] containing 135 drawings of the life of women with children by Rembrandt",[7] which Van de Capelle had probably bought at the sale of the older artist's effects in 1657–58. It seems likely that Rembrandt compiled the portfolio as useful reference material, and the Courtauld drawing could well have been among the contents. C W

FIG. 54 Rembrandt van Rijn,
Saskia in bed, c. 1635
Red chalk, 130 × 175 mm
Amsterdam, Rijksprentenkabinet,
inv. no. A 4520r

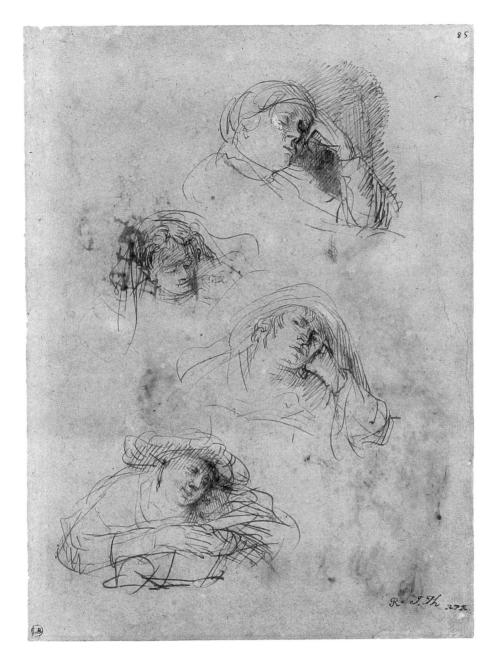

85

NOTES

1 De Winkel in Edinburgh and London 2001,
  p. 56 and n. 15.
2 Berlin, Kupferstichkabinett, KdZ 1152;
  Benesch 1954–57, vol. 2, no. 427.
3 Strauss and van der Meulen 1979, no. 1636/3.
4 Pen and brown ink, with some grey wash,
  corrected with white, 990 × 620 mm;
  Benesch 1954–57, vol. 2, no. 360.

5 Benesch 1954–57, vol. 2, no. 280b.
6 For example, Helena as herself in the portrait
  in Munich, Alte Pinakothek (Jaffé 1989,
  no. 1044), and Helena serving as the model
  for the figure of Venus in the *Judgement of*
  Paris in Madrid, Museo del Prado (*ibid.*,
  no. 1371).
7 Schatborn 1981, pp. 10–12, item no. 17.

REMBRANDT VAN RIJN
Leiden 1606–1669 Amsterdam

26 *Two men in discussion*, 1641

Quill and reed pen in brown ink, with corrections in white bodycolour (darkened),
on laid paper; inscribed by the artist in pen and brown ink at bottom centre *Rembrand… f. 1641*;
extensive overall foxing; losses at left, top and bottom edges, centre left and lower left,
mostly repaired; framing line in pen and brown ink, partially trimmed
229 × 183/185 mm

WATERMARK
Post horn in shield

Samuel Courtauld Trust, D.1978.PG.190

This dramatic drawing of two men in conversation – one
leaning over a wall, with his hand out in forceful gesture,
the other standing back receiving the message in a resolute
stance – poses the question of what, if any, subject was at
the back of the artist's mind. A general resemblance has
been noted with an etching of the same year, generally
known as *Three oriental figures* (fig. 56). Before a doorway,
three men exotically dressed are in earnest conversation,
which seems to portend more than general chat. But since
it is uncertain what the subject of the etching is – *Jacob
and Laban* and *Job and His Three Friends* have both been
unconvincing suggestions – we are no nearer to the answer
about this drawing. Perhaps one should not seek any
further than supposing that it is a study from everyday
life. There were many exotic inhabitants in Amsterdam at
the time, and these two men would fit very naturally into
the general ambience. Although their costume is usually
described as being Oriental, Marieke de Winkel has kindly
pointed out that the man on the left, with frogging down
his tunic and a high cap instead of a turban, is more likely
to be Russian than Turkish; the costume of the man on
the right is indeterminate.[1] Rembrandt showed genius in
imbuing the everyday with unaccustomed meaning.

FIG. 56 Rembrandt van Rijn, *Three oriental figures*,
signed and dated 1641 (in reverse)
Etching, 145 × 114 mm
London, British Museum, inv. no. 1848,0911.59

PROVENANCE
Private collection, France; Mrs O'Rooney,
Ireland, by descent; Patrick de Bayser; Count
Antoine Seilern (1901–1978), acquired from
Arthur Goldschmidt, Paris, 21 October 1952;
Princes Gate Bequest, 1978

SELECTED LITERATURE
Benesch 1954–57, vol. 3, no. 500a; Drost 1957,
p. 184; Rosenberg 1959, p. 112; Seilern 1961,
no. 190; Haverkamp Begemann 1961, p. 17;
Sumowski 1961, p. 9; Slive 1964, p. 275;
Royalton-Kisch 1992, p. 99 under no. 37;
Royalton-Kisch and Schatborn 2011, p. 338,
no. 49, fig. 123

SELECTED EXHIBITIONS
London 1983a, no. 18; Los Angeles 2010,
no. 21.1

It is symptomatic of its somewhat unusual character that Jakob Rosenberg at first doubted the attribution of this drawing to Rembrandt. It has since been accepted unequivocally, an opinion enforced by the signature and date. There are, in fact, only a handful of signed and dated works in the artist's drawn oeuvre – four the year before the Courtauld sheet, one in 1643, a charming drawing of a man smoking, and one in 1644, an unusually large and imposing landscape, and thereafter none.[2] It is, therefore, surprising that this sheet should be among the group. Although lively and vigorously drawn, it is not a refined drawing in the normal terms of that description. For this reason, one might wonder whether the artist would have given it to a friend or admirer, like the other two drawings just mentioned. Holm Bevers has suggested that the artist used it as an example for his pupils.[3] One might ask, as an example of what – a demonstration of combining quill and reed pens? Perhaps one must accept that an artist is not bound to submit to any laws of logic, and he signs and dates a work when he feels like it.

The technique of this drawing is distinguished by the extensive use of the reed pen worked over the initial lay-in of the composition with the quill pen, a combination that Rembrandt was to use regularly after this date. The quill, earlier his favourite instrument for drawing, offers precision, fluency and flexibility, brilliantly displaying the individuality of the artist's hand. The reed pen, first used in Italy in the sixteenth century by such artists as Luca Cambiaso, is less adaptable to quick changes in breadth and direction of line. Its broader, blunter-ended stroke articulates and monumentalises figures surrounded by space; at the same time, it establishes soft tonal accents, recording the fluctuating play of light and shadow, which create a magical atmosphere throughout a composition.

By his mid career, Rembrandt had developed a feeling for the communality of interest in whichever of the three basic media – painting, drawing and etching – he was

FIG. 57 Rembrandt van Rijn,
The Triumph of Mordecai, c. 1641
Etching and drypoint, 174 × 215 mm
London, British Museum, inv. no. 1868,0822.661

working.[4] In this respect, one can equate the use of the reed pen with the increasing appearance of drypoint in his etchings to create a broadness of tone at the same time as a greater emphasis on individual figures. Maybe done in the same year as the Courtauld drawing, *The Triumph of Mordecai* (fig. 57) shows very similar reworking of the outlines of the figures first established in etching with rich accents of burr created by the drypoint, added only after the artist had removed the plate from the acid. The figure of the discomforted and humiliated Haman, reworked in drypoint, stands out in the left foreground of the print in much the same way as the standing man, overdrawn with the reed pen, dominates the left of the drawing. Thereafter, both the reed pen and the drypoint needle were to assume increasing importance in the artist's work, often being the only technique employed in a particular work. CW

NOTES
1 E-mail to the author, 19 September 2011.
2 The two dated drawings are respectively in a private collection (Benesch 1954–57, vol. 4, no. 686) and New York, The Metropolitan Museum of Art (*ibid.*, no. 815).
3 Bevers in Los Angeles 2010, p. 142.
4 For further exploration of this theme, see Rosenberg 1940, pp. 193–206.

PIETER SAENREDAM
Assendelft 1597–1665 Haarlem

27 *The south ambulatory of St Bavokerk, Haarlem*, 1634

Pen and brown ink with grey wash, with some black-chalk shading, heightened with white,
on blue laid paper, laid down, backing partially removed; traces of fixative; later framing line
in pen and black ink; overall foxing.

Verso: numbered in pen and dark brown ink at lower left *No 995*; in graphite at centre *405*
338 × 235/238 mm

Samuel Courtauld Trust, D.1952. RW.2010

The spire, with its lantern, of the Grote Kerk of St Bavo is as much a recognisable landmark of the town of Haarlem when seen from the dunes as the north spire of the cathedral is of Antwerp seen from across the river Schelde (or Scheldt). Built between about 1390 and 1550, the Dutch Gothic church is as imposing on the inside as it is on the outside. It was natural that it should attract the intense admiration of the leading local architectural painter, Pieter Saenredam, who had lived in the town since the age of eleven.

With the single exception of Hendrik Goltzius's engraving of *The Circumcision* of 1594,[1] which used the Brewer's Chapel as a background, Saenredam was the first artist to portray the interior, but curiously never the exterior, of the great church of his home town. He first turned his attention to the building in the mid to late 1620s, producing drawings and paintings, and then returned for what became his last campaign in the years 1634 to 1637, when he produced six paintings and a number of related drawings, including this one.

Here the artist depicts the south ambulatory, seen from west to east beginning at the crossing. A more distant view of the ambulatory can be found in the *Interior of St Bavo: View from the south aisle looking east,* painted about 1690 by a follower, Isaac van Nickelen (active *c.* 1655–1703), which is now in a Dutch private collection.[2] Apart from the organ emerging from the Brewer's Chapel on the right, one of three in the church, and two chandeliers hanging in the centre, it is a scene of unencumbered architecture, with only a solitary walking figure to humanise the scene.

Having decided on a viewpoint, Saenredam tended to work in a set pattern, first making a drawing 'from the life', which may have been kept for reference or sold to a collector. This was followed by a construction drawing, before committing the subject to a panel; panel was the support he invariably used for painting, because it allowed him the precision of detail he sought in his work. In this case the natural view, recorded in the Courtauld sheet, was followed by a large construction drawing (fig. 58), dated November 1634, in the Municipal Archives, Haarlem, which corrects the perspective, rounds the arches and measures the architecture. Following what had become his regular – though unusual – practice, which from the nature of the information provided seems intended more for posterity than for the artist's own purposes, he inscribed his drawing in an empty space on the left: "This so drawn as you see it in November 1634. [It] is the south ambulatory of the Great Church in Haarlem in Holland. This was completed in painting, equally large, on 20 June 1635."[3] This painting, executed on panel (fig. 59), signed and dated 1635, is in the Gemäldegalerie, Berlin, and, despite what the artist wrote on his construction drawing, is in fact slightly smaller.

An intriguing aspect of the sequence of works is the way Saenredam developed the story line from the general to the particular. From one solitary loitering male figure in

PROVENANCE
Arnal collection; Sir Robert Witt (1872–1952;
L. 2228b), acquired at Arnal sale, Sotheby's,
London, 24 February 1925, lot 87; Robert Witt
Bequest, 1952

SELECTED LITERATURE
Schwartz and Bok, p. 110, no. 53, fig. 118

SELECTED EXHIBITIONS
Utrecht 1961, no. 53; Edinburgh 1984, no. 24;
London 1991, no. 63

FIG. 58 Pieter Saenredam, *The south ambulatory of St Bavokerk, Haarlem*, dated 1634
Construction drawing in pen, graphite, red chalk and watercolour, 550 × 423 mm
Haarlem, Municipal Archives

FIG. 59 Pieter Saenredam, *The south ambulatory of St Bavokerk, Haarlem, with the Presentation in the Temple*, signed and dated 1635
Oil on panel, 46 × 35 cm
Berlin, Staatliche Museen, Gemäldegalerie

the Courtauld drawing, he proceeded to two small unspecific groups of figures in the construction drawing, and finally, almost surreptitiously, introduced a religious subject into the painting. So secular in feel is the staffage in the last work that it takes a moment to realise that the few people casually wandering about are in fact acting out the Presentation in the Temple. In the centre of the ambulatory, the elderly bearded figure of Simeon, carrying the Christ Child and followed by Joseph and Mary, advance towards the right, where the high priest can be partially seen emerging from behind a column to receive them. Anna hurries forth from the choir on the left to play her part in the event about to happen. When it came to the composition, Saenredam cut off the top of the vault in the immediate foreground in the panel, so that instead of a detached view

taken from the crossing, as in the preliminary drawings, the spectator feels himself drawn into the space of the ambulatory and overawed by the height of the vault.

The daylight in the present sheet floods in from the tall clear-glass windows, casting, through a combination of wash and short diagonal pen-strokes, a subtly fluctuating range of shadows on the ripple of vaults above and on the stone floor below. Enhanced by the warmth of the blue paper, the drawing succeeds in becoming a masterly study in luminosity. From the spontaneity with which the artist recorded what he saw before him, it not surprisingly offers a much livelier image than that seen in the dry execution of the construction drawing and, when compared with the stronger tonal contrasts in the painting, portrays a more naturalistic pattern of light flooding the church. C W

NOTES

1 Strauss 1977, no. 322, repr.

2 Edinburgh 1984, no. 32, repr.

3 Schwartz and Bok 1990, p. 261, no. 54: 'Dit aldus geteijckent in November 1634. is de Zuijder gangh groote kerck binnen Haerlem in Hollant. Dit gedaen met schilderen Den 20ᵉ. Junij Aᵒ. 1635. even dus groot geschildert.'

PIETER DE MOLYN
London 1595–1661 Haarlem

28 *Landscape with travellers on a road*, mid 1650s

Red chalk over black chalk, with grey and brown wash and additional drawing in black chalk, on laid paper; inscribed by the artist at lower right *PMolyn* (PM interlinked); flattened diagonal paper fold at lower right; overall slight discolouration, brown stain at bottom left corner, slight water stain at top right corner; later framing line in pen and brown ink over an earlier one in red chalk

Verso: inscribed at top centre in graphite *3* (crossed out in brown ink) *B7* and in black chalk *89*; in centre in graphite *… –40*; left of centre *65* (crossed out)

189/187 × 303 mm

Samuel Courtauld Trust, D.1952. RW.4015

Landscape with travellers on a road shows a winding road leading to the dunes, bordering a fenced property; mounted travellers appear on the horizon. On the right an open gateway leads to what is probably a distant farmhouse; a portly figure lies slumped on the ground at the extreme right. The drawing has all the appearance of the simple scene that might have greeted the artist as he walked towards the coast from his home town of Haarlem, where, from the age of twenty-one, he spent his life.

The Courtauld sheet was probably drawn in the mid 1650s, which was a prolific period for Molyn as a draughtsman. It can, for example, be compared with a similar subject, *Cottage amid a clump of trees at the edge of a road*, signed and dated 16[5?]4, in the Morgan Library and Museum, New York.[1] Perhaps acknowledging the limited opportunities presented by the terrain, the composition is a variation on that in a painting produced many years earlier, *Dune Landscape*, signed and dated 1626, in the Herzog Anton Ulrich-Museum, Brunswick (fig. 60). This re-use of his earlier repertoire of landscape forms was a feature of the artist's later work, which had lost some of the innovative drive and inspiration of his earlier paintings and drawings.

The extensive use of red chalk in the present drawing is most unusual. Almost invariably, Molyn limited himself to black chalk and grey wash. Moreover, the artist appears to

FIG. 60 Pieter de Molyn, *Dune landscape*, 1626
Oil on panel, 26 × 36.5 cm
Brunswick, Herzog Anton Ulrich-Museum

have introduced technical refinements to his usually straightforward method of drawing. He seems to have applied a light wash of water over some of the chalk areas to create a light tint – for example, over the group of figures coming over the horizon on the left and across the figure resting on the ground at the right. In the foreground the chalk was applied wet over the grey wash to get a denser, more intense black. Such care argues that it was a drawing executed as a finished work of art destined for a collector's album and not just as a preparatory study.

PROVENANCE
Sir Robert Witt (1872–1952), acquired from Colnaghi; Robert Witt Bequest, 1952

SELECTED EXHIBITIONS
New York and London 1986, no. 52; London 1991, no. 51

Made up of small mountains of sand, large pools of water and gnarled vegetation, the dunes run parallel to the Dutch coast from Zeeland in the south to the Frisian Islands in the north and form a vital protective barrier between the sea and the inland countryside. They are an essential and distinctive part of the Dutch landscape with their own ecosystem of wildlife and vegetation. In the seventeenth century they spoke deeply to the Dutch psyche. People recognised and praised the particular qualities of the dunes, enjoying the distant views of surrounding flat country that could be gained from climbing their heights. Hunting, although limited to the upper echelons of society, was an especial pastime that took place there. And, on a more practical level, the dunes provided an essential source of water for neighbouring towns, catering to, for example, the breweries and bleaching fields, essential to the linen industry; both of these activities played an important part in the commercial life of Haarlem.[2]

Artists notably responded to the unique pictorial attractions of the dunes. An early awareness of the homely scenes to be found outside Haarlem can be seen in the set of etchings made about 1611–12 by Claes Jansz. Visscher, bearing the evocative title *Plaisante Plaetsen* (Pleasant places) and revealing the Dutch taste for the homely and the rustic (see, for example, fig. 61).[3] What Molyn has drawn here is essentially the same as the farmsteads portrayed by Visscher, but Visscher's work and that of his contemporaries Jan van Goyen and Salomon van Ruisdael differ from Molyn's in their appreciation of the particular quality of light, air and colour. This unique feature of the dunes is one to which numerous Dutch artists from then onwards, above all Philip Wouwerman and Jan Wijnants, both Haarlem artists, responded.

The early trio of Haarlem artists, Molyn, Van Goyen, and Salomon van Ruisdael, led what was in effect a revolution in landscape painting, practising the so-called tonal phase in reaction to the earlier realist period of Dutch art. By contrast to those works, in these all local colour was removed in order to concentrate on the depiction of atmosphere. Working with the strong diagonal arrangement of the motif – the way the track starts on the right and, after a brief dogleg turn, continues over the hill to the left, as emphasised by the straight line of the fence – Molyn produced dramatic contrasts of light and shade, limiting his palette to a few basic colours. He successfully imbued a simple natural setting with a stature it does not inherently possess. c w

FIG. 61 Claes Jansz. Visscher, *Paters herbergh* (Father's inn), from *Plaisante Plaetsen* Etching, 103 × 158 mm London, British Museum, inv. no. 1987.1003.14

NOTES
1 Shoaf Turner 2006, no. 160, repr.
2 For the cultural significance of the dunes in the seventeenth century, see Gibson 2000, pp. 85–116.
3 *New Hollstein* 1991 (Luijten, vols. 38–39), nos. 149–60, repr.

CLAUDE LORRAIN (CLAUDE GELLÉE)
Chamagne, Lorraine 1600–1682 Rome

29 *Landscape with trees and buildings, c. 1640–46*

Graphite, brown and grey wash, black chalk, brush and dark brown ink, on laid paper;
original freehand framing line in black chalk; inscribed by the artist in pen and
brown ink in lower right corner 27, and on verso in red chalk, at lower centre left *Claud/Ro IV*;
overall slight undulation and discolouration; extensive foxing; numerous light creases.

Verso: localised adhesive stains in the corners showing through to the recto

224 × 321 mm

Samuel Courtauld Trust, D.1978.PG.214

This sheet comes from the so-called Tivoli Book, which was either a sketchbook belonging to Claude, as argued by Marcel Röthlisberger, or an album of separate drawings that he compiled later, as proposed by Jon Whiteley.[2] Like the other pages of the book, this one is inscribed by the artist with his monogram and a page number. The group originally consisted of sixty-nine or seventy sheets, of which thirty-five have been identified; this one numbers among the thirty-two nature drawings.[3] It was subsequently bound into an album of eighty-one drawings by Claude distinguished for their exceptional quality and identified in the 1713 inventory of Prince Livio Odescalchi.[4] The last family member who owned it was Princess Maria Ausiliatrice, whose husband, Donato Sanminiatelli, sold eight of its sheets to the art dealer Hans Calmann in 1958, including the Courtauld drawing, before the rest were acquired by Georges Wildenstein in 1960.[5]

Michael Kitson, followed by Röthlisberger, plausibly dated this drawing to about 1640–46, on the basis of comparison with a view of St Peter's, also from the Tivoli Book, that can be dated to 1640–41.[6] By this time, Claude had been in Rome for more than twenty years and was

established as a painter for an elite, international clientele. Continual innovation may have been important to his sustained success in the specialised field of landscape painting, and Filippo Baldinucci praised Claude's remarkably versatile approach to the genre.[7] Drawing played a significant role in this creative process, and this small sheet demonstrates his wide range of drawing techniques.

The artist first sketched framing lines in black chalk, and with this medium also underpinned the sloping foreground features and at least four different types of trees in the distant forest. As in many of his other landscape drawings, however, Claude sought pictorial effect rather than botanical or topographic accuracy.[8] This approach extends to the two larger trees in the right foreground and middle ground, whose outlines he defined in graphite. Graphite was an expensive material which Claude rarely used as his principal medium, but he employed it here extensively, to outstanding effect.[9]

Helen Braham has observed that Claude varied his media to depict distance, and he also relied on contrasts between them to convey different effects of light.[10] In the

PROVENANCE
Prince Livio Odescalchi (1653–1713), before 1713;[1] by descent until 1957; Hans M. Calmann (1899–1982), 1958; Count Antoine Seilern (1901–1978), acquired from Colnaghi, November 1958; Princes Gate Bequest, 1978

SELECTED LITERATURE
Kitson 1961, p. 253; Seilern 1961, no. 241; Röthlisberger 1962, p. 9; Calmann 1976, pp. 71–72; Röthlisberger 1968, vol. 1, no. 471

SELECTED EXHIBITIONS
London 1958, no. 18; London 1969, no. 73; London 1981a, no. 147; London 1991, no. 22

147

pine tree in front of a building to the right, the tiny, dense strokes of graphite that establish the inner masses of needles also contribute volume to its canopy. The sparkling graphite particles are surrounded by a halo of matt chalk outlines, creating the impression of warm sunlight reflecting off the foliage, helping to define the tree's location within the composition by the strength of light that illuminates it.

In the forest, Claude employed brown and grey washes in a wide range of tones to evoke the impression of diffused light. Warm, sunlit patches throughout the centre of this area are picked out in varying shades of golden-brown wash, and a light-grey wash was applied to the longest elevation of the wall as well as to select patches of foreground shrubbery. Subtly differentiated passages of light and shade, which can be difficult to discern in many of his paintings owing to their fugitive pigments, are also found in the pictorial features both nearest to and farthest from the viewer. For example, pale brown wash envelops the distant tower, and the large tree trunk in the right foreground is modelled with a darker mixture. Both objects contrast with the tones surrounding them as well as with the large swathe of white paper that was reserved for the sky and suggest the broad spectrum of sunlight and shadow that Claude sought to simulate.

Claude's technical facility in multiple media also enabled him to express texture, such as the serrated outline of pointed needles that silhouettes the voluminous pine tree against the sky. Remarkably descriptive surfaces can also be found elsewhere. In the immediate foreground, Claude reworked the trunk of a large tree, defined in brush and brown wash, with zigzagging horizontal strokes of black chalk that contribute a rough, dry, barklike finish. The dense, almost impenetrable form created here also serves as an effective foil to the empty outlines of each tree trunk in the distance, made visible by the surrounding shadows of the forest.

Despite the many individually successful pictorial effects seen here, the composition as a whole is not entirely resolved. Claude's uneven application of golden-brown wash to the foliage above and beyond the wall makes its distance from the viewer difficult to ascertain. Equally, the pine tree's short branches are so densely distributed that they blur into solid masses of wash.

Even if Claude did not fully realise the representational potential of this landscape sketch, he executed it in diverse media on a single small sheet that may be interpreted as an experiment in which the artist pushed the limits of his drawing technique. N S

NOTES
1 Röthlisberger 1968, vol. 1, pp. 65–66. In Röthlisberger 1962, pp. 9–10, the author claimed that both Queen Christina of Sweden (1626–1689) and Cardinal Decio Azzolini (1623–1689) were previous owners of the album from which this drawing was extracted, but this cannot be confirmed.
2 Röthlisberger 1968, vol. 1, pp. 65–66; Whiteley in Oxford 1998, pp. 24–25.
3 Whiteley in Oxford 1998, p. 15.
4 Röthlisberger 1968, vol. 1, p. 55.
5 Calmann 1976, pp. 71–72.
6 Kitson in Seilern 1961, p. 68; Röthlisberger 1968, vol. 1, p. 200.
7 Baldinucci quoted in Röthlisberger 1961, vol. 1, p. 56.
8 Williamstown 2006, p. 64.
9 De la Chapelle and Van Gulik in Paris 2011, p. 56.
10 Braham in London 1991, p. 52.

GIAN LORENZO BERNINI
Naples 1589–1680 Rome

30   *The Louvre, east façade* (study for the First Project), 1664

Pen and brown ink, on laid paper, laid down; considerable degrading of iron-gall ink
with noticeable lateral migration; overall uneven discolouration, damaged areas across lower
half of the sheet; paper crease across lower left corner; later framing-line in pen and brown ink,
sheet unevenly trimmed, and edged again (noticeable at top and bottom edges); inscribed with
pen and brown ink, at lower left *CAV. Bernini*, and in pen and carbon black ink in a different
hand *N.˚ 42 110.V.* Verso (migrating through to recto) at lower right *G.L. Bernino*
165/169 × 278 mm

Samuel Courtauld Trust, D.1984.AB.51.1

This study for the east façade of a projected design for the
Louvre palace in Paris was first attributed to Bernini by
Anthony Blunt.[1] His opinion is accepted by most scholars,
though not by Jörg Martin Merz.[2] Despite later damage,
the inherent delicacy of this lightweight paper was well
suited to capturing the exceptionally fine details that
Bernini recorded in pen and ink. Multiple tiny flicks and
squiggles describe the foliage of each Corinthian capital
and convey the form of each balustrade figure efficiently
but with confidence. As in many architectural engravings
of symmetrical elevations, the entire façade of this
building terminates abruptly before the left edge of the
sheet – another shorthand technique. Stylistic features
of architectural sketches by Bernini include, as in this
drawing, long, crooked lines that articulate channelled
rustication on the foundation walls.[3]

The only other surviving drawing for this initial version
of Bernini's design for King Louis XIV, today in the Musée
du Louvre, depicts the entire east façade (fig. 62). It is
more finished than the Courtauld sketch, and their
compositions also differ in that its frieze is decorated with

pairs of sphinxes, creatures that often guarded entrances.
If this Louvre elevation was part of the first proposal that
Bernini sent to the king, then the Courtauld's smaller and
quickly executed study was perhaps preparatory for it,
even though the London sheet was probably not his
first attempt.[4]

Bernini was addressing the king's desire to complete
his unfinished palace by encasing the extant structure,
designed by Pierre Lescot, in a new façade that would
present an official, ceremonial entrance. He introduced
architectural elements not previously used in the building
but that recall his own earlier work.[5] For example, the flat
roof edged by a balustrade decorated with figural sculpture
is similar to Bernini's design of the colonnade surrounding
the Piazza of St Peter's in Rome, begun in 1656. In both
projects, monumental engaged columns or pilasters link
the main floors.

The two levels are expressed in this façade by means
of a loggia. Although his central pavilion gives on to the
Cour Carrée and its ground-floor bays would have offered
views of the courtyard beyond, a pre-existing moat limited

PROVENANCE
Anthony Blunt (1907–1983), received as a gift
from Margaret Whinney; Blunt Bequest, 1984
(via the Art Fund)

SELECTED LITERATURE
Blunt 1953, p. 231; Pesco 1984, p. 13; Merz 1993,
p. 844; Hall 2007, p. 478

SELECTED EXHIBITIONS
Farr (ed.) 1987, p. 160; London 1991, no. 9;
Stuttgart 1993, no. 30

Cav. Bernini ... A° 42 ... 110 ...

physical access to a single point of entry through its central portal. The upper floor of this structure offered the ruler a location from which to address his subjects, like the benediction loggias found, for example, at St Peter's or at St John Lateran in Rome. Here the loggia's multiple bays may have framed not only the king but also his retinue, whose appearance signalled the royal presence.

Each bay in the upper loggia of the façade is articulated by a Serlian arch (an arch flanked by a pair of columns). Bernini had deployed a single monumental example to frame the Scala Regia, the formal entrance to Vatican Palace.[6] His series of smaller Serlian arches similarly adorns the threshold of a ruler's principal residence and indicates the importance of the inhabitant whose apartment is located behind.

Although scholars have frequently pointed out that elements of Bernini's design recall Roman precedents, such as the oval room in the Palazzo Barberini (1633) and the double movement of the façade of Santa Maria della Pace by Pietro da Cortona (1656), some of these features had already been employed in France.[7] Hillary Ballon plausibly argued that the first proposal by Bernini did not reject an idea submitted by the king's architect, Louis Le Vau, but instead endorsed it.[8] In his design for the east façade that the king did not use, Le Vau included a projecting central pavilion containing an oval room. While Bernini claimed ignorance of these plans, they had been sent to Rome for his inspection, and the artist maintained this feature in the Courtauld drawing.[9] In fact, he enhanced its expression in the façade, thereby increasing the dramatic impact implicit in Le Vau's scheme.

The London sheet is also compatible with precedents designed by French architects, both hypothetical and then under construction. In his 1652 engraving of an ideal château, Antoine Lepautre introduced a convex-concave elevation with monumental pilasters, also topped by a drum (fig. 63).[10] The two designs share curving wings, which are also a feature of the Collège des Quatre Nations

FIG. 63 Antoine Lepautre, Project for an ideal château,
from *Desseins de plusieurs palais*, Paris, 1652
Engraving, 240 × 363 mm
New York, Columbia University, Avery Architectural
and Fine Arts Library

by Le Vau, begun in 1662 and situated directly across
the river from the Louvre.[11] Whether or not Bernini was
familiar with these projects when the king solicited his
advice two years later, he cast the east façade in an
innovative idiom but one already introduced in France
with some success. Perhaps his approach, visible at this
early stage in the design process, can be interpreted as
a tactic deployed in response to the competitive nature
of this prestigious commission. NS

NOTES

1   Blunt 1953, p. 231. I would like to thank
    Louise Rice for discussing this drawing
    with me.

2   Davies in Farr (ed.) 1987, p. 160; Bradford
    in London 1991, p. 26; Merz 1993, p. 844;
    Kieven in Stuttgart 1993, p. 108; Hall 2007,
    p. 480.

3   Hall 2007, p. 480.

4   Bradford in London 1991, p. 26.

5   Bresc-Bautier 2008, pp. 42 and 62;
    Marder 1998, p. 264.

6   Marder 1997, pp. 213–34.

7   Davies in Farr (ed.) 1987, p. 160; Bradford
    in London 1991, p. 26.

8   Ballon 1999, p. 78.

9   Chantelou (Blunt) 1985, pp. 326–27.

10 Berger 1966, pp. 170–71.

11 Ballon 1999, p. 78.

JEAN-ANTOINE WATTEAU
Valenciennes 1684–1721 Nogent-sur-Marne

31 *Carmelite friar, standing, c. 1715*

Black and red chalk, on laid paper; overall extensive foxing
and slight discolouration; horizontal flattened fold
334/336 × 225/232 mm

WATERMARK
Letters *J D* (?) linked by horizontal lines, separated by a heart

Samuel Courtauld Trust, D.1978.PG.220

In this vigorous, densely worked costume study –
undoubtedly drawn from the life – Watteau presents a
young friar, with something of a 'baby face', who appears
almost overwhelmed by his capacious garments and
extravagant hat.[1] The compact treatment of the clerical
apparel, the shading of the upturned brim and the rich
deposits of red and black chalk on the folds and shadows of
the voluminous mantle and scapular recall the technique
of Watteau's studies of Persians and Savoyards of 1715,
the date to which this drawing should be assigned.[2]

As was customary, Watteau first outlined his figure
faintly in red, reworking his initial contours in chalks of
black and red manipulated with the greatest assurance. He
used the neutral tone of the paper almost as a third colour
to evoke the light falling across the model's downcast eyes
and fleshy chin as well as to suggest the brighter fabric
of the saddlebag, or *sacoche*, slung over his left shoulder.
Watteau rose to the challenge of reproducing the various
layers of the friar's woollen costume – the outer folds of
the mantle, the wide sleeves and striped patterning of
the tunic, and the protective scapular, draped down the
front and back.

Watteau's friar is a lay brother – or *frère convers* – of
the Discalced Carmelite order, perhaps about to set out to
collect alms for the monastery. (His fastidious expression

FIG. 64 Unknown artist, 'A lay brother of the Carmelites
seeking alms', from Pierre Hélyot, *Histoire des ordres
monastiques, religieux et militaires*, Paris, 1714, vol. 1, p. 361
New York, The New York Public Library

PROVENANCE
Jean de Jullienne (1686–1766), sold at auction
30 March–22 May 1767, lot 769; Brisart
collection; Andrew James (d. before 1857); Sarah
Ann James, London; Christie's, London, 22 June
1891, lot 304; John Postle Heseltine (1843–1929;
L.1507); Adrien Fauchier-Magnan (1873–1965);
Count Antoine Seilern (1901–1978), acquired
at Fauchier-Magnan sale, Sotheby's, London, 4
December 1935, lot 65; Princes Gate Bequest, 1978

SELECTED LITERATURE
Washington and elsewhere 1984, p. 321;
Rosenberg and Prat 1996, vol. 1, pp. 214, 486,
vol. 2, no. 368; Roland Michel 1998, p. 752;
Grasselli 2001, p. 333 n. 24

SELECTED EXHIBITIONS
London 1968a, no. 747; London 1983, no. 77;
London 2011, no. 36

155

and empty bag suggest that he goes forth with a certain reluctance.) Comparison with contemporary illustrations in two compendia chronicling the history of clerical orders confirms the specificity (and accuracy) of Watteau's portrayal.[3] In Pierre Hélyot's *Histoire des ordres monastiques, religieux, et militaries* (Paris, 1714), the lay brother is shown in similar apparel, with open-toed leather sandals and a full bag over his shoulder (fig. 64). Lest there be any doubt of his actions, the engraving confirms what his gesture and expression convey, namely, that he is begging for alms – "*faisant la queste*".[4] The cruder engraving in Filippo Buonanni's *Histoire du clergé séculier et régulier* (Amsterdam, 1716) shows a lay brother closer in age to Watteau's more youthful protagonist (fig. 65), whose high collar, floppy hat with dangling leather straps and open-toed sandals – a symbol of the order's austerity – reappear with considerably more elegance in Watteau's drawing.[5]

Founded in Spain at the end of the sixteenth century by Saint Theresa of Ávila, in France the reformed order of the Discalced Carmelites received the protection of Marie de' Medici, who in 1613 laid the first stone of the church of St-Joseph-des-Carmes on the rue de Vaugirard, near the Luxembourg Gardens. In the century to come, a convent and its associated buildings were also erected. By the first decade of the eighteenth century, the Carmelites, renowned for their scholasticism and austerity, were property owners in a booming sector of Paris. The main source of their income, however, came from the manufacture and sale of *eau de Mélisse* or *eau des Carmes* – a medicinal balm used for migraines and other ailments.[6] Within the hierarchy of the order, lay brothers – the figure represented by Watteau – occupied the lowest rank. Unlike those destined for clerical service from infancy, these were less well-educated men, who entered the convent later in life and were dedicated to serving the monastery through manual labour and the collecting of alms, as well as through prayer and study.[7] If Watteau's well-fed lay brother seems

FIG. 65. D. Jonckmann, *A Carmelite lay brother*, from Filippo Buonanni (and others), *Histoire du clergé seculier et regulier*, Amsterdam, 1716, p. 337 New York, The Burke Library, Columbia University at Union Theological Seminary

to lack humility, there is no question of his affiliation. The church and group of buildings hastily sketched in the background, under a cloudy sky – *pace* Pierre Rosenberg, they are not the same as those that appear in the wintry *Marmot* of 1715–16 (St Petersburg, State Hermitage Museum)[8] – recall the façade of St-Joseph des Carmes, surmounted by its cupola and lantern (the second highest in Paris at this time).[9] Even though it is omitted in François Boucher's engraving of this drawing in the first volume of *Figures de différents caractères*, announced in 1726, there is no reason to doubt that this motif is by Watteau's hand.[10] Indeed, given Watteau's earlier apprenticeship with Claude III Audran (1658–1734), concierge of the Luxembourg palace, as well as his continuing affection for the public gardens there, both the mendicant and his convent represented in Watteau's drawing must have been intensely familiar sights. The artist's achievement here was to have portrayed the lay brother with the same freshness and originality that he brought to his more exotic confrontations with Persians and Savoyards. CBB

NOTES

1 Rosenberg in London 2011, p. 98.
2 As noted in Roland Michel 1998, p. 752.
3 I am indebted to Aimee Ng for her tenacious investigations into the history of the Discalced Carmelites and in particular the costume of the order.
4 Hélyot 1714–19, vol. 1, p. 362.
5 Buonanni 1716, vol. 2, p. 337.

6 See Lebeuf 1867, pp. 161–64; Pisani 1891, pp. 1–26.
7 See the definition of '*Frere convers*' in Diderot and d'Alembert's *Encyclopédie*, vol. 15, p. 403.
8 Washington and elsewhere 1984, p. 321.
9 Hillairet 1997, vol. 2, pp. 603–04.
10 For Boucher's engraving, see Jean-Richard 1978, no. 48, p. 38. Grasselli 2001, p. 333,

considered these "scribbled landscape elements" to be by another hand, citing their absence from Boucher's engraving as additional evidence. As Eidelberg 1977, p. 163, had noted, "... the omission of landscape backgrounds was a regular part of the program of the *Figures de différents caractères*".

JEAN-ANTOINE WATTEAU
Valenciennes 1684–1721 Nogent-sur-Marne

32 *Satyr pouring wine*, 1717

Black, red and white chalk, on laid paper; later framing line in pen and brown ink,
partially trimmed; overall undulation and discolouration with several stains and localised foxing;
small holes near centre left edge repaired and retouched and small loss at top edge
285 × 211 mm

WATERMARK
Letters *C* (?) *C* linked by horizontal lines, separated by a heart and unidentifiable countermark

Samuel Courtauld Trust, D.1978.PG.221

Satyr pouring wine is one of four – or possibly five –
surviving preparatory drawings for *Autumn* (fig. 66) in
Watteau's series the Four Seasons, overdoor decorations for
the dining room of Pierre Crozat's *hôtel particulier* on the
rue de Richelieu.[1] The banker and Maecenas had initially
awarded this commission to the former director of the
Royal Academy of Painting and Sculpture, Charles de La
Fosse, a tenant of the *hôtel* Crozat since 1706, who painted
a large *Birth of Minerva* for the ceiling of Crozat's gallery.
When La Fosse died in December 1716, without having
completed the dining room decorations, his widow was
obliged to return the four oval canvases on their stretchers
to Crozat's household.[2] Watteau, whom La Fosse had
befriended and championed, received this unexpected
commission early in 1717 and took up residence in the
hôtel to work on it.

Satyr pouring wine is the second study that Watteau
made for the background figure who stands behind the
reclining Bacchus as he fills his cup. In the first preparatory
drawing (fig. 67) Watteau shows the figure in profile, hair
tied back, with his right arm outstretched as he tilts his
flask.[3] The Courtauld sheet, which has darkened through
exposure to light but in which the handling is even more
vigorous and exuberant, shows the figure posed precisely
as he will appear in the final composition. Watteau took

L'AUTONNE
*Gravé d'Aprés le Tableau original Point en ovale par Watteau chez
M. Crozat haut de 4 pieds 3. pouces sur 3. pieds 9. pouces de large.*

FIG. 66 Étienne Fessard after Jean-Antoine Watteau,
Autumn, no. 106 of *L'Œuvre d'Antoine Watteau*, 1726–35
Etching with engraving, 450 × 340 mm
London, British Museum, inv. no. 1838,0526.1.106

PROVENANCE
Mounted by François Renaud (L. 1042); Jean-
Antoine Vassal de Saint-Hubert (1741–1782),
sale, Paris, 23 March–17 April 1779, possibly
part of lot 94; Jules-Robert Auguste (1789–1850)
(?); possibly his sale, Hôtel Drouot, Paris, 28–31
May 1850, lots 100–103 (lots are not described);
Baron Louis-Auguste de Schwiter (1805–1889;
L. 1768), sale, Hôtel Drouot, Paris, 20 April 1883;
Henri Michel-Lévy (1845–1914), sale, Paris,

12–13 May 1919, lot 116; Adrien Fauchier-
Magnan (1873–1965); Count Antoine Seilern
(1901–1978), acquired at Fauchier-Magnan sale,
Sotheby's, 4 December 1935, lot 66; Princes
Gate Bequest, 1978

SELECTED LITERATURE
Seilern 1961, no. 221 and p. 76; Grasselli 1987,
vol. 1, no. 181 and pp. 252ff.; Rosenberg and Prat
1996, vol. 2, no. 374; Hattori 2001, pp. 64 n. 13,
65 n. 40; Conisbee 2009, p. 471 n. 14

SELECTED EXHIBITIONS
London 1981, no. 153 (repr. reversed); London
1983, no. 76; London 1991, no. 78; London 2011,
no. 41

into account both the function and the location of his decorations, which, inserted into panelling, were to be seen at a certain height. In both drawings the figure of the wine-pouring satyr looks down at us from above.

The two sheets were probably made during the same session and after the same model: note his large ears and somewhat flaccid stomach. In both, Watteau first lightly outlined the contours of the figure's head and upper body in red chalk, changing to a faint black for the thighs and legs, which taper away. In the Courtauld sheet, Watteau went back over the head and torso in stabbing accents of black, endowing his model with a V-shaped face, more chiselled features and an intense downward gaze – all of which he would assume in the finished painting. Although no horns are indicated on the forehead, in this drawing Watteau initiated the transformation of his model into the bestial demigod. The figure in the Courtauld sheet appears more hirsute than in the other; greater attention is paid to his nipples, pubic hair and genitals. Also noteworthy are the vibrancy of the rippling black lines of the upper body and the syncopated black strokes that define his chin, clavicle and left arm. White chalk is used extensively on the figure's forehead and upper body: even the knuckles and fingers of his left hand are highlighted in white. We sense the weight and pressure of these large hands as they grasp the spectral (and empty) flagons, indicated in the briefest of black lines, almost as afterthoughts.

In crafting his allegorical representation of Autumn Watteau recalled an array of venerable sources. The composition as a whole may have been inspired by Rubens's *Bacchus on a Barrel* (1636–40; St Petersburg, Hermitage Museum), then in Crozat's collection.[4] Titian's *Andrians* (Madrid, Museo del Prado) provided the figure of the reclining bacchante in the foreground and inspired that of the satyr pouring wine.[5] Watteau's familiarity with Titian's composition may also have been indebted to La Fosse, whose collection included "a large painting on canvas in its gilded

FIG.67 Jean-Antoine Watteau, Study of a nude man holding bottles, 1717; red, black and white chalk, 277 × 226 mm New York, The Metropolitan Museum of Art, Walter C. Baker Bequest, inv. no. 1972.118.238

frame representing a Bacchanal of Bacchus after Titian".[6]

Watteau's studies of the nude were dismissed by Caylus as deficient, since they were quite unlike the muscular, classically proportioned *académies* produced by the senior history painters of his generation. "Having no knowledge of human anatomy, and having almost never drawn the nude figure, he knew neither how to read nor express it; so much so that undertaking a male nude was onerous for him and gave him no pleasure".[7] With Watteau's *fêtes galantes* in mind, Caylus also claimed that the artist "generally drew without a purpose, for he never made sketches or preparatory studies for any of his paintings".[8] For Crozat's allegories, Watteau proved more orthodox in his practice. As Count Seilern noted, the Crozat drawings "are rare instances of studies made by Watteau with a specific painting or set of paintings in mind".[9] CBB

NOTES

1 Conisbee 2009, pp. 466–70. See also Hattori 2001. The preparatory drawings for *Autumn* are catalogued in Rosenberg and Prat 1996, nos. 371–74 and no. 378, *Standing satyr*, which has been cut down and whose relationship to this group is less secure.

2 Hattori 2001, p. 57, established the secure dating of 1717 for Watteau's studies for the Crozat Seasons, previously assigned by all authors to *c*. 1715–16.

3 New York 1999, pp. 8–10.

4 Posner 1984, pp. 78–80; Hattori 2001, pp. 60–61.

5 Washington and elsewhere 1984, pp. 133–34. I am less convinced by Hattori's suggestion (Hattori 2001, pp. 61–62, 65 n. 41) that the figure of the satyr was derived from Van Dyck's *Bacchanal of Children* (Zurich, Kunsthaus).

6 See Gustin-Gomez 2006, vol. 1, p. 255, for this picture in La Fosse's posthumous inventory of 23 December 1716.

7 Rosenberg 1984, p. 72.

8 *Ibid.*, p. 78.

9 Seilern 1961, p. 77.

CHARLES-JOSEPH NATOIRE
Nîmes 1700–1777 Castel Gandolfo

33 *The Life Class at the Royal Academy of Painting and Sculpture*, 1746

Pen, black and brown ink, grey wash and watercolour and traces of graphite, over black chalk,
on laid paper, lined with Japanese paper; minor foxing; inscribed by the artist in pen and
dark grey ink at lower centre *C. NATOIRE f. 1746*
453 × 322 mm

Samuel Courtauld Trust, D.1952.RW.3973

In December 1778 this drawing was described as "very detailed ... lightly coloured, and executed on white paper", representing "a group of students drawing" at the Academy of Painting's life class from models "posed by Charles Natoire, the professor in charge".[1] Dated 1746 on the box in the centre foreground, it is a large, complex drawing that the artist kept for more than thirty years.[2]

Black chalk, the beginner's choice because of its ease of manipulation, was Natoire's instrument of every day. Lightly drawn across the paper of the Courtauld sheet, chalk established a graphic foundation for the virtuoso pen and brush work that partly covers and fills it in.[3] For Natoire, drawing prepared the way for painting. As Susanna Caviglia-Brunel has demonstrated, he first produced a sketch of the composition.[4] Studies of the principal figures then refined contours and clarified gestures, before he made a finished drawing to which the planned painting conformed almost exactly. Most of the drawings Natoire produced before he took up the post of director of the French School in Rome in 1751 belong to one of these three categories. Not so *The Life Class*. Although it resembles in format and preparation the *modelli* Natoire made for paintings in the 1730s and 1740s, no painting of

this design exists or is recorded. However, in 1745 he was completing a pair of paintings for the collector Jean de Jullienne, representing *Drawing and Painting* (fig. 69) and *Music and Lyric Poetry*.[5] In the first, Drawing stands and shows her work to Painting with a gesture not unrelated to the students at Natoire's knee in *The Life Class*. Perhaps this commission inspired the Courtauld's drawing, which in other respects – as a genre scene, notably – remains unique in the painter's oeuvre.

The paintings depicted on the walls are not the ones that actually hung there: in 1746 Charles Le Brun's *Alexander at the Tent of Darius* (1661) was at Versailles; Jean Jouvenet's *Deposition* (1697) at the Capucines in Paris; Eustache Le Sueur's *Solomon and the Queen of Sheba* (1650) at Devonshire House in London; and François Lemoine's *Annunciation* (1725) at St-Sulpice.[6] However, the plan and elevation of the Life Class Room (fig. 68) that illustrates Nicolas Guérin's 1715 description of the Academy's rooms at the Louvre suggest that Natoire's scene is not completely imaginary. The room was hung wainscot to ceiling with pictures whose sizes and shapes are consistent with Natoire's re-creation; moreover, at the lower levels Natoire depicts precisely the kind of drawings and bas-reliefs after

PROVENANCE
Charles Louis Clérisseau (1721–1820), acquired at artist's sale, Paris, 14 December 1778, lot 100; Gilbert Paignon-Dijonval (1708–1792); Sir Robert Witt (1872–1952), acquired at Walker Gallery; Robert Witt Bequest, 1952

SELECTED LITERATURE
Bénard 1810, no. 3348; Mirimonde 1958, p. 282, fig. 3; Princeton 1977, pp. 22–23, fig. 3; Troyes and elsewhere 1977, p. 80; Bordeaux 1984, p. 108; Roland Michel 1987, p. 58, fig. 45; Forster 1998, pp. 48–85; Paris 2003, p. 85; Paris 2009, p. 40, fig. 13; Petherbridge 2010, p. 222, pl. 152

SELECTED EXHIBITIONS
London 1950, no. 54; London and elsewhere 1953, no. 79; London 1953, no. 391; London 1958a, no. 68; Los Angeles 1961, no. 25; London 1962, no. 37; Swansea 1962, no. 63; Nottingham 1966 (unnumbered); London 1968a, no. 490; King's Lynn 1985, no. 33; London 1991d, no. 35

the model produced by the professors to aid the student that are described in Guérin's text.[7] The models are posed on the table that occupied the centre of the room; the light entered from windows to the left; and the table had hooks at its corners to enable the professors to manoeuvre stage and model into an advantageous relation to the angle of sunlight.[8] Two models were available to hold an interactive pose one week in every month[9] and, finally, the students distributed themselves on three tiers of seating that wrapped around the table on three sides. Only the casts of antique statues – the Farnese *Hercules*, the *Laocoön* and the Medici *Venus* – are utterly out of place, recruited from elsewhere in the Academy's apartments.[10]

While the Jullienne commission may have prompted the drawing, the politics of the moment certainly marked it. Made in the year that Le Normand de Tournehem arrived at the Bâtiments du Roi with a programme for the regeneration of French history painting, Natoire's drawing makes a case for the centrality of *disegno* to that endeavour. Natoire presents the scene with the *gravitas* of modern history, and its narrative provides a moral: copying leads to emulation and emulation to invention in a causal chain that links practice today to a place on the walls tomorrow. In the Courtauld drawing, Natoire both invented a new subject for French art[11] and asserted that the inventiveness of drawing depended on skills honed by copying.[12] KS

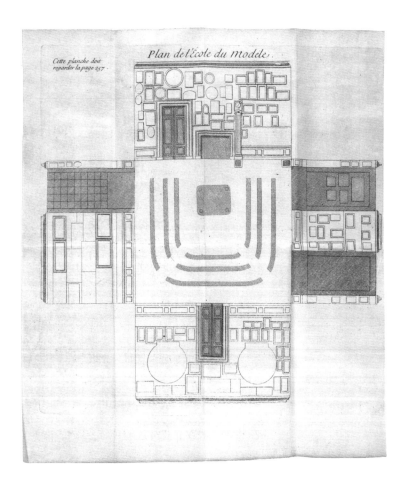

FIG. 68 Unknown artist, Plan of the Life Class Room, from Nicolas Guérin, *Description de l'Académie royale de peinture et de sculpture*, 1715, engraving London, British Library, General Reference Collection 7807.e.3

163

C. NATOIRE
f. 1746.

FIG. 69 Jean Pelletier after
Charles-Joseph Natoire,
*The Union of Painting and
Drawing*, 1750
Etching and engraving,
353 × 395 mm
Dijon, Musée des Beaux Arts

NOTES

1 *Catalogue de vente de feu M. Natoire, directeur de l'Académie de France à Rome*, Paris, 14 December 1778 (L. 2928), lot 100.

2 Another, somewhat less detailed version is at the Musée Atget in Montpellier (album M34, fol. 9), and a drawing of the same subject in a related scene transposed to antiquity and allegorised to illustrate the Horatian maxim *ut pictura poesis* is in the Cleveland Museum of Art (acc. no. 1998.76). Meanwhile, a number of black-chalk studies of individual figures, six in all, survive, for the professor and some of the students. The preparatory drawing for the professor is at Amsterdam, Rijksprentenkabinet, inv. no 1975:89, and a sketch for the seated student at the centre is at Harvard, Fogg Museum, Bequest of Frances L. Hofer, 1979.94; both were formerly in the Bernard Houthakker collection. A drawing in the Ashmolean in Oxford relates to the figure of the boy showing his drawing in the foreground;

another of the same figure was sold at Colnaghi, London, in 1954. A preparatory drawing for the servant in the right foreground is recorded but its whereabouts are unknown; a variant of this, of a boy with his hands in a satchel, is at the Bibliothèque Jacques Villon at Rouen. For a recent discussion, see Paris 2003, no 25.

3 Natoire's first recorded use of watercolour dates from 1739, in the composition drawing for *Calypso's Nymphs burning Telemachus's Ships* (Stockholm, Nationalmuseum). See Bjurström 1984, no. 1073.

4 Caviglia-Brunel 2004, pp. 35–48.

5 See Tillerot 2010, pp. 165–66, nos. 131–32. The picture's location is unknown. The portrait of Raphael is an addition of the print.

6 Kennedy in London 1991, no. 35, notes that the images are reversed, drawn from reproductive prints.

7 Guérin 1715, p. 258.

8 However, in the winter months (including February), the students drew by lamplight.

9 The second model was transferred from the Gobelins for the week in question.

10 Casts of the *Hercules* and the *Laocoön* were in the adjacent Salle des Assemblées and of the *Venus Pudica* in the third room of the apartment. See Guérin 1715, pp. 105–06, 185.

11 It was preceded by images of the draughtsman and of the private academy; it very possibly inspired later depictions of the Royal Academy, notably by Charles-Nicolas Cochin in the illustration of 'Dessein' for Diderot and d'Alembert's *Encyclopédie* (1751–78).

12 On Natoire's own practice of copying, see Stein 2000, pp. 167–86.

34 *Terrace in an Italian Garden, c.* 1760

Red chalk, vertical fold in centre with an original compressed crease to its left; minor foxing; small hole with retouching in centre. Verso: inscribed in pencil *II 19*

325 × 441 mm

WATERMARK
Three lines of letters, largely illegible, a fleur-de-lys within an oval surmounted by a crown

Samuel Courtauld Trust, D.1978.PG.232

What does it mean to speak of a 'master drawing' if the drawing is the outcome of a collaboration, conceptual and manual, between two artists? The present drawing, ascribed since 1961 to Robert, was long attributed to Jean-Honoré Fragonard (see cat. no. 35).[1] The two artists drew and sketched from nature next to one another in the environs of Rome.[2] The enjoyable activity was both a pedagogic exercise and a visceral exploration through drawing of the exciting new territory that was Italy. The red-chalk drawings they produced between 1758 and 1761, such as this one, are self-consciously virtuosic but have proved puzzlingly indistinguishable: rather than artistic competition or individuality, the emerging master's hands exhibit an unusually sympathetic correspondence (see fig. 70).[3]

In spite of the difficulty of attribution, comparisons are frequently drawn between the early works of these two artists. Where the landscape drawings of Fragonard are said to be inventive, those of Robert are supposedly banally faithful to the motif; where Fragonard's views are extensive and spacious, Robert's tend to be close and constricted. If Fragonard's landscape is of a prodigious originality, Robert's repeats a narrow range of motifs. Images of unbounded generative nature erupt in one and theatrical artifice stultifies the other. Fragonard's landscape is imaginative poetry, whereas Robert's is worldly prose.[4]

On the basis of this drawing, we beg to differ. In fact, in 1760 Robert, at twenty-six, was the more precocious of the two. In 1759 Abel Poisson, marquis de Marigny, director of the Bâtiments du Roi, wrote from Paris to Charles-Joseph Natoire (see cat. no. 33), director of the French Academy in Rome, advising him to exhort the young *pensionnaires* to follow the path of Robert, "*… car il me revient de tous les côtes de grandes éloges de ce jeune home*" (for from every quarter I hear great praise for this young man). In 1760 Natoire reported, "*Robert travaille*" (Robert is working), and three years later, "*C'est un artiste laborieux*" (he's an arduous artist).[5]

The Courtauld drawing, in its brilliant technical virtuosity and great pictorial intelligence, encapsulates this extraordinary early achievement. The variety and heterogeneity of calligraphic marks are as effective in rendering different textures as they are masterly in conveying the effect of nature's vibrant mobility. The dynamism of the looping strokes of the trees evoke a nervous rustling; beyond this proscenium, Robert conveys the blinding stillness and silence of a summer afternoon through the graduated, revealed blankness of

PROVENANCE
Lippmann-Mayer, acquired at Georges Petit, Paris, 26 June 1924, lot 6; Adrien Fauchier-Magnan (d. 1965); Count Antoine Seilern (1901–1978), acquired at Fauchier-Magnan sale, Sotheby's, London, 4 December 1935, lot 15; Princes Gate Bequest, 1978

SELECTED LITERATURE
Seilern 1961, no. 232; Ananoff 1961–70, vol. 1, no. 368; New York 1990, pp. 206, fig. 1, 208; Rome 1990, pp. 26, 28

SELECTED EXHIBITIONS
London 1968a, no. 600; London 1991, no. 60

FIG. 70 Jean-Honoré Fragonard, *Stairway of the Villa d'Este, Tivoli* Red chalk, 350 × 487 mm Besançon, Musée des Beaux Arts et d'Archéologie, D 2844

the white of the paper. The dark, almost wet application of sanguine on the more heavily worked right margin conveys a heavy, dense humidity, just as the light, dry touch of the lightly sketched clump of trees at the drawing's centre – wavery and shimmering, Van Gogh-like – transmits a hallucinatory noonday dryness.

Robert shows us here four figures – or five, if one includes the statue beneath the bower, whose classical drapery contrasts with the modernity of the costume of the diminutive laundresses and the child in the foreground and imparts to the drawing a sense of enduring time and matronly authority. Robert's deployment of figures in the landscape is rhetorically effective. The outstretched foreshortened arm of the standing laundress in the foreground resonates with the gesture of the artist himself, sizing up and drawing the landscape that he beholds. This ostensive gesture, combined with her alert posture, encourages us, if not exactly to reach

out and touch, to enter alertly into this imaginary world.

The gazes and gestures of the mother and child direct us towards the crux of the image. The natural tunnel – a small hole of white seen through a circular dense smudge of red chalk – pulls the viewer deep into the bold perspectival construction. Robert cleverly places there the subtlest of hints of human presences looking back at us. Throughout the rest of his career, Robert obsessively returned to the motif of a tunnel or passageway.[6] The limitless gaze penetrating darkness in search of light was a classic trope of the Enlightenment. Robert also admits the figure of the sleep of reason – a young man (or two?) lying unconscious on the ground at the foot of the statue and immersed in light. Through this figure of male reverie, Robert indicates this seductive landscape as one of fantasy, a dreamworld produced by an artist (or two) in the celebrated passage through Italy – drawing in a state of transit. S P

NOTES

1 See Seilern 1961 and Ananoff 1961–70, vol. 1, no. 368. On the drawing's testifying to a "collaborative relationship", see Rome 1990, p. 28. On the general confusion in attribution of their red-chalk drawings, see Williams in Washington and elsewhere 1978, p. 29; and Paris and New York 1987, p. 65.
2 See Paris 1983 and Rome 1990.
3 The date of the Courtauld sheet is based on similarity, in both style and motif, to drawings

Fragonard executed at the Villa d'Este in Tivoli during his summer stay there in 1760, in the company of the abbé de Saint-Non (but possibly not Robert). Although known by Seilern as *The Tivoli Gardens*, it is more likely an entirely imaginary construction. Cuzin and Rosenberg in Rome 1990 view the year 1760 as the most productive – and in terms of signature, densely problematic – moment of the collaboration. They speculate that

this could be a counterproof produced by Fragonard over which Robert drew. Fragonard left Italy for Paris in 1761; Robert remained there four more years.
4 These value judgements are subtly pervasive in discussions of the comparisons between these two artists.
5 Gabillot 1895, p. 74.
6 Corboz 1978.

JEAN-HONORÉ FRAGONARD
Grasse 1732–1806 Paris

35 *Young girl seated*, 1785

Red chalk, on laid paper; laid down on an 18th(?)-century mount; framing line in pen and black ink; inscribed at lower left in pen and brown ink *frago. 178[6?]5*; overall slight discolouration and foxing, with a light stain at upper left

225 × 172 mm

Samuel Courtauld Trust, D.1978.PG.229

Edmond and Jules de Goncourt described Fragonard's remarkable chalk technique:

> [Fragonard's] effects suggest that he used chalk without a holder, that he rubbed it flat for the masses, that he was continually turning it between his thumb and forefinger in risky, but inspired, wheelings and twistings; that he rolled and contorted it over the branches of his trees, that he broke it on the zigzags of his foliage. Every irregularity of the chalk's point, which he left unsharpened, was pressed into service. When it blunted, he drew fully and broadly . . . when it sharpened, he turned it to the subtleties, the lines and the lights.[1]

This vivid description suggests that Fragonard did not so much master the medium as freely capitulate to it. The heterogeneity of marks seen in the present drawing – from the sharp, emphatic strokes of the folds of the bodice to the languorous lines of the shawl – exemplify Fragonard's adaptation to the plastic transformations of the chalk, even if this is a relatively restrained performance.

Both the date of the drawing and the identification of the sitter – it is clearly a portrait – are contentious.[2] As Pierre Rosenberg noted, the writing in pen and ink at the lower left of the sheet is not a signature but an inscription.[3] The date there is indistinct, 1765 or 1785. Reading it as 1765, as did Anita Brookner and the maker of the possibly eighteenth-century mount, renders the drawing an anomaly in Fragonard's practice when he was wavering between making grand history paintings and fantastic heads inspired by Rembrandt.[4] If we accept the later date, following Eunice Williams, the sitter can tentatively be identified as the artist's daughter Rosalie, born in 1769.[5] In the 1770s and 1780s Fragonard executed what are undoubtedly portrait drawings of members of his family as well as drawings of seated young women (see fig. 71).[6] The identification as Rosalie imbues it with

PROVENANCE
M. Marcille senior, by 1857; Edmond and Jules de Goncourt (1822–1896 and 1830–1870; L. 1089), acquired at sale, Paris, 4–7 March 1857; Pierre Decourcelle, acquired at de Goncourt sale, Paris, 15–17 February 1897, lot 83; E. M. Hodgkins (1892–1917), acquired at Georges Petit, Paris, 29–30 May 1911, lot 89; Hodgkins sale, Paris, 30 April 1914, lot 26; Dufois, acquired at Sotheby's, London, 9 December 1936, lot 50; Count Antoine Seilern (1901–1978), 1936; Princes Gate Bequest, 1978

SELECTED LITERATURE
Ananoff 1961–70, vol. 1, no. 199; Seilern 1961, no. 229, p. 93; Washington and elsewhere 1978, p. 136; Paris and New York 1987, p. 568, fig. 1; Brookner in Farr (ed.) 1987, pp. 176–77; Launay 1991, pp. 291–92

SELECTED EXHIBITION
London 1981, no. 135; London 1983, no. 67; London 1991d, no. 21

FIG. 71 Jean-Honoré Fragonard, *Young girl dozing*
Red chalk, 241 × 188 mm
New York, private collection

a gloomy significance. In 1788 she died at age nineteen, to Fragonard's devastation. In drawing forth the sickly girl does Fragonard draw her imminent withdrawal from life? In the attitude of resignation and posture of passivity might we detect a certain vulnerable vitality?

Biographical speculation aside, this late Rococo sheet reprises a richly variegated motif in French drawing of the eighteenth century – the seated female figure, whose most famous early eighteenth-century exponent was Watteau.[8] Watteau may have been inspired by engraved fashion plates of the 1690s, which, with their extrovert poses and modish self-presentation, had contributed to the sexual liberation of French women.[9] Executed in the more censorious years around 1780, Fragonard's drawings of this motif are rather different in their sexual politics:

this young woman is not confidently sensual but wistful, passive and withdrawn. It is easy to reject the title given to it only in the twentieth century as unsubstantiated, yet it correctly responds to a quality in the drawing – *La Resignée* (Resigned).[7]

The darkish brown hue of Fragonard's chalk imparts an overall sombreness, relieved by a lighter vivacious red, most prominent in the darkest shadows on the right and across the girl's lap. Fragonard used the white of the sheet (now discoloured) to establish the luminosity of youthful skin, particularly on the broad expanse of the side of the tilted face. The bold disruption of form at the bottom of the sheet focuses our attention on the restless drama towards its centre – the exposed hand that distractedly fumbles with the shawl.

The most intense and nervous graphic activity is reserved for the slightly twisting upper body. Fragonard's lines here shift from a relative economy on the left of the page to density and depth of shadow on the right, suggesting some affecting presence towards which the smiling head above is turned in greeting. The most active business of drawing occurs at the centre of the sheet, around the girl's heart. Coincidentally, in the years around 1780 Fragonard was painting small, dark cabinet paintings on the theme of the vows of love, in which young female figures are released into a state of erotic frenzy.[10]

Although he continued to draw, Fragonard soon virtually stopped painting. Yet in 1790–91, when he completed the Progress of Love series (New York, Frick Collection) with the canvas 'L'Abandonnée' (fig. 72), he reprised the seated female figure one last time. Here, the turning woman with an air of resignation is transformed into a late and melancholic permutation of the motif. SP

FIG. 72 Jean-Honoré Fragonard, 'L'Abandonée' (also called 'La Reverie'), 1790–91
Oil on canvas, 317.8 × 197.2 cm
New York, Frick Collection, Henry Clay Frick Bequest

NOTES

1 Goncourt 1856–75, pp. 301–02. The Goncourts acquired two drawings by Fragonard of seated young women in 1857, of which this is one. See Launay 1991, pp. 291–92, and note 6 below.

2 Between 1775 and 1785 Fragonard made drawings of young women seated or standing, with individuated faces. At this time, he was living with his wife, Marie-Anne; her younger sister, Marguerite Gérard; and his daughter, Rosalie, and it is not easy to identify each sitter. On comparable standing portrait figures, see Besançon 2006, pp. 166–68, nos. 91 and 92.

3 Rosenberg in Paris and New York 1987, p. 568.

4 Brookner in Farr (ed.) 1987, pp. 176–77.

5 Washington and elsewhere 1978, p. 136. Rosenberg in Paris and New York 1987, p. 568, concurs with the later date but is agnostic on the identity of the sitter.

6 See also Young Girl seated on the ground (London, British Museum), which features the same mantle dress. For these drawings as a coherent group, see Washington and elsewhere 1978, no. 54; Paris and New York 1987, nos. 298 and 299; and New York and London 2005, no. 58. On the medallion

drawings of the Fragonard family, see Paris and New York 1987, nos. 287–96.

7 This title first appeared in Berlin 1910. See Seilern 1961, no. 229.

8 See, for example, Watteau's Woman lying on a sofa (c. 1717–18; Paris, Fondation Custodia), in Washington and elsewhere 1984, no. 114.

9 De Jean in Conisbee (ed.) 2007.

10 The Invocation to Love focuses on a young girl, turned to the right, in a headlong rush towards the figure of Eros. See Paris and New York 1987, nos. 280–82.

GIOVANNI BATTISTA PIAZZETTA
Venice 1683–1754 Venice

36 *The head of a boy and of an old man, c. 1739–40*

Black chalk heightened with white chalk, on laid grey paper;
overall undulation and slight discolouration; extensive abrasion on raised areas;
heavy vertical creases along left and right edges; diagonal rope mark at lower right;
minor tears at left edge and centre right, repaired
336/342 × 274 mm

Samuel Courtauld Trust, D.1952.RW.1645

Piazzetta began, like his father, as a wood-carver and then worked in the studio of Antonio Molinari (1665–1727). He became deeply influenced by Giuseppe Maria Crespi's works when he went to Bologna to complete his education in the first decade of the 1700s. He was especially attracted by Crespi's treatment of colour dominated by dramatic chiaroscuro, indebted to the Carracci and Guercino. Crespi's cultivation of genre scenes also helped him abandon almost entirely large-scale history painting, as he evolved new forms of psychological close-ups or character heads. This was a response to the demand for small, unpretentious pictures made for comfortable rooms, which followed the Rococo trend for informality that reached Venice around 1720. Up to this time drawings had been conserved in portfolios or pasted into albums of amateurs, who showed them to their peers at exclusive parties at which each person had the opportunity to make brilliant observations in elegantly turned phrases. But now drawings became works of art in their own right, on a par with paintings, to be glazed and framed and hung on the wall alongside frail pastels and engravings, adding to the intimacy and luxuriousness of the rooms. The Venetian invention of costly crystal glass, used for the glazing and often specified in inventories, was a crucial factor in this development.

The present drawing belongs to this category of character heads made for the open market as independent works of art. They are Piazzetta's most celebrated and most familiar works. They secured his reputation from the very beginning, as demonstrated by a letter from the Venetian painter Antonio Balestra to the Florentine collector Niccolò Gabburri (see cat. no. 9) of 1717 and by subsequent letters to Gabburri from Marco Ricci from 1723.[1] The drawings were so popular that they were often imitated by members of Piazzetta's circle many years after his death, which has caused serious problems of attribution. Since they show little stylistic development and very few of them bear dates, any proposed chronology remains tentative.

A scrutiny of these character heads reveals that Piazzetta, apparently, worked from a very small number of live models, often members of his family, whom he drew from different angles and combined in many different ways. The old man in the Courtauld drawing recurs, dressed as an ecclesiastic, in a drawing in the Albertina in Vienna and in two sheets that were on the art market in

PROVENANCE
Prince W. Argoutinsky-Dolgoroukoff (1875–1941; L. 2602d); Sir Robert Witt (1872–1952; L. 2228b), acquired at Argoutinsky-Dolgoroukoff sale, Sotheby's, London, 4 July 1923, lot 17; Robert Witt Bequest, 1952

SELECTED EXHIBITION
London 1991, no. 55

FIG. 73 Giovanni Battista
Piazzetta, *The head of a boy and
an old man*
Graphite, charcoal and stumping
with white highlights on
grey paper, 390 × 560 mm
Bergamo, Accademia Carrara,
AC 2000

1960, and, as proposed by Helen Braham, he might also have been the sitter for studies in Bergamo (fig. 73) and Milan.[2] The boy is re-encountered in the drawing at Bergamo, in one belonging to the Museo Correr, in a sheet sold in Berne in 1960, and in *Boy and a girl with a trap* in the Accademia in Venice.[3] He is also present, now wearing a hat, in a study in Milan for the painting *Pastorale* in the Art Institute in Chicago of 1739–40,[4] which might be taken as an approximate date for this group of works, including the Courtauld's sheet.

Like so many of these character heads, the Courtauld drawing is conceived like a snapshot, showing the interruption of an interaction between two figures. A boy seen in profile from behind is studying a book with immobile concentration, while his tutor, an old bearded man, has become distracted by something outside the picture field and turns away. Youth and old age, engagement and disengagement, stability and movement, front and rear, all are depicted within a construction of an open rhomboid created from the parallel, opposing angles of the boy's shoulder and crown of head, three-quarter profile, and hand. However, one cannot rid oneself of the feeling that there is something more at work here. This is not a depiction of a schoolteacher and his pupil. What is the boy reading? What has attracted the attention of the tutor, and who is he? The answer may lie in Giovanni Battista Tiepolo's *Scherzi* etchings from approximately the same time. Many of these scenes feature young boys who appear to be instructed in the secrets of witchcraft by bearded magi, often of Oriental origin. Apart from being evocative images of mysteries beyond reason, no satisfactory explanation of their deeper meaning has been given so far, and it is indeed a question if there is any.[5] C F

NOTES

1 Bottari 1757, II, p. 100.

2 Vienna, Albertina, inv. no. 1792, Birke and Kertész 1992–97, vol. 2, p. 943, no. 1792, repr.; art market, London, Koetser Gallery, photo Witt Library, and Berne 1960, lot 196 (a variant of the Vienna drawing); Bergamo, Accademia Carrara, AC 2000, Ruggieri 1967, p. 9, pl. 1; Milan, Castello Sforzesco, Coll. E 82/3 Gen. 4882/3, Milan 1971, no. 13.

3 Venice, Museo Correr, inv. no. 7058, Pignatti 1980–96, vol. 5, pp. 132–33, no. 1323; Berne 1960, lot 198; Venice, Accademia, inv. no. 15123.

4 Milan, Castello Sforzesco, Coll. D 223/1 Gen. 4884/1, Milan 1971, no. 2.

5 For various proposals of interpretations, see Fischer in Copenhagen 1992, pp. 18–20.

GIOVANNI BATTISTA TIEPOLO
Venice 1696–1770 Madrid

37 *The Holy Family with Saint Joseph Reading, c.* 1757

Pen, brown ink and grey brown wash, on laid paper; partially laid down;
overall undulation and localised staining at lower corners
285 × 211/215 mm

WATERMARK
Three crescents

Samuel Courtauld Trust, D.1978.PG.159

This drawing belongs to a large and homogeneous group of almost seventy pen-and-wash variations on the theme of the Holy Family. Like others of this series, it shows us Giovanni Battista Tiepolo's formidable virtuosity in this medium: the subject almost floats on the page like an exquisite arabesque. Two other sheets from the series are in The Courtauld collection, and closely related compositions are in public collections in Rotterdam, Los Angeles and Berlin, while others have been on the art market.[1] George Knox dates the group in the "later 1750s",[2] and in the present case this is supported by Count Seilern's observation that the Child resembles the small boys in the sheet of studies of children playing used for the decorations in the *foresteria* of the Villa Valmarana, executed about 1757.[3]

Although some of these drawings are clearly depictions of the Rest on the Flight into Egypt, most of them, including the Courtauld sheet, are simply variations on the theme of the Holy Family. Thus, Giambattista's concern does not seem to have been so much with the iconography as with the composition and its ability to transmit moods and atmosphere to the spectator, much like the musical variations on a theme of Johann Sebastian Bach's

Musikalisches Opfer composed ten years earlier. In the present drawing Giambattista has represented Saint Joseph turning his back to the Virgin and Child, absorbed in reading instead of assisting them with concern as he does in the idealised versions of the theme that we are used to seeing. In this way Giambattista has given the holy scene an unexpected humorous and mundane twist typical of the unique combination of lively spirit and intelligence noticed by his contemporaries.[4]

Before Giovanni Battista left Venice for Madrid in 1762, he had many of his drawings bound into volumes, which he left behind. At least two of these volumes, one containing studies of heads, the other studies for the Holy Family, were apparently given to his son Giuseppe, who was a friar in the convent of the Somaschi at Santa Maria della Salute; from there they came into the possession of Antonio Canova, the sculptor. Canova was an avid collector of Tiepolo and had already bought four volumes of the master's drawings from Giambattista's heir, Domenico Tiepolo's widow, in 1810.[5] There can be little doubt that the Courtauld drawing belonged to the volume containing variations on the theme of the Holy Family.

PROVENANCE
Giuseppe Tiepolo, son of the artist and friar in the convent of the Somaschi, Santa Maria della Salute, Venice, given by the artist mounted in an album, 1762; kept in convent of the Somaschi until its suppression, 1810; Count Leopoldo Cicognara (1767–1834); Antonio Canova (1754–1822); Monsignor Giovanni Battista Sartori-Canova (1775–1858), by descent; Francesco Pesaro, Venice, purchased from Sartori-Canova; Edward Cheney (1803–1884), Badger Hall, Shropshire, purchased from

Pesaro, 1842; Colonel Alfred Capel Cure (1826–1896), Blake Hall, Ongar, Essex, by descent; Parson's, acquired at Sotheby's, London, 29 April 1885, lot 1024; Tomás Harris (1908–1964), acquired at Sotheby's, London, 31 May 1932, lot 16; Albert Paul Rudolf and Carl Robert Rudolf (1884–1974; L. 2811b); Count Antoine Seilern (1901–1978), acquired at Rudolf sale, Sotheby's, London, 2 November 1949, lot 39; Princes Gate Bequest, 1978

SELECTED LITERATURE
Seilern 1959, no. 159; Pavanello 1996, p. 45

SELECTED EXHIBITIONS
London 1936a, no. 86; London 1939a, no. 120; London 1981, no. 151; London 1983, no. 72

Members of the Tiepolo workshop commonly pasted their drawings into albums organised according to themes or techniques, such as dressed figures, single figures for ceilings, heads or caricatures, or studies and *ricordi* in red chalk on blue paper, which survived intact till the very end of the nineteenth century and even beyond. This was apparently done with a view to later use, so that elements from different volumes could easily be arranged together.[6] Similar organisation of material seems to have been in use in Rubens's studio, as attested by a large number of drawings from his workshop – the so-called Rubens Cantoor – in the Department of Prints and Drawings at the Statens Museum for Kunst in Copenhagen.[7]

It has been argued that Giovanni Battista Tiepolo's drawings of the Holy Family were intended as models for the sons, although none of them is known to have been transferred into paintings. It has, however, been demonstrated that Domenico's drawings of variations on the theme of Saint Antony and the Christ Child were inspired by them.[8] C F

NOTES

1 London, The Courtauld Gallery, D 1978 PG 158 and D 1935 SC 250; Rotterdam, Museum Boijmans Van Beuningen, I 440, Rotterdam 1996, pp. 86–87, no. 36; New York, The Metropolitan Museum of Art, inv. no. 59.23.81, Bean and Griswold 1990, pp. 242–243, no. 234; Los Angeles County Museum of Art, *Gazette des Beaux-Arts* 1970, fig. 326; Berlin, Kupferstichkabinett, inv. no. 127-1928, Schulze Altcappenberg in Berlin 1996, pp. 46–48, no. 26; art market: Baroni 1980; Sotheby's, London, 2 July 1984, lot 121; Paris 1991a, no. 20.

2 Knox 1975, p. 92 under no. 275.

3 *Ibid.*, p. 88, no. 259.

4 For example, Anton Maria Zanetti in 1732 spoke of *"il vivacissimo spirito del quale unito all'intelligenza é infatti singolare"*(his vivid spirit united with intelligence is in fact quite unique); see Pallucchini 1960, p. 86.

5 Pavanello 1996, pp. 37–38 and 75 n. 56.

6 Schulze Altcappenberg in Berlin 1996, pp. 7–11.

7 The original order of the material has been tentatively reconstructed by Jesper Svenningsen in an unpublished paper for Copenhagen University in 2009.

8 Schulz 1978, pp. 63–73.

CANALETTO (GIOVANNI ANTONIO CANAL)

Venice 1697–1768 Venice

38 A view from Somerset Gardens looking towards London Bridge, c. 1746–55

Pen, brown ink and grey wash, on laid paper; lined with Japanese paper; overall uneven discolouration,
extensive abrasion towards the edges; several tears along edges, repaired, loss at bottom left corner;
old repair at centre left edge where piece was cut out and replaced by rectangle of laid paper (71 × 66 mm)
retouched with brush; two later framing lines in pen and ink (grey and black)
234/236 × 736/731 mm (single sheet)

WATERMARK
Fragment of fleur-de-lys surmounted by crown and countermark of fragments of letters

Samuel Courtauld Trust, D.1978.PG.131

Canaletto, the renowned painter of *vedute* from Venice
and darling of the British tourists, went to England in 1746
because his income at home was seriously affected by the
War of the Austrian Succession, which started in 1741 and
kept tourists from visiting his city. Apart from two return
visits to Venice in 1750–51 and 1753, he remained in
England for nine years, painting mainly views of London
and the Thames and making drawings for printers and
for the free market. When he returned to Venice in 1755
or 1756, Canaletto left behind a number of works, which
constitute the most complete survey of mid-Georgian
London by any one artist.

This view towards the city is seen from an imaginary
point above the terrace of Old Somerset House, soon to be
destroyed to make way for William Chambers's Somerset
House as it is preserved today. In the drawing Inigo Jones's
river stairs lead down to the Thames, which is busy with
boats. The skyline with the spires of the city churches is
dominated by St Paul's on the left and, behind the monument commemorating the Great Fire, in the far distance
on the right we see Old London Bridge, leading towards
a short stretch of the south bank.

The rapidly developing city of London was described by
contemporaries as heir to the legacy of ancient Rome and
Renaissance Venice, and Canaletto must have been aware
of this.[1] English optimism and pride in London's growing
power and beauty are cleverly matched by Canaletto's
clarity of light and his display of the metropolis's classical
architecture and buzzing commerce. The broad sweep of
the river calls to mind his views of the Grand Canal, which,
like the Thames, was a busy public thoroughfare framed
by privately owned houses, gardens and terraces brought
to life by the play of light and atmospheric effect.

Panoramic views like this one are often thought to
have been made with the use of a *camera obscura*, a
mechanical aid to drawing that Canaletto is reported to
have used. Within a darkened tent, the artist traced on a
sheet of paper the outlines of an image that was projected
by a moveable system of lenses and mirrors, resulting in
a distortion of the buildings close to the *camera*. A few
fragments of *vedute* drawings that apparently extended
over several sheets of paper are extant and are sometimes
said to have been made by Canaletto with the aid of the
camera.[2] But, as J.G. Links concluded, Canaletto's

PROVENANCE
Thomas Moore Slade (1771-1824), sale, London,
5 July 1810; Mrs Heywood Johnstone; Ellis and
Smith, acquired at Heywood Johnstone sale,
Christie's, 20 February 1925, lot 20; Adrien
Fauchier-Magnan (1873–1965); Count Antoine
Seilern (1901-1978), acquired at Fauchier-
Magnan sale, Sotheby's, 4 December 1935, lot 3;
Princes Gate Bequest, 1978

SELECTED LITERATURE
Constable 1927, p. 18; Parker 1948, p. 53 under
no. 114; Seilern 1959, no. 131; Venice 1962, p. 36
under no. 40; Constable 1962, p. 528 under
no. 745; Seilern 1971, no. 131; Constable (Links)
1976, pp. 143, 418f., 421, 575 under no. 745;
London 1980, p. 73 under no. 38 and p. 113
under no. 86; Farr (ed.) 1987, p. 168; Frankfurt
and elsewhere 1989, p. 151 (Italian edn, p. 153)

SELECTED EXHIBITIONS
London 1981, no. 129; London 1983, no. 65;
London 1991, no. 19

purported viewpoint here was about twelve feet above
and far out in the river, a vantage that no one could have
had before the construction of Waterloo Bridge in 1817.
Use of the *camera obscura* can thus be excluded in this
case.[3] Helen Braham proposed that the drawing was more
likely to have been composed in the studio using a number
of sketches, now lost, from different viewpoints on the
river as well as from the river stairs and the terrace.[4] By
making the viewer a floating spectator, Canaletto offers
him a wider perspective of the commercial life on the
river and in the capital, an approach that no doubt
appealed to the new class of trading aristocrats for
whom Canaletto worked.

Finished drawings like this one – in which Canaletto combined the use of a ruler and pencil with pen and ink and final touches of several layers of wash for the depiction of atmosphere and light instead of hatchings – did not appear in the artist's work before the late 1730s. By the time of his visit to England, he had developed this technique to an unrivalled degree of mastery.[5]

The view was apparently a success. W.G. Constable lists six autograph painted versions, one drawing and several pictures of the view by Canaletto imitators. Among the autograph paintings is one at Windsor, painted for Canaletto's patron the Venetian resident Consul Smith, presumably executed during Canaletto's eight months' visit to his native city in 1750–51; it includes more sky and foreground than we see here. Another picture, now in the Mellon Collection, was owned by Thomas West in 1850, when it was engraved by Edward Rooker (fig. 74). Consul Smith also owned a drawing, now at Windsor, which is smaller and of lesser quality (fig. 75). Despite showing more of the sky, it is clearly based on the Courtauld version, which may therefore be considered the earliest.[6] Since none of the drawings corresponds with the paintings, they were probably made as independent works of art. Canaletto also painted a corresponding view upstream towards Westminster for Consul Smith,[7] and he probably also made a comparable drawing, now lost. CF

NOTES

1 Hallett in Birmingham 1993, pp. 46–54.
2 For the *camera obscura* in general, see Meder 1923, p. 550; for discussion of Canaletto's use of it, see Links 1982, pp. 104–06; Moschini 1963, pp. 6–7; Gioseffi 1959.
3 Letter of 2 February 1974 in The Courtauld Gallery archives referred to in Seilern 1959.
4 Braham in London 1991, no. 19.
5 On Canaletto's drawings in general, see especially Hadeln 1929 and Parker 1948.
6 For the paintings, see Constable 1962, vol. 2, pp. 388–89, no. 428; on the drawing at Windsor, Royal Library, RL 7560, see Parker 1948, p. 53, no. 114, pl. 69.
7 Constable 1962, vol. 1, p. 389, no. 429, pl. 79.

JOHN ROBERT COZENS
London 1752-1799 London

39 *Castel Sant'Angelo, Rome*, 1780

Watercolour, and grey ink washes, with some drawing with the point of the brush in dark grey ink,
over graphite, and traces of squaring up with graphite, on laid paper; laid down on artist's laid paper mount
with a design of five ruled bands in pen, two tinted with grey ink wash, 416 × 580 mm; inscribed by the artist
in pen and black ink at lower edge left of centre *Jnº Cozens 1780*; overall uneven slight discolouration; minor
retouchings. Verso: inscribed in a later hand in pencil *Castle of St Angelo Rome I J:R Cozens 1780* and *£40*
362 × 526 mm

WATERMARK
Drawing: fleur-de-lys within a shield surmounted by a crown, the letter W below;
mount: J WHATMAN

Samuel Courtauld Trust, D.1967.WS.31

Following in the footsteps of the landscape painter Richard
Wilson (1713/14–1782), a number of British artists, among
them Francis Towne (see cat. no. 42) and John Robert
Cozens, based themselves in Rome during the 1770s and
1780s. Cozens made his first journey to Italy in April 1776
in the company of the collector and connoisseur Richard
Payne Knight (1750–1824). *Castel Sant'Angelo* is one of
around forty similarly large watercolours that he executed
following his return to England in 1779.[1] The vast circular
fortress situated on the banks of the river Tiber traces
its origins back to the mausoleum of Emperor Hadrian
(built AD 130–39).[2] It was one of the most conspicuous
of the city's monuments, and a favourite subject for
eighteenth-century *vedutisti* (view painters), notably
Giovanni Battista Piranesi (1720–1778), whose dramatic
architectural landscapes epitomising the sublime image
of Rome affected Cozens's vision of its topography.

Whereas the majority of artists, including Piranesi,
depicted the castle and the full span of the Ponte
Sant'Angelo (fig. 76) with the dome of St Peter's beyond,
Cozens's composition, viewed from a closer, sideways
angle, is less extensive, with only two arches of the bridge

FIG. 76 Giovanni Battista Piranesi, *View of the bridge and
of Castel Sant'Angelo*, from the series *Vedute di Roma*, 1754
Etching, 377 × 484 mm
London, British Museum, inv. no. 1914,0216.93

visible. No preliminary drawing for the present watercolour
is known, although faint traces of ruled graphite lines
underlying the area above the building suggest it might
have been squared up from an earlier study or conceivably
from an etching attributed to his father, Alexander Cozens
(1717–1786), which presents a similar, but reversed image
of the castle with plume of smoke (fig. 77).[3] Significant

PROVENANCE
Sir Thomas Barlow Bt (1845–1945); Guy D.
Harvey Samuel; Fine Art Society, 1946; William
Wycliffe Spooner (1882–1967) and Mrs Spooner;
Spooner Bequest, 1967

SELECTED LITERATURE
Bell and Girtin 1934–35, no. 117; Oppé 1952a,
p. 115; Troutman 1968, p. 51

SELECTED EXHIBITIONS
London 1968, no. 10; Bath 1969, no. 241;
Manchester and London 1971, no. 19; Bristol
1973, no. 17; London 1974, no. 9; London 1977a,
no. 6; London 1979, no. 25; New Haven 1980,
no. 3; New York and London 1986, no. 84;
Manchester 1988, no. 9; London 1991, no. 30;
London and elsewhere 2005, no. 17

FIG. 77 Alexander Cozens,
Castel Sant'Angelo, 1746 (?)
Etching, 276 × 377 mm
London, British Museum,
inv. no. 1858,0417.325

additions to the watercolour are the house wall at the far left and protruding riverbank in the foreground, which form an L-shaped framing device, and a ferryboat and two small fishermen on the shore, the angle of one of their rods echoed in the pole of washing above. These compositional elements could well have been inspired by Piranesi's fanciful architectural view, which, designed for the tourist market, bustles with human activity. In contrast, Cozens's sparse scene is a more introspective vision: silhouetted against an overcast sky, the monolithic cylinder is mirrored in the glassy water. *The Colosseum from the North* (Edinburgh, National Gallery of Scotland), another 1780 watercolour of a monumental Roman building, is in a similar vein.[3] These two drawings provide evidence for the claim that Cozens effected the transition from

topographical view-making to Romantic watercolour painting in Britain.[4] His ability to capture both the emotional and the meteorological atmosphere was unique among watercolourists of the time and was greatly admired by J.M.W. Turner and John Constable, who famously described the artist's work as "all poetry".[5]

Cozens was also largely instrumental in transforming watercolour from 'tinted' drawing into a more expressive and painterly medium,[6] as demonstrated in this work, where colour is built up from successive layers of pure watercolour wash. His limited palette of grey, blue, brown and soft green was developed during this first Italian visit.[7] William Bradford considered that the singularly muted colours in this drawing were deliberately chosen "to arouse in the spectator a spirit of solitary contemplation and sombre, even fearful sentiments".[8] The earliest British watercolour painter consistently to model form using colour rather than line,[9] Cozens has here built up tonal contrasts in the sky, water and riverbanks with touches of grey, blue and black. His concern for outline shapes, whether of clouds, buildings or other objects, was probably affected by his father's 'blot' method, by which forms made by blotting monochrome washes acted as the basis for landscape paintings, although John Robert's views were always of actual places.[10]

Cozens was prey to depressive tendencies and in his final years was confined to an asylum. John Murdoch notes "the overwhelming solemnity" of the artist's image of a former prison. He maintains that, though not a depressive drawing, "it is as a work of art occupying a place in the discourse of melancholy as a creative force since the sixteenth century that we should try to grapple with its significance".[12] JS

NOTES

1 On the influence of his father's large-scale drawings, see Bradford in London 1991, no. 30, p. 68. The artist's integral line mount in grey wash suggests that this drawing was destined for a portfolio.

2 For the history of the building, see Hawcroft in Manchester 1988, no. 9, p. 14.

3 For further discussion, see Oppé 1952, p. 115; Godfrey 1978, p. 62; Wilton in New Haven 1980, no. 3, p. 23; Hawcroft in Manchester 1988, and Bradford in London 1991. Hawcroft suggests that Alexander's etching might derive from his son's watercolour.

4 See Lyles in London 1997, no. 60, p. 156.

5 Constable to John Fisher, 1821, quoted in Constable (Beckett) 1968, vol. 6, p. 72.

6 Also known as 'stained' drawing, whereby watercolour is laid over a neutral grey or brown underwash. See also cat. no. 42.

7 His restrained colouring was influenced by his father's use of monochrome washes. For further discussion on Cozens's use of colour, see Wilton in New Haven 1980, pp. 10–12.

8 Bradford in London 1991. He noted that they "may be seen to extend his father's

research into the impact upon the emotions of certain landscape configurations".

9 For further discussion, see Lyles in London 1997, p. 27.

10 See Wilton in New Haven 1980, p. 31, for further information on Alexander Cozens's 'New Method'.

11 London and elsewhere 2005, p. 50.

THOMAS GAINSBOROUGH
Sudbury 1727–1788 London

40 *Landscape with cattle on a road running through a wooded valley,*
mid to late 1780s

Black chalks, Indian ink wash and white bodycolour, on laid light-brown tinted paper;
slight overall discolouration; diagonal crease across upper left; small tear at bottom left repaired
278 × 394/391 mm

WATERMARK
Fleur-de-lys in shield

Samuel Courtauld Trust, D.1952.RW.2428

Despite – or perhaps because of – the fact that Thomas Gainsborough hardly ever sold or exhibited any of his drawings, no eighteenth-century British oil painter enjoyed more celebrity as a draughtsman. A decade after his death, the artist's good friend William Jackson wrote,

> If I were to rest his reputation upon one point, it should be on his Drawings. No man ever possessed methods so various in producing effect, and all excellent – his washy, hatching style, was here in its proper element. The subject which is scarce enough for a picture, is sufficient for a drawing, and the hasty loose handling, which in painting is poor, is rich in a transparent wash of bistre and Indian ink.

Many of Gainsborough's paintings, Jackson went on to say, might have had no merit beyond the "facility of [their] execution", which by itself may have made them valuable, but perhaps not valuable enough. By contrast, "His drawings almost rest on this quality alone … but possessing it in an eminent degree (and no drawing can have any merit where it is wanting) his works, therefore,

in this branch of the art, approach nearer than his paintings to perfection".[1]

Gainsborough had begun producing the type of drawing to which Jackson was referring – of which the Courtauld sheet is a fine and characteristic example – shortly after moving from his native Suffolk to the fashionable spa resort of Bath, where he established himself as a portraitist (and occasional landscape painter) in 1759. Most of his sketching before this time had taken the form of detailed pencil or chalk studies done directly from nature, executed with a view to mastering the realistic landscape idiom associated with Jacob van Ruisdael, Jan Wijnants and other painters of the seventeenth-century Dutch school. When he moved to Bath, however, Gainsborough rejected this approach (condemned by academic theorists as laborious and mindless copying) in favour of using landscape as a vehicle for expressing his creative imagination, which (not by coincidence) he complained was stifled by the demands of his portrait patrons. If as a portraitist he was compelled to play the part of a glorified servant, who had to flatter to succeed, in landscape (and landscape drawing especially)

PROVENANCE
Sir Robert Witt (1872–1952; L. 2228b), received as a gift from Lord Duveen; Robert Witt Bequest, 1952

SELECTED LITERATURE
Witt 1935, p. 380, repr.; Woodall 1949, no. 373; Hayes 1970, no. 760

SELECTED EXHIBITIONS
London 1934, no. 1144; London 1936, no. 40; London and elsewhere 1953, no. 12; London 1958a, no. 54; Auckland 1960, no. 10; York and elsewhere 1960, no. 52; Manchester 1962, no. 6; London 1965, no. 11; London 1977a, no. 9; Tokyo 1978, no. 41

Gainsborough discovered an artistic arena where, during his leisure hours, he could display the superior knowledge and easy freedom that were the hallmarks of the true gentleman. In pursuit of this aim, he embraced the representation of a generalised nature, broadly evocative of the pastoral Golden Age celebrated by generations of poets going back to the ancient Romans Ovid and Virgil, and at the same time he shifted his artistic allegiance away from the Dutch naturalists, initially to Peter Paul Rubens and later to the great seventeenth-century Franco-Roman masters of classical landscape art, Claude Lorrain and Gaspard Dughet.

In composition the Courtauld drawing owes less to Claude than it does to a Gaspard such as one in the National Gallery, London (fig. 78).[2] But for all that its design may invoke the Old Masters, its fluently calli-graphic handling proclaims that it is first and foremost a Gainsborough, the product of a sensibility uniquely his own. "Mr Gainsborough's manner of penciling", wrote his early biographer Edward Edwards, "was so peculiar to himself, that his works needed no signature." Like Jackson, Edwards had the artist's later drawings in mind, which he said,

... were executed by a process rather capricious, truly deserving the epithet bestowed upon them by a witty lady, who called them moppings.

Many of these were in black and white, which colours were applied in the following manner: a small bit of sponge tied to a bit of stick, served as a pencil for the shadows, and a small lump of whiting, held by a pair of tea-tongs was the instrument by which the high lights were applied; beside these, there were others in black and white chalks, India ink, bister, and some in a slight tint of oil colours; with these various materials, he struck out a vast number of bold, free sketches of landscape and cattle, all of which have a most captivating effect to the eye of an artist, or connoisseur of real taste.[3]

'Moppings' like the Courtauld's were not intended for ordinary viewers, in other words. Instead, their sketchy and indeterminate qualities could only be properly appreciated – at least so Gainsborough's early champions confidently assumed – by those select few who prized executive and imaginative freedom as the sign of great art. D S

FIG. 78 Gaspard Dughet, *Landscape with a shepherd and his flock*, c. 1670
Oil on canvas, 48.6 × 65.3 cm
London, National Gallery

NOTES

1 Jackson 1798, pp. 157–58. For a useful discussion of Jackson's views on Gainsborough, see Rempel 1997, pp. 150–70.

2 During the mid 1780s Gainsborough's interest in Gaspard extended to the production of a series of drawings inspired by another landscape type devised by the seventeenth-century master, in which rustic architectural motifs such as houses, mills, and farm buildings played a prominent role; see Hayes 1970a.

3 Edwards 1808, pp. 142, 138.

THOMAS GIRTIN
London 1775–1802 London

41 *View of Appledore, North Devon, from Instow Sands, c.* 1798 (or *c.* 1800?)

Brown ink and watercolour with touches of bodycolour over graphite, on coarse laid wrapping paper; inscribed by the artist in pen and dark grey ink at bottom edge, left of centre *Girtin –*; overall slight discolouration with some foxing; minor loss at upper left edge and top right corner.

Verso: areas of skinning

245/242 × 472 mm

Samuel Courtauld Trust, D.1952.RW.846

During the later 1790s Girtin, alongside his exact contemporary J.M.W. Turner, emerged as one of the most promising of England's landscape watercolourists. Of the two youths, Girtin, the offspring of a London brushmaker, remained closer to his artisanal roots, undertaking an old-fashioned formal apprenticeship with the topographical watercolour artist Edward Dayes and keeping his distance from the Royal Academy. Academic theorists promoted the intellectual character of art production, notably the mind's ability to abstract general, ideal truths from the particular appearances of nature, at the expense of its manual dimension, which they felt hindered efforts by painters and sculptors to raise the social status of their profession.

Girtin's *Appledore* shows just how out of sympathy he was with academic doctrines. His view eschews any tendency to idealise in favour of providing a detailed visual record of the actual appearance of its North Devon locale, which looks much the same even now (fig. 79). An additional guarantee of topographical accuracy is implied by the use of a panoramic format borrowed from seventeenth-century Dutch art – a school of painting that the Royal Academy's first president, Sir Joshua Reynolds, denigrated for its unimaginative, "portrait-like representation of nature".[1] Together with *Appledore*'s reasonably high level of finish, its close compositional similarities to the works of Salomon van Ruysdael or Jan van Goyen (fig. 80) tell us that Girtin's sheet is a studio product. In all likelihood it

FIG. 79
Appledore, North Devon,
photographed from Instow Sands

PROVENANCE
Commissioned by Rowland Calvert (*c.* 1750–1813) (?); Katherine Calvert, by descent; Palser, 1913; Agnew's, 1914; Sir Robert Witt (1872–1952), acquired from Agnew's; Robert Witt Bequest, 1952

SELECTED LITERATURE
See 1919, p. 201; Mayne 1949, p. 107; Girtin and Loshak 1954, pp. 66, 68, 168, no. 254, fig. 37 (before 1975, misidentified in all twentieth-century literature and exhibitions as a view of Exmouth)

SELECTED EXHIBITIONS
Plymouth 1821, no. 91; London 1934, no. 752; Amsterdam 1936, no. 222; London 1953a, no. 29; London and elsewhere 1953, no. 15; London 1958a, no. 50; Calais 1961, no. 68; London 1965, no. 52; London 1973, no. 186; Manchester and London 1975, no. 36; Exeter and Nottingham 1995, no. 24; London 2002a, no. 110

FIG. 80 Jan van Goyen, *River landscape*, 1645
Oil on oak, 66 × 96.5 cm
London, National Gallery

was based on an untraced sketch (in either pencil or watercolour) made on the spot some months earlier, during his tour of the West Country in the late autumn of 1797.[2] His portrayal nevertheless has a remarkable freshness that suggests the immediacy of a direct encounter.

This impression is due in large part to the sense that the watercolour was painted at some speed, leaving the process of its manufacture plainly evident to the eye. Taking full advantage of the transparent nature of his medium, Girtin built up the design in layers that resolutely refuse to blend into one another, thus encouraging us to track the successive movements of his hand. Hence, rather than trying to erase the evidence of his labour and materials, as the Academy urged its students to do, here the artist has done precisely the opposite, starting from the very moment when he chose the paper. From the outset of his independent career, Girtin deliberately sought out relatively coarse and softly textured sheets, the irregularities in which permitted him to achieve greater richness in his washes than a finer paper would have allowed. The tiny

flecks of brown and grey that feature so prominently in *Appledore* (especially in the more thinly washed passages, such as the sky) may have become more visible over time – though the sheet remains in superb condition – but they will have always left their imprint on the image's appearance, not just by giving the surface greater warmth and tonal variation but also by demarcating a material point of origin for the complex act of portrayal that subsequently took place. To a greater extent than any of his predecessors, and well beyond any steps in the same direction that his friend Turner took only much later in his career, Girtin was prepared to let the bare paper play a remarkably active part in his finished compositions: here the houses, sails, clouds, and reflections on the River Torridge have in the main been defined simply by having been left untouched.

The glow of the off-white paper suffuses the scene with light and helps create an all-embracing unity of atmosphere. But Girtin's highly personal watercolour technique also throws into question the spatial relationships that seventeenth- and eighteenth-century landscape pictures rarely if ever asked their viewers to consider. Although we invariably conceive of clouds, for example, as standing out against an infinite expanse of blue sky, in *Appledore* Girtin's handling makes it clear that the passages of deepest blue have in fact been freely applied on top of the paler blue-greys and whites, while elsewhere it is equally obvious that certain elements – notably the nearby figures – have been drawn in only after the areas behind them have been completed. In conjunction with a brushwork that insistently draws attention to itself as brushwork, these features acknowledge a disjunction between nature and its pictorial representation, creating a gap that allows the artist to assert his presence as a creative individual. No wonder that, in the late 1790s, English critics and connoisseurs began to salute Girtin for the boldness that they took to be an unmistakable indicator of artistic genius. DS

NOTES
1 Reynolds (Wark) 1975, p. 254.
2 While this two-stage process would have been broadly in line with the standard academic argument for a strict separation between sketching from nature and the production of finished works of art, the same doctrines also equated finish with the representation of abstract, general truths – which Girtin made no effort to convey. Gregory Smith has kindly informed me, in private correspondence, of his recent discovery of documentary evidence proving that Girtin was travelling in Devon in late November 1797, and not during the summer, as has previously been assumed. If *Appledore* was based on materials gathered during this tour, then the artist's depiction of a bright summer's day must be understood as a further imaginative transformation wrought in the studio. Smith believes, however, that the Courtauld watercolour and *View on the River Taw, North Devon, looking from Braunton Marsh towards Instow and Appledore* (Washington, DC, National Gallery of Art) may derive from a subsequent (but undocumented) trip to Devon, which may have taken place in 1800 or thereabouts. I am extremely grateful to Dr Smith for his help.

FRANCIS TOWNE
Isleworth, Middlesex 1739–1816 Exeter

42 *The Forest of Radnor, with the Black Mountains in the distance*, 1810

Watercolour, bodycolour and grey-ink washes, with some drawing with the point of
the brush and pen in dark grey ink, over graphite, on two sheets of wove paper,
joined vertically at the centre; lined with Japanese paper.

Verso: inscribed in pen and brown ink by the artist on the right sheet
The Forest of Radnor. the black Mountains in the left-hand distance;
both sheets numbered 3 & 4
171 × 506 mm (two single sheets joined, 171 × 253 mm each)

WATERMARK (on both sheets)
[WH]ATMAN / 1808

Samuel Courtauld Trust, D.1967.WS.92

At an early age Towne was apprenticed to a London coach-painter. He subsequently attended William Shipley's drawing school in the Strand and the St Martin's Lane Academy. Edward Edwards in *Anecdotes of Painters* noted the "sharpness of touch, which is peculiar to all those who have been bred coach-painters".[1] In 1759 Towne won a premium for the best landscape drawing from the Society of Arts, and later acknowledged the apprenticeship as his first step towards becoming a landscape painter.[2] Although he exhibited oils at the Society of Artists from 1762 to 1773, he could earn a more comfortable living as a drawing master in Exeter, where he stayed for periods every year. In 1777 he took up watercolour painting full time and on a tour of Wales that year began to evolve his distinctive, linear approach to landscape.

Towne's reputation rests largely on the drawings he made during his single journey abroad. In 1780 he travelled to Italy, one of the first English landscape artists to do so,[3] returning through Switzerland the following year with John 'Warwick' Smith (1749–1831). As Martin Hardie has observed, Towne's "power of realising structure and simplifying mass found ideal scope in the superb mountain scenery .... With unerring line he preserves the essential sublimity of mountain form, and with his brush adds quiet colour of enamelled clarity."[4] Hardie's words perfectly describe this view of the Forest of Radnor, a broad, featureless upland area used as a royal hunting forest in the early mediaeval period. The long, narrow format with no framing device and a succession of receding diagonals accentuate the vastness of the bleak landscape, as do the tiny figures that appear to suggest man's insignificance in the presence of untamed nature. The view may well have been taken from the southwestern edge of the forest, possibly from a point slightly higher than where the present-day A44 main road skirts it.[5] The road follows a route that has been used for centuries.

The clarity and precision of the drawing exemplify Towne's watercolour practice. Closely observing the landscape, he delineated the scene in graphite or ink, or often in ink over graphite. Sometime later he would add pure coloured washes, rather than colouring over grey-ink wash, as was the standard 'stained' drawing practice.[6]

PROVENANCE
John Herman Merivale (1779–1844); Mr and Mrs Sutton, by descent; Fine Art Society, 1961; William Wycliffe Spooner (1882–1967) and Mrs Spooner, 1964; Spooner Bequest, 1967

SELECTED LITERATURE
Oppé 1920, p. 121, no. 1

SELECTED EXHIBITIONS
London 1968, no. 20; London 1968b, no. 666; Bath 1969, no. 70; Bristol 1973, no. 54; London 1974, no. 25; Wellington and elsewhere 1976, no. 16; London 1983, no. 94; New York and London 1986, no. 108; London and Leeds 1997, no. 68; London and elsewhere 2005, no. 17

FIG. 81 Francis Towne, *Near Devil's Bridge, Wales*, 1810
Graphite, watercolour, gouache and ink, 171 × 512 mm
London, The Courtauld Gallery D.1967.WS.93

Finally, he strengthened the lines in pen and ink – an emphasis on outline that differentiates his work from that of his contemporaries. As in many of his watercolours, the restricted palette – here grey-blue, green, buff and blue tones – is as abstract as the form, the colours skilfully modulated to create the effect of light and shadow. Contrast, for instance, the yellow line of sky with the louring grey clouds above, or the shaded peaks with the clear blue crest beyond.

All Towne's surviving work after 1808 was made in sketchbooks.[7] Both this drawing and another in The Courtauld Gallery, *Near Devil's Bridge, Wales* (fig. 81), come from one dated 19 August 1810, which records a tour in mid Wales and concludes with views made on his return to Devon early in September.[8] The evident join in the sheets gives the effect of immediacy and authenticity of drawings made on the spot – Towne's main claim to originality[9]

– even though they lack the artist's usual annotations recording the date and precise time of day they were drawn. The sketchbook was still complete when it was acquired by the Fine Art Society in 1963, and the fact that the sheets were left blank on the reverse side suggests that Towne anticipated removing them for display. The artist's idiosyncratic style was unappreciated in his time, and he was never elected a member of the Royal Academy. His name languished in obscurity until the emergence in 1915 of a large number of his drawings (among them these two sheets) from the descendents of his heir, John Herman Merivale, and the publication of an article by the scholar-collector Paul Oppé in 1920.[10] The simplicity and austerity of Towne's designs showed a marked affinity with Japanese colour prints that struck a chord in the early twentieth century, when Towne's work was hailed as revolutionary for its time.[11] JS

NOTES

1 Edwards [1808], p. 260.
2 Towne to Ozias Humphrey, 23 November 1803, Paul Oppé Archive, private collection. For further biographical information, see Stephens 1996, pp. 500–01, and Wilcox in London and Leeds 1997, p. 30.
3 See cat. no. 39.
4 Hardie 1966, pp. 121–22.
5 See Clarke in London and elsewhere 2005, no. 17, p. 106. The author is indebted to Will Adams, Curator of Radnorshire Museum, for his opinion on the topography.

6 Numbered and dated drawings from this tour were frequently made on a double sheet of a sketchbook with a fold in the middle, or on two or more sheets pieced together, as is the present work.
7 See cat. no. 39, note 6.
8 See Wilcox in London and Leeds 1997, no. 68, p. 140. Watercolours of Devil's Bridge and Radnor from the same sketchbook are reproduced by Wilcox in London 2005, nos. 13 and 14 respectively. *New Radnor*, also from the sketchbook, is held at the

Yale Center for British Art, New Haven, B.1975.4.960. The author is grateful to Timothy Wilcox for information on these and other drawings made in the vicinity.
9 See Wilcox in London and Leeds 1997, p. 11.
10 Oppé 1920.
11 Murdoch 1997, p. 711.

JOHN CONSTABLE
East Bergholt 1776–1837 London

43 *East Bergholt Church, from the south-west, c. 1815–17*

Graphite, on wove paper, traces of a framing line in graphite, trimmed, at upper left;
minor foxing; small loss at top right corner; loss at top left corner repaired;
small tear at centre right, repaired
318 × 240/238 mm

Samuel Courtauld Trust, D.1967.WS.16

Constable was born in East Bergholt in Suffolk. The family
home was only a short distance from St Mary's Church,
where his father, a wealthy miller, was one of the wardens.
Constable made over forty drawings and paintings of the
church, more than of any other specific subject. The
picturesque, unfinished tower, seen here, is a feature in
many of them.[1]

For Constable, perspective was "the whole grammar
of Painting & drawing".[2] A watercolour of East Bergholt
church made about 1797 and squared for transfer was an
attempt to master the building's perspective.[3] Ian Fleming-
Williams observed the artist's later use of traced outlines
made on glass and transferred to paper.[4] He noted, in
particular, a tracing of the church porch, viewed from the
south-east, which, according to the artist's inscription on
the verso, was a lesson in two-point perspective.[5] This 1814
outline became the basis for a finished work (San Marino,
Huntington Library and Art Gallery).[6] The Courtauld
drawing is remarkably similar in detail and perspective
to a modern-day photograph of the west end, taken from
more or less the same viewpoint (fig. 82). Compare, for
instance, the complex pattern of arches beyond the Gothic
doorway and the multifaceted walls of the buttress. The
Courtauld sheet may also have evolved from a tracing,

FIG. 82 St Mary's Church, East Bergholt,
photographed from the south-west

PROVENANCE
Charles Golding Constable (1821–1879), by
descent; Anna Maria Constable, by descent;
Sir William Cuthbert Quilter (1841–1911),
acquired at C.G. Constable sale, Christie's,
London, 11 July 1887, lot 23; P.M. Turner;
Gilbert Davis; Mr and Mrs William Wycliffe
Spooner (1882–1967), by 1963; Spooner
Bequest, 1967

SELECTED LITERATURE
MS. list of Captain Charles G. Constable's
collection compiled by W.W. May for the legal
action Constable v. Blundell (Public Records
Office, 1980, C.1621); Day 1975, p. 117, pl. 120;
Reynolds 1984, no. 17.32, pl. 32

SELECTED EXHIBITIONS
London 1880, no. 109; London 1963a, no. 56;
London 1968, no. 71; Harrogate 1968, no. 51;
Bath 1969, no. 1; Bristol 1973, no. 9; London
1976a, no. 155; Sudbury 1976, no. 18; London
1983, no. 114; New York and London 1986,
no. 74, p. 172; London 1998, p. 4, pl. 7; London
and elsewhere 2005, no. 57, p. 186

199

which could have been squared for enlargement, although the details would probably have been drawn from first-hand observation.[7]

Large-scale graphite pencil drawings such as this are rare in Constable's oeuvre, since he mostly made on-the-spot studies in sketchbooks. The present work is one of several elaborate drawings he executed from 1815 to 1817. Six of these were exhibited at the Royal Academy, in 1815 and 1818, but their imprecise descriptions in the catalogues mean that their identities and dates can only be surmised.[8] *Elm Trees in Old Hall Park, East Bergholt* (London, Victoria and Albert Museum) may be said with reasonable confidence to have been exhibited in 1818.[9] The Huntington drawing is almost certainly *A Gothic Porch*, displayed the same year.[10] Although the Courtauld sheet has been dated about 1817 on the basis of its stylistic likeness with the Huntington view,[11] Fleming-Williams notes its similarity also with *East Bergholt Church: South Archway of the Tower* (London, Victoria and Albert Museum),[12] which is believed to have been exhibited in 1815, together with *View over the Gardens from East Bergholt House* (London, Victoria and Albert Museum).[13] Both are mounted with their original lined borders and were in the artist's possession at his death, as was the Courtauld drawing. The third Royal Academy exhibition drawing from 1815 is unaccounted for. Could the present drawing, which shows traces of a ruled line, be the missing exhibit, or else one that the artist decided not to display? A freely handled, on-the-spot study (fig. 83),[14] dated 1814, shows a section of the tower from a different angle; this composition demonstrates Constable's interest at this time in the rich pattern of architecture as seen from the west end of the church.

FIG. 83 John Constable, *East Bergholt Church*, 1814
Black chalk, 251 × 201 mm
London, The Courtauld Gallery D.1952.RW.1007

Constable excelled in the treatment of building materials. Picturesquely decayed masonry – rubble, brick, flint and stone, depicted with a network of parallel hatching and short curves and dashes – is portrayed as if a form found in nature. Using hard and soft graphite pencil, both freehand and with ruled lines, Constable emphasised the various textures and patterns through strong contrasts of light, working heavily in places and leaving untouched paper elsewhere. The length and direction of the shadows confirm the time of day as shown on the clock – ten past five. Dwarfed by the ruined tower, three local characters add a human dimension to the ancient monument. J S

NOTES

1 For further information on the building, see Elam 1986, and Pevsner 1974, pp. 195–96.

2 Parris, Shields, and Fleming-Williams 1975, p. 86.

3 *East Bergholt Church: The Exterior from the South-West*, London, Victoria and Albert Museum, Reynolds 1996, vol. 1, no. 15; see London 1976a, no. 10, p. 40.

4 For a fuller discussion, see Fleming-Williams 1990, pp. 118–23.

5 *East Bergholt Church: The Porch*, Munich, Staatliche Graphische Sammlung, Reynolds 1996, vol. 1, no. 14.59. The same view is also

seen in the 1814 *Sketch-book Used in Suffolk and Essex*, Reynolds 1996, vol. 1, no. 14.32, and in two drawings, *ibidem*, vol. 1, nos. 14.60 (private collection) and a replica, 14.67 (Cambridge, Fitzwilliam Museum). See *ibidem*, p. 202.

6 Reynolds 1984, vol. 1, no. 17.31.

7 Anne Lyles supports the author's suggestion and has kindly provided further information on the drawing.

8 See, in particular, London 1976a, no. 156, p. 105, and London 1991, no. 26, p. 60 and fn 7, p. 177.

9 Reynolds 1984, vol. 1, no. 17.21 and fn. 10, and London 1976a, no. 156, p. 105.

10 See Reynolds 1984, p. 12, no. 17.32, London 1976a, no. 155, p. 104, and London 1991.

11 Reynolds 1984, vol. 1, no. 17.32. See Fleming-Williams 1991, no. 278, p. 433, and London 1991, no. 26, p. 60 and fn.7, p. 177.

12 Reynolds 1984, vol. 1, no. 17.33. See also London 1991a, no. 254, p. 417, and London and Toronto 1994, no. 44.

13 See London 1991a, no. 254, p. 417.

14 Reynolds 1996, vol. 1, no. 14.66.

JOSEPH MALLORD WILLIAM TURNER
London 1775–1851 London

44 *Colchester, Essex, c. 1825–26*

Watercolour, with some drawing with the point of the brush, white and coloured chalks and bodycolour, with scraping out, over traces of graphite, on wove paper,[1] lined with Japanese paper
287 × 407 mm

Samuel Courtauld Trust, D.1974.STC.11

The popularity of the picturesque tour and topographical illustration in Turner's early years encouraged him to look to prints for promoting his work. *Colchester* is one of his subjects for *Picturesque Views in England and Wales*,[2] the largest and most ambitious series of engravings ever produced from his designs.[3] Probably in 1825, the print publisher Charles Heath commissioned a large number of watercolours, 120 of which were to be engraved in sets of four. Despite the high quality and technical excellence of the plates, disappointing sales meant that only ninety-six were published, between 1827 and 1838.[4] Robert Wallis's engraving of *Colchester* (fig. 85) was one of the first views to appear. Turner's annotations on a trial proof – detailed instructions on the changes he required[5] – reveal the control he had over the engravers, whose prints, he believed, should be considered works of art in their own right and not reproductive images.[6]

The subjects in *England and Wales* were entirely Turner's choice, mostly based on old sketchbook material.

As seen from the sketch of Middle Mill (fig. 84),[7] he adhered to them only loosely. Many of the scenes feature imposing monuments such as castles and cathedrals. In this drawing, however, a humble working mill, solidly cast in shades of brown, sets the scene. Turner's interest in the newly industrialised landscapes of England is apparent in this edge-of-town scene, where the densely packed houses next to open countryside convey a sense of creeping urbanisation. He skilfully describes the atmospheric effects of smoking chimneys and fresh air, evoking their mood and tone by contrasting chalky pinks and yellows with purer, more natural colours – green, brown and orange for vegetation and earth and opposing shades of blue for sky and water. A bright beam, scratched into the paper in places, bisects the pond, imbuing the scene with a mysterious quality, as does a shaft of light in a similar position on the sheet in *Dawn after the Wreck* (cat. no. 45). The time of day represented in these two works has long been a matter of debate, initiated in both instances by John Ruskin.[8]

PROVENANCE
John Hornby Maw (1800–1885), by 1829; Miss James; Agnew's, acquired at James sale, Christie's, London, 22 June 1891, lot 160; William Lockett Agnew (1858–1918), 1893; Thomas Agnew, by descent; Agnew's, acquired at sale, Christie's, London, 16 June 1906, lot 58; Charles Fairfax Murray (1849–1919), acquired from Agnew's, 1906; Agnew's, acquired from Charles Fairfax Murray; Sir Stephen Courtauld (1883–1967), acquired from Agnew's, 11 February 1918; gift in memory of Sir Stephen Courtauld, 1974

SELECTED LITERATURE
Ruskin (Cook and Wedderburn) 1903–12, vol. 3 (1903), pp. 266, n.1, 298 and n. 2, and vol. 15 (1904), p. 75 note; Armstrong 1902, p. 247; Rawlinson 1908, vol. 1, no. 213, pp. 121–22; Finberg 1961, pp. 297, 344, no. 326, 488, no. 390, 494; Shanes 1979, no. 6, pp. 25 and 157; Wilton 1979, no. 789, p. 392; Herrmann 1990, pp. 114 and 116

SELECTED EXHIBITIONS
London 1829, no. 34; Birmingham Society of Artists, 1829, no. 388, 'Modern Works of Art'; London 1833, no. 56; London 1891, no. 84; London 1913, no. 67; London 1924, no. 33; London 1951, no. 71; London 1974, no. 8; London 1977, no. 29; London 1979a, no. 6; London 1980a, no. 9; London 1983, no. 123; New York and London 1986, no. 113; London 1991, no. 72; Tulsa 1998, no. 25; Birmingham 2003, pp. 164–65; London and Grasmere 2008, no. 23

FIG. 84 J.M.W. Turner, *Colchester, c.* 1824,
from the Norfolk, Suffolk and Essex Sketchbook,
graphite, 115 × 188 mm
London, Tate TB CCIX 6a; D.18169

For Turner, the inclusion of figures was a vital aspect of his watercolour landscapes, particularly those for *England and Wales*, which was intended as an exploration of human life rather than as a purely topographical survey. The narrative element in *Colchester* is exceptionally dramatic. On the far side of the pond a dark figure seated on a horse waves frantically at a hare pursued by three men and a dog. Turner's interest in visual metaphor is evident in this complex allusion to the infamous witch hunts carried out during the Civil War and the subsequent trials that took place at Colchester Castle.[9] Though disproportionate in scale, the figures are perfectly integrated into the linear structure of the work, their raised arms, echoed in the two small willows, creating a circular movement around the pond.[10]

The challenge of providing watercolours for intricately engraved plates stimulated many of Turner's advances in the medium. The transition from a mature to a late style can be seen most clearly in the *England and Wales* watercolours.[11] The artist's system of superimposing careful finish, fine stippling especially, over structured colour underwashes was perfected in this series.[12] Ruskin praised Turner's minute and subtle variations of tone with specific reference to the Courtauld work: "The drawing of Colchester, in the England series, is an example of this delicacy and fulness of tint, together with which nothing but nature can be compared".[13] A selection of the watercolours and prints were shown in exhibitions in 1829 and 1833. *Colchester*, considered among the finest of the group, was one of the few displayed in both.[14] J S

FIG. 85 Robert Wallis after J.M.W. Turner, *Colchester, Essex*, from *Picturesque Views in England and Wales*, Part 2, no. 1, 1827
Engraving, 250 × 297 mm
London, The Courtauld Gallery, G.2007.XX.2

NOTES

1 Lightweight wove writing paper, made by William Balston at Springfield Mill, Maidstone, Kent. The author is indebted to Peter Bower for this information.

2 See Wilton 1979, no. 789, p. 392.

3 Shanes 1979.

4 This watercolour is datable to 1825–26, since drawings preparatory to it were executed in 1824, and the engraving after it was published on 1 June 1827.

5 Yale Center for British Art, New Haven: "Lines of the hills too much seen tho they are laid the right way. Try and blend them but *not* by a cross line. Burnish the sky round the sun etc. etc. *Dont top up,* and try some [here some marks] at x x x, and I shall see how they will answer."

6 For more on Turner's approach to print-making, see Lee in New Haven 1993, pp. 7–8, and Herrmann 1990, pp. 247–51.

7 See Finberg 1909, pp. 631–34: Norfolk, Suffolk and Essex Sketchbook (TB CCIX), nos. 4a–7, 61, 62 and 71 held at Tate Britain. Drawing 6v (here fig. 84) is closest to the present composition.

8 Selborne in London and Grasmere 2008, pp. 122 and 146–47.

9 According to rural tradition, witches turned themselves into hares. For more on the running hare in Turner's work, notably in *Rain, Steam and Speed* (1844; London, National Gallery), see Shanes in London 1979, no. 6, p. 25, and Hamilton in Birmingham 2003, pp. 164–65.

10 See Shanes 1990, pp. 174–75, for Turner's use of the visual simile in this drawing.

11 See Gage 1987, p. 89.

12 A minute trace of strong yellow pigment at the lower right edge reveals the original undiluted colour of the underwash. For a discussion on Turner's use of "colour beginnings" in this series, see Shanes in London 1997a, pp. 23–27.

13 Ruskin (Cook and Wedderburn) 1903–12, vol. 3, 9 (1903), p. 298 n. 2.

14 See list of exhibits in both venues in Shanes 1979, p. 157.

JOSEPH MALLORD WILLIAM TURNER
London 1775-1851 London

45 *Dawn after the Wreck, c.* 1841

Watercolour, with some drawing with the point of the brush, bodycolour
and touches of red chalk with some rubbing out and scraping out,
over traces of graphite, on wove paper,[1] lined with Japanese paper;
later framing line in pen and brown ink, trimmed;
overall slight discolouration, loss at top right corner
251 × 368 mm

Samuel Courtauld Trust, D. 1974.STC.9

Many of Turner's marine watercolour studies throughout the 1830s and 1840s resulted from his frequent visits to Margate, on the north-eastern tip of the Kent coast, where he was attracted by the long stretches of sand and spectacular skies.[2] The Courtauld watercolour is probably set there, considering its similarity to *The New Moon* (1840; London, Tate), which supposedly depicts the beach at Margate.[3] Turner's major contribution to maritime painting was his expressive portrayal of changing weather conditions and man's struggle against the elements. In *Modern Painters* John Ruskin famously described this scene as "a small space of level sea shore; beyond it a fair, soft light in the east; the last storm-clouds melting away, oblique into the morning air; some little vessel – a collier, probably – has gone down in the night, all hands lost; a single dog has come ashore. Utterly exhausted, its limbs failing under it, and sinking in the sand, it stands howling and shivering."[4]

The perils of the Kentish shores were renowned, and capsizing boats and battered hulks were a regular feature of Turner's seascapes.[5] Although this image does not directly depict a shipwreck, faint puffs of lilac-grey on the horizon might indicate smoke from a sinking ship. Turner's oil paintings and watercolours of the beaches around Margate are invariably populated, but the figures are generally blurred and unresolved.[6] A finely delineated dog, alone on an empty beach, is therefore an unusual element.[7] The howling animal is possibly a reference to a disaster at sea and, by implication, to death. Turner's intense colour scheme is redolent of such meaning. In Ruskin's opinion, "the scarlet of the clouds" – "reflected with the same feeble blood-stain on the sand" – was Turner's "symbol of destruction."[8] The artist used the same "colour of blood " for such cataclysmic subjects as *Slavers throwing overboard the Dead and Dying – Typhoon Coming On* (exhibited 1829; London, The National Gallery) and *The Fighting 'Temeraire'* (exhibited 1839; London, The National Gallery).[9] The mood appears to be one of solitude, loss and despair, introspective and pessimistic sentiments no doubt coloured by Turner's declining health and awareness of his mortality.[10]

The numerous sketches and studies Turner made throughout his career reveal his continuing urge to explore the nature and mood of the skies and sea.[11] Such early

PROVENANCE
Revd William Kingsley (1815–1916); Mrs Kingsley, by descent; Agnew's, acquired at Kingsley sale, Christie's, London, 14 July 1916, lot 27; Sir Stephen Courtauld (1883–1967), acquired from Agnew's, 1917; gift in memory of Sir Stephen Courtauld, 1974

SELECTED LITERATURE
Ruskin (Cook and Wedderburn) 1903–12, vol. 7 (1905), p. 438; Armstrong 1902, p. 249; Oppé 1925, p. 20; Wilton 1979, no. 1398, p. 467; Gage 1987, pp. 6–7

SELECTED EXHIBITIONS
London 1892, no. 3; London 1924, no. 91; Brussels 1929, no. 26; London 1934, no. 887; London 1951, no. 94; London 1974a, no. 11;

Hamburg 1976, no. 121; London 1977a, no. 32; London 1980a, no. 12; London 1983, no. 122; Paris 1983a, no. 228; New York and London 1986, no. 114; London 1995, no. 67; Tulsa 1998, no. 35; London 2000, no. 64; Williamstown and elsewhere 2003, unpaginated (fig. 88); London and Grasmere 2008, no. 30

watercolour exercises as *Pink and yellow sky* (fig. 86) laid the foundations for the more vibrant paintings of his later years, including the present work. Unlike many exploratory studies made for their own sake, this highly finished watercolour was probably intended for a prospective buyer. Jewel-like shades of blue, red and yellow are immaculately handled. The crescent moon is painted with the point of a brush in white bodycolour, and light, formed by rubbing and scratching through the paper's surface, glistens on the wet sands and tips of breaking waves.

Ruskin's poignant description of this "little sketch of dawn" – "one of the saddest and most tender" of Turner's "momentary dreams" [12] – has perpetuated the myth enshrined in the Courtauld drawing's traditional title.

Recent scholarship has questioned the critic's assumption about the dawn setting. The drawing may be similar to *The New Moon*, but that painting shows the onset of dusk. If the Courtauld sheet represents Margate at sunrise, then the lunar crescent should face the opposite way. [13] As I have observed elsewhere, the time of day remains a matter of conjecture, since Turner regularly disregarded astronomical correctness, using artistic licence to make a compositional or symbolic point. [14] Ruskin produced an etching of the drawing to illustrate his descriptive passage in *Modern Painters* (fig. 87). [15] There, he reversed the direction of the moon, to indicate a dawn scene – an extreme case of his insistence on representational accuracy, perhaps. [16] JS

NOTES

1. A half sheet of handmade white wove writing paper, made by Bally, Ellen & Steart at De Montalt Mill, near Bath, Somerset. The author is indebted to Peter Bower for this information.
2. For Turner and Margate, see Selborne in London and Grasmere 2008, pp. 132–49.
3. The author is grateful to Ian Warrell for information on this drawing.
4. *Modern Painters*, 1860, vol. 5, reprinted in Ruskin (Cook and Wedderburn) 1903–12, vol. 7, 1905, p. 438 and n. 3.
5. See, for instance, *A Boat on a rough sea, c.* 1840, London, The Courtauld Gallery, D.1952.RW.4022; Selborne in London and Grasmere 2008, no. 29, pp. 144–45.
6. Compare, for example, *Margate Pier, c.* 1835–40, London, The Courtauld Gallery, D.2007.DS.46 (W.1397); Selborne in London and Grasmere 2008, no. 26, pp. 134–37.

Warrell in Washington and elsewhere 2007, p. 191, no. 135.

7. The drawing is also known as *The Baying Hound*. See London 2000, no. 64, p. 85.
8. *Modern Painters*, 1860, vol. 5, reprinted in Ruskin (Cook and Wedderburn) 1903–12, vol. 7, 1905, p. 438.
9. See Egerton in London 1995, p. 64.
10. Warrell in Washington and elsewhere 2007, no. 140, p. 196. See also Wilton in Toronto and elsewhere 1980, no. 68, p. 153.
11. See, for instance, *Heaped thundercloud over sand and sea* and *Storm on Margate Sands, c.* 1835–40, London, The Courtauld Gallery, D.1952.STC.3 and D.1952.STC.2. See Selborne in London and Grasmere 2008, nos. 27 and 18, pp. 138–43.
12. See note 3 above. The drawing was possibly named by the owner, William Kingsley, or his friend Ruskin.

13. See Davis 1996, pp. 10–12, and Davis 2009, pp. 6–11; Shanes 2009, pp. 8–10.
14. Selborne in London and Grasmere 2008, p. 146. Davis 2009, p. 10, supports the author's conclusion.
15. Ruskin first etched the plate in 1859. It was eventually published in the 'Complete Edition' issued in 1888 and reprinted in Ruskin (Cook and Wedderburn) 1903–12, vol. 7, 1905, pl. 86.
16. Davis 1996, p. 11.

46 *Singing and Dancing (Cantar y bailar), c.* 1819–20

Point of the brush and black ink, with scraping, on laid paper; overall slight discolouration, light foxing; inscribed by the artist in black chalk near bottom edge *Cantar y bailar*; in light-brown ink at top edge centre *3*; in dark-brown ink *23* (by a later hand)[1] 235 × 145 mm

Samuel Courtauld Trust, D.1978.PG.256

Goya's drawings often relate to his celebrated prints, published in series between 1799 and 1820.[2] In the later 1790s, he began filling the pages of albums with drawings of figures, some observed from life, others originating in the artist's imagination, an unprecedented practice in Spain. Eleanor Sayre wrote of these albums: "Goya in his fifties … evolved a singular use for drawing albums …. They had been transmuted by him into journals – drawn not written – whose pictorial entries of varying length pertained predominantly to what Goya thought rather than what he saw."[3]

Goya's intentions for the album drawings have never been reconstructed fully, although he may have had in mind the light-hearted drawings depicting contemporary life by Giovanni Battista Tiepolo, whose work he saw in Madrid, and even English caricature. The drawings may also reflect social and historical conditions in Goya's Spain, and some may interpret popular Spanish proverbs or lyrics, emblems or visual puns. Many of his drawings, however, seem unconnected with any concrete cultural or visual reference. The artist's numbering of most of the album pages has aided the reconstruction of their original order, following the disassembly and dispersal of the albums in the nineteenth and twentieth centuries.[4]

The albums were begun in the years following Goya's major illness in 1792–93, which left him with lifelong deafness. Perhaps this experience triggered an even more marked acuity in his observation of human behaviour. Throughout his mature and late career Goya explored a visionary world at times threatening and sinister, at other times ironical and detached.

The Courtauld drawing comes from Album D, the so-called Witches and Old Women Album, and is datable about 1819–20.[5] Two crones are placed against an un-differentiated background; their interaction conveys a sense of narrative and makes it clear that this is a carefully considered work. In the air one woman grasps a guitar and sings with wide-open mouth, while her legs suggest an awkward, raucous dance step that permits the second figure, seated on the ground and (perhaps) holding her nose, to gaze up the other's skirts. The seated woman may be dressed as a masked nun, and the spoon and bowl on the ground at left may imply that a magical substance was used to achieve levitation.[6] A slightly sinister carnival air is

PROVENANCE
Javier Goya y Bayeu (1784–1854); Mariano Goya y Goicoechea (1806–1874); Federico de Madrazo and / or Román Garreta y Huerta (c. 1855–60); Paul Lebas, Paris; Émile Calando (d. 1899; L. 837), acquired at sale, Drouot, Paris, 3 April 1877, lot 22; Emile Calando sale, Drouot, Paris, 11–12 December 1899, lot 75; Émile Pierre Calando (d. 1953; L. 426b); Arthur Goldschmidt, Paris; Count Antoine Seilern (1901–1978), London, 1953; Princes Gate Bequest, 1978

SELECTED LITERATURE
Seilern 1961, no. 256, pl. 82; Gassier 1972, p. 112; Véliz 2011, pp. 279–81, no. 103

SELECTED EXHIBITIONS
London 1963, no. 166; London 2001, no. 87; London 2011a, no. 36

Cantar y bailar

FIG. 88 Francisco de Goya,
Pesadilla (Nightmare)
Brush and Indian ink, with
scraping, 234 × 144 mm
New York, The Metropolitan
Museum of Art, inv. no. 19.27

FIG. 89 Francisco de Goya,
Suben alegres (Happy they rise)
Ink and point of brush,
232 × 140 mm
Paris, Musée du Louvre,
Département des Arts Graphiques,
RF 29772

produced by the mask of the seated woman, the frilly dress worn by the airborne figure, and the large flower adorning her hair. Goya's terse note, *Cantar y bailar* (Singing and dancing), ironically points out that his characters express neither the grace nor the joy usually associated with these activities.

The apparent freshness of the brushwork belies the fact that Goya reworked this sheet with care. Areas of scraping around the seated figure and the levitating singer's hem are witness to his creative process. The most dramatic change occurred at lower right, where faint outlines of a standing figure can be seen. This section has been scraped extensively, presumably to eliminate traces of the upright figure, whose form appears to have begun much farther down the page. The artist also scraped away some of the wash in the singer's mouth to define the concavity of that orifice. The vocabulary of texture and density of ink in *Cantar y bailar* are remarkable in their range and subtlety.[7]

From overlaying fluid layers of ink in different densities, to scraping to increase contrast, to using a nearly dry brush for broken light tones, the artist exploited fully the potential of expressive drawing in ink. Other drawings from Album D, such as *Pesadilla* (Nightmare; fig. 88), show similar reworking.[8]

The Courtauld drawing is number 3 in the series of Witches and Old Women, and the drawing nearest to it in sequence is *Visión: bajan riñendo* (A vision: arguing they descend), inscribed initially as number 2 by Goya, subsequently changed to 1 in an autograph correction.[9] The drawing that then became number 2 is *Suben alegres* (Happy, they rise; fig. 89). Thus, in the three drawings opening Album D, Goya explored several interpretations of floating figures: they are effortlessly airborne creatures synonymous with a happy state while those on the ground or falling have lost the elevating force of (deceptive?) joy and are literally down to earth. z v

NOTES

1 Many of Goya's drawings were given numbers when they were owned by Federico Madrazo after 1854; *23* is one of these numbers. The *3* is presumed to be in Goya's hand and relates to its original sequence in the album. See London 2001, pp. 24–25.

2 The closest correlation exists between *Los caprichos* series and Albums A and B.

3 Sayre 1958, p. 120. Sayre's observations in turn owe a debt to Gassier 1947 and the efforts of Malraux 1947.

4 Wilson-Bareau in London 2001, pp. 12–14.

5 *Ibid.*, pp. 135–37.

6 *Ibid.*, p. 194.

7 For an insightful discussion of the technical characteristics of the album drawings, see London 2001, pp. 20–21.

8 *Ibid.*, p. 23, fig. 14; also p. 196, no. 93.

9 Christie's, London, Old Master Drawings, 8 July 2008, pp. 100–05, lot 65, repr.

JEAN-AUGUSTE-DOMINIQUE INGRES
Montauban 1780–1867 Paris

47 Study for *La Grande Odalisque*, 1814

Graphite, on wove paper; extensive discolouration;
top left corner repaired
211 × 272/270 mm

Samuel Courtauld Trust, D.1995.XX.1

The Courtauld's headless and exquisitely elongated female *académie* is one of three surviving studies for Ingres's *Grande Odalisque* (1814; fig. 90), commissioned by Queen Caroline Murat of Naples as a pendant to the artist's earlier *Sleeping Woman of Naples* (1808; location unknown, presumed destroyed) – the extraordinarily sensuous figure painting that her husband, Joachim Murat, had acquired in November 1809.[1] Ingres had probably been promoted to the queen by her "distinguished architect" François Mazois, a close friend of the painter.[2] In the early spring of 1814 Ingres left Rome for Naples, where he spent nearly two months working on a portrait of the queen and a group portrait of her family.[3] He also revisited his *Sleeping Woman of Naples* in the royal palace, where he noted that his "beautiful figure of a woman was indeed well placed in the *petits appartements*".[4]

After returning to Rome in the last week of May 1814, Ingres divided his time between completing the royal portraits and starting work on the *Grande Odalisque*, which, by early July, was "*très avancée*".[5] The painting was probably completed and sent to Naples by the autumn. Unaware, perhaps, of the turmoil brought about by Murat's defection to the Allies in January 1814 and Napoleon's abdication three months later, Ingres was dismayed when his patrons failed to remit his fee of fifty

louis (1,200 francs). In December 1814 Ingres was reassured by the sculptor Pierre-Jean David d'Angers that a mutual friend in Naples had seen "his latest female figure" and greatly admired it.[6] Through considerable persistence, Ingres reclaimed the painting, which was back in Rome by 1816. It was one of the three pictures he sent to Paris in August 1819 for the second Salon of the Restauration, where it was vilified by all the critics. Charles Landon's celebrated squib – "One realises that there is neither bones, nor muscles, nor blood, nor life in this figure" – is characteristic of the cruel and uncomprehending response.[7]

The three preparatory drawings for the *Grande Odalisque* were probably made in Rome in the late spring of 1814, after Ingres had seen its companion, *The Sleeping Woman of Naples, in situ* and had an idea of the room in which both pictures would be displayed. He seems to have begun with the upper drawing on the double sheet in the Louvre (fig. 91), in which the model's presence is most keenly felt.[8] She poses on her left elbow and is shown with her right arm crooked and her right leg placed over her left. Ingres made summary notations of her eyes, nose and mouth, as well as of the divan on which she sat. In the lower part of the Louvre sheets, the figure begins to assume a more spectral presence: her left shoulder and the fabric on the bed are only minimally indicated. Her left leg is now

PROVENANCE

Louis-Joseph-Auguste Coutan (1779–1830; L. 464); Lucienne Coutan, née Hauguet (1788–1838), by descent; Ferdinand Hauguet (d. 1860), by descent; Maurice-Jacques-Albert Hauguet (d. 1889), by descent; M.-T. Hauguet (d. 1889), by descent; Jean Schubert and Mme Gustave Milliet, acquired at Coutan-Haguet sale, Paris, 16–17 December 1889, lot 239; Edgar Degas (1834–1917; L. 657), sold in Paris, 26–27 March 1918, lot 204; Walter Halvorsen, Oslo; Samuel Courtauld (1876–1947), acquired from Leicester Galleries, 1925; Charles Morgan (1894–1958), by descent, 1947; Roger Morgan (b. 1926), by descent; The Samuel Courtauld Trust, acquired from Roger Morgan, 1995 (with the assistance of the Victoria and Albert Museum / Museums and Galleries Commission Purchase Grant Fund)

SELECTED LITERATURE

Dumas 1996, p. 24; Bajou 1999, pp. 137, 358 n. 77; Prat 2004, p. 78; Salmon 2006, p. 15; New York 2011, p. 70 under no. 25

SELECTED EXHIBITIONS

London 1938, no. 87; London 1948, no. 110; Paris 1955, no. 81; Paris 1967, no. 72; London 1991d, no. 27; Sydney 1999, no. 201

placed over the right and her right arm extends almost to her ankle, intimations of the final pose. Ingres is still experimenting with the placement of the right hand and left foot; a tiny, illegible annotation is also barely visible at the bottom of the sheet.[9]

In the Courtauld study Ingres concentrated on the weight and mass of the model's back, breast, buttocks, thigh and feet. At first glance, his odalisque is faceless, although closer inspection reveals that just the scantest of attention has been paid to the band of her headdress and the lines of her neck and chin. There is no indication of the model's left arm or of the structure on which she is seated. Instead, Ingres lingers on her pert nipple, the delicate folds of her stomach and the shadow cast by her absent hand on her left leg. The model's taut back, expansive haunch and feet are described in intricate

cross-hatchings. For all its linearity, this is the most sculptural and volumetric of the preparatory studies.[10]

It has been suggested that the pose of the *Grande Odalisque* was inspired by Ingres's recollection of David's portrait of *Juliette Récamier* (1800; Paris, Musée du Louvre).[11] Canova's *Pauline Borghese as Venus Victorious* (1804–08; Rome, Palazzo Borghese) also hovers over the purity and stylisation of Ingres' figure.[12] Another unexpected – if disturbing – source of inspiration may have come from the very young model whom Ingres used for this composition. In his efforts to recuperate the *Grande Odalisque* from Naples in September 1815, Ingres was at pains to deny the rumour that he had given his odalisque the facial features of Caroline Murat. "This is an absolute falsehood," he insisted; "the model in Rome whose services I used was a little girl, ten years of age."[13]
CBB

FIG. 90 Jean-Auguste-Dominique Ingres,
La Grande Odalisque, 1814
Oil on canvas, 91 × 162 cm
Paris, Musée du Louvre

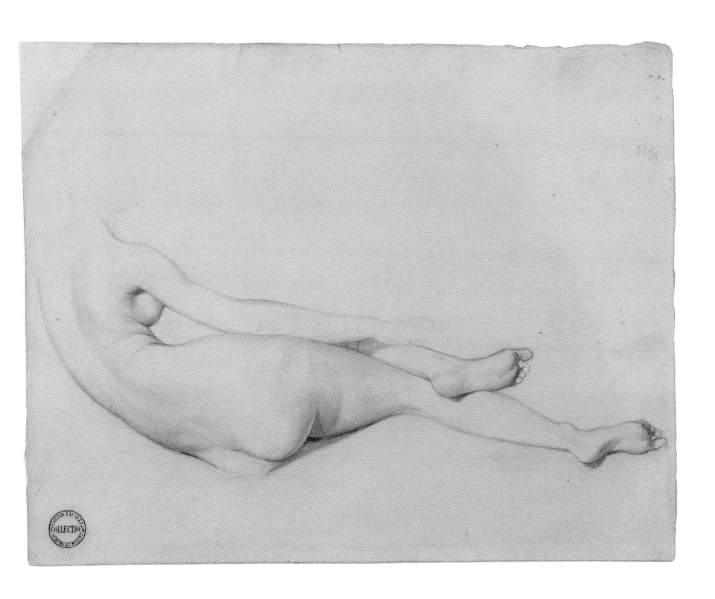

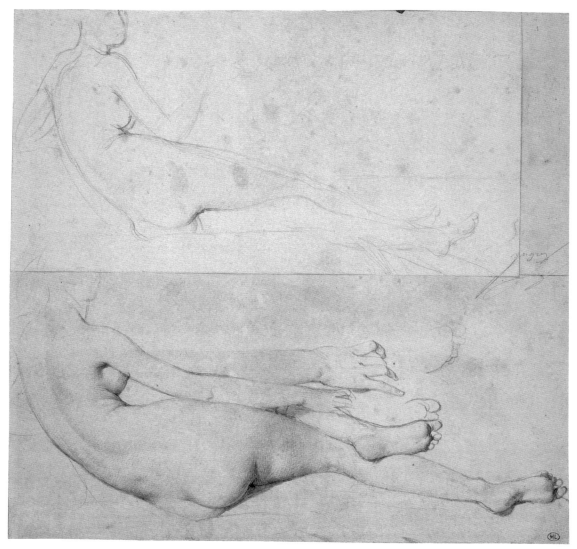

FIG. 91 Jean-Auguste-Dominique Ingres,
Two studies for *La Grande Odalisque*, 1814
Graphite, 254 × 265 mm
Paris, Musée du Louvre, RF 1451r

NOTES

1 Conisbee in London and elsewhere 1999,
 pp. 101–11; Bajou 1999, pp. 134–37; Salmon
 2006, pp. 14–20.
2 Ternois 1999, p. 57.
3 Naef 1977–80, vol. 1 (1977), pp. 379–97;
 Conisbee in London and elsewhere 1999,
 pp. 144–47.
4 Ternois 1999, p. 58.
5 Salmon 2006, p. 20, citing Ingres's undated
 letter to Mazois, likely written in July 1814.
6 *Ibid.*, pp. 20–21, citing David d'Angers's
 letter of 19 December 1814 to the painter
 Louis Dupré.

7 Salmon 2006, pp. 23–33. As Shelton 2008,
 p. 60, has noted, "Reviewers tripped over
 one another in their rush to ridicule the
 painting".
8 Prat 2004, p. 78; New York 2011, pp. 70–71.
9 Prat 2004, p. 78, deciphers this graphic
 annotation as ... *noir.*
10 The different qualities of the Louvre and
 Courtauld sheets are well discussed by
 Gillian Kennedy in London 1991, pp. 60, 62.
11 *Ibid.*, p. 60.
12 Conisbee in London and elsewhere 1999,
 pp. 99, 101.

13 Salmon 2006, pp. 22–23. Salmon identifies
 the ten-year-old model as Atala Stamaty,
 daughter of a vice consul in Civitavecchia
 whose family Ingres recorded in a memo-
 rable group portrait drawing now in the
 Louvre. It is unlikely that she would have
 been allowed to pose for any part of the
 composition.

THÉODORE GÉRICAULT
Rouen 1791–1824 Paris

48 Sheet of figure studies, *c*. 1817–18

Pen and two shades of brown ink over graphite, on laid paper;
laid on Japanese paper; overall discolouration and foxing;
numerous losses including bottom left corner repaired,
with water staining
216 × 340 mm

WATERMARK
Dragon

Samuel Courtauld Trust, D.1952.RW.714

Possibly from a dismantled sketchbook of considerable size, the Courtauld sheet of figure studies contains ten vignettes in pen and ink, meticulously arranged on three registers. Reading from left to right on the uppermost register, a muscular nude male is shown pulling up (or lowering) a large container attached to a pulley.[1] The rope is cut off by the top of the page, an unexpected truncation that suggests the sheet may initially have been several centimetres higher. Next to this Michelangelesque nude is a group of four figures – two women, a young boy and an infant – that relate loosely to *The Italian Family* of 1816–17 (Stuttgart, Staatsgalerie), a genre painting with allegorical resonances securely dated to Géricault's yearlong sojourn in Rome.[2] Only the old woman with her traditional Roman headdress derives from that painting; the composition more closely invokes the Virgin and Child with Saint John the Baptist and Saint Anne.[3] Except for the vignette of the seated man in classical dress at far left of the middle register – probably drawn at the same time as the two previously mentioned motifs – the remaining seven compositions are of military subjects, although the relationship of these motifs to Géricault's painted and lithographic projects in the early years of the restored Bourbon monarchy is far from clear.[4]

The hatless figure on the uppermost register, standing on a slight hillock and gesturing with his right hand, his troops far behind him, may relate to the elaborate wash-and-bistre drawing of either General Kléber or the future *maréchal* Lannes at the Battle of Acre or Saint-Jean d'Acre (fig. 92). This episode of Bonaparte's Syrian campaign of 1799 was among the military subjects from recent French history that Géricault tackled following his return to Paris in the autumn of 1817.[5] Pen-and-ink studies for the Courtauld's standing soldier and the adjacent vignette of the mounted officer appear on the verso of a drawing that is preparatory for the kneeling man in *The Raft of the Medusa* (1819; Paris, Musée du Louvre), the Salon submission that dominated Géricault's production between the autumn of 1818 and the summer of 1819.[6]

The largest vignette in the second tier shows five bareheaded soldiers reclining in various poses on rocky terrain. Beside them, in the background, a mounted guard sounds his trumpet, while in the foreground a mameluke holding a long pike, seen from behind, steadies a saddled

PROVENANCE
Théodore Sauvé (1792–1869), by 1867; P. Huart (L. 2084) (?); Aimé-Charles-Horace His de la Salle (1795–1878; L. 1333); Sir Robert Witt (1872–1952), acquired from Barnard; Robert Witt Bequest, 1952

SELECTED LITERATURE
Clément 1867, no. 19; New York and elsewhere 1985, under no. 24; Bazin 1987, vol. 5, no. 1540; Paris 1991, under no. 103; Prendeville 1995, pp. 104 and 110ff.; Whitney 1997, pp. 68ff. and 183

SELECTED EXHIBITIONS
London 1962, no. 62; Los Angeles and elsewhere 1971, no. 60; San Francisco 1989, no. 23, London 1991, no. 24

horse. Often considered casualties of war, these soldiers are more probably sleeping; Géricault may have intended this sequence to represent a reveille.[7] He re-used the pose of the sleeping soldier seen from behind at right for the figure of the half-naked plague victim in *The Epidemic of Yellow Fever at Cadiz* (1819; Richmond, Virginia Museum of Fine Arts).[8]

On the lowest register, the first sketch shows a mounted officer on a rearing horse arriving before a group of standing figures; the graphite underdrawing that continues beyond the frame makes clear that this vignette was conceived as a larger composition. The central frieze of figures at the bottom of the sheet shows a group of soldiers – some turbaned, others bareheaded – straining to transport large blocks of stones roped to a makeshift cart. The soldiers behind them are ascending to the terrain with ladders; one of them, bent over, carries stones on his back. Charles Clément considered this the principal vignette of the sheet, but he did not illuminate its subject.[9] Might this scene also relate to the unsuccessful storming of the fortified citadel of Acre at the beginning of Bonaparte's Egyptian campaign (see fig. 92)?

The Courtauld drawing dates to Géricault's return to Paris and has notable affinities with a similarly elaborate and vigorous sheet of studies in a New York private

FIG. 93 Theodore Géricault, Sheet of studies, 1817
Pen and ink, 230 × 260 mm
New York, private collection

collection, dominated by a Michaelangelesque nude and a group of female figures relating to *The Italian Family* in Stuttgart (fig. 93).[10] As has been noted, it is possible that both these large sheets initially belonged to the same sketchbook, although, unlike the Courtauld's drawing, the vignettes in the New York sheet were sketched directly on the page, without any underdrawing.[11] Whereas the New York sheet shows a certain disorder in the placement of its vignettes, which appear in all directions and are of various sizes, the Courtauld's drawing is a disciplined exercise in combining scenes from antiquity, the Old Masters and, above all, Bonapartist military life. It is a palimpsest of Géricault's preoccupations and experiments at this time, as well as announcing the themes that would dominate his production in the new medium of lithography. CBB

NOTES

1 It is suggested in San Francisco 1989, p. 53, that water is being drawn from a well; this seems unlikely.

2 Whitney 1997, pp. 63–70.

3 *Ibid.*, p. 69. Géricault made an elaborate pen-and-ink and wash copy of Andrea del Sarto's composition in the Galleria Borghese in his Roman sketchbook (Zurich, Kunsthaus).

4 The seated male in a stock melancholic pose may have been a later addition; his cloak is drawn over the background of the reclining figure that begins the second group of military figures.

5 Bazin 1987, vol. 5, p. 169; Paris 1991, pp. 181, 396.

6 New York and elsewhere 1985, p. 153.

7 First suggested in Prendeville 1995, p. 110.

8 Bruno Chenique recently identified the picture traditionally entitled *Scene from the Greek War of Independence* in Lyons 2006, pp. 155–62. Aimee Ng brought to my attention the relationship between the Courtauld vignette and this painting.

9 Clément 1867, p. 366, no. 19: "*Deux hommes qui traînent une voiture chargée de grosses pierres. Sur la meme feuille, neuf autres sujets moins importants.*"

10 Paris 1991, pp. 69, 356–57; Whitney 1997, pp. 68–70.

11 Lüthy 1985–86, p. 565.

EUGÈNE DELACROIX
Charenton 1798–1863 Paris

49 Sheet with two studies of a female nude, 1847

Graphite, on laid paper; sheet formerly cut into two parts and rejoined on the verso;[1] traces of
blue offset media at upper right of centre; overall undulation and slight discolouration with ingrained dirt;
brown staining at top edge and some minor foxing; small losses at centre left and centre right, repaired
and retouched, pinholes at upper left and centre top edge; inscribed by the artist in graphite (left half)
ou bien elle tient la pomme./ la maladie, les maux, le peché les attendent. la mort dans l'arbre de la science;
(right half) *les faire après la faute. appuyés tristement à l'arbre / Adam consterné et assis*
257/262 × 392/384 mm (257 × 212 mm (left part) and 257 × 180 mm (right part))

Samuel Courtauld Trust, D.1978.PG.234

In this evanescent sheet of studies, word and image are
given equal weight. Along the lower edge, Delacroix
outlines a subject relating to the Fall of Man: "Or perhaps
she holds the apple. Illness, misfortune and sin await
them. Death in the Tree of Knowledge. Show them after
the Fall, leaning sadly against the Tree. Adam distressed
and seated."[2] On the right, Delacroix shows a standing
nude combing her hair. He lingers over the curve of the
figure's arms and hands, repeating the right arm and
shoulder in an adjacent vignette. He describes the model's
ample breasts, wide waist and generous haunches but
indicates little of her physiognomy.

The standing figure at right relates more directly to
the inscription. This study of a nude woman of similar
proportions and with the same abundant *chevelure*
shows her holding an object aloft in her right hand while
cradling her head with her left. She probably represents
Eve reaching for the apple from the Tree of Knowledge.
In the faintest of lines in between these two nudes is the
figure of a supplicating man, nude to the waist and seen
from behind. Larger in scale and outlined extremely
tentatively, this figure, unlikely to represent Adam,
seems to be an idea that Delacroix soon abandoned.[3]

As Gillian Kennedy first noted in 1991, the inscription
on the Courtauld drawing also relates to the sheet of
studies with various nude figures in the Musée du Louvre
(fig. 95) – a sheet that is comparable in dimensions but

FIG. 94 Eugène Delacroix, *Le Lever*, 1849–50
Oil on canvas, 47 × 38 cm
Private collection

PROVENANCE
Delacroix sale (L. 838a, three stamps), Paris,
17–29 February 1864; Count Antoine Seilern
(1901–1978), 1954; Princes Gate Bequest, 1978

SELECTED LITERATURE
Seilern 1961, no. 234; Clark 1973, pp. 137–38;
Johnson 1986, vol. 3, p. 7 under no. 168

SELECTED EXHIBITIONS
Edinburgh and London 1964, no. 159;
London 1991d, no. 15

ou bien elle tient la pomme.
la malade, les mains le guide les attendent. la mort dans l'arbre de la science

86

les bras après le fruit. appuyé tu dans à l'arbre
Adam constern et affli

89

89

more crowded and more summary in execution. Here the figure of Eve appears again at far right, in a similar pose. A muscular, if despondent, Adam is seated to her left, and this nude male figure is twice reprised in slightly different poses. In the background at left appears a hastily sketched Tree of Knowledge, with three ghoulish figures, one of whom – the farthest on the right – brandishes a scythe.[4]

The drawing in The Courtauld has been related to a journal entry, written in Paris on 3 May 1847, in which Delacroix listed subjects for allegorical paintings. (The entry also applies to the drawing in the Louvre.) "A nude woman, standing. Death prepares to seize her. / A woman combing her hair; Death prepares his rake. / Adam and Eve. Misfortune and Death in the background, at the moment when they are about to eat the fruit, grouped among the fatal branches and on the point of bearing down upon humanity."[5] The week before, Delacroix had leafed through his illustrated edition of Achille Bocchi's ironic poems, *Symbolicarum quaestionum de universo genere libri quinque* (1555), with engraved emblems – ravishing in their elegance – by Giulio Bonasone.[6] This quest for moralising subjects continued into the first week of May, when, during a visit to the engraver and curator Frédéric Villot, Delacroix noted two allegories of death in an illustrated anatomical manual from the late eighteenth century.[7]

More than two years later, in mid September 1849, Delacroix returned to the themes of Sin and the Fall, now filtered through Goethe's *Faust*. In the studio of his country house at Champrosay, a village twenty kilometres south of Paris, he began work on a picture (fig. 94) based quite clearly on the left-hand nude in the Courtauld drawing.[8] He made a second preparatory drawing (Cambridge, Fitzwilliam Museum), in which all the elements of the final composition appear.[9] In the painting, the standing woman, naked but for her earring, combs her golden hair while the Devil crouches behind the mirror on her dressing table. Roses, perfume and various jewels are arrayed before her. As T.J. Clark noted, the woman has become Gretchen from *Faust*, discovering the casket of jewels planted by Mephistopheles.[10] After two sessions, on 16 and 17 September 1849, the painting was fully sketched in grisaille.[11] It was further advanced by February 1850, when a Polish princess visiting Delacroix in his Parisian studio remarked on the brazenness of the figure's nudity.[12] Delacroix put the finishing touches to his

painting in Champrosay in mid May 1850, when he feared
that he might be spoiling it.[13] Now entitled *Le Lever*, it was
among the five paintings that he submitted to the Salon
of 1850–51. Despite their reservations about the figure
behind the mirror – which Théophile Gautier considered
"*un souvenir de faux romantisme*" – critics responded
enthusiastically to the sensuousness and luxuriance of
Delacroix's composition.[14] CBB

FIG. 95 Eugène Delacroix,
Sheet of studies with various
nude figures, 1847
Graphite, 264 × 395 mm
Paris, Musée du Louvre,
RF 9942r

NOTES

1 Seilern 1961, p. 99, speculated that it was "Delacroix himself who cut the sheet".

2 See the inscription; also transcribed in London 1991, p. 38.

3 Kennedy in London 1991, p. 38, identified this "lightly inscribed figure" as Adam.

4 *Ibid*. For the Louvre's sheet, which Maurice Sérullaz associated with the hordes of Attila but correctly assigned to the period 1840–50, see Sérullaz 1984, vol. 1, pp. 262–63, no. 563.

5 *Journal* 2009, vol. 1, p. 378, 3 May 1847.

6 *Ibid*., p. 373, 24 April 1847. On Delacroix's copies after Bonasone's engravings, see Lichtenstein 1976.

7 *Journal* 2009, vol. 1, p. 380, 6 May 1847; Delacroix examined Jacques Gamelin's *Nouveau recueil d'ostéologie et de myologie*, Toulouse, 1779.

8 *Ibid*., p. 459, 16 September 1849.

9 See Edinburgh and London 1964, p. 61 and pl. 86.

10 Clark 1973, p. 138; London 1991, p. 38.

11 *Journal* 2009, vol. 1, p. 459, 16, 17 September 1849.

12 *Ibid*., p. 487, 16 February 1850.

13 *Ibid*., p. 510, 17, 18 May 1850.

14 Johnson 1986, vol. 3, pp. 6–7, for the most thorough review of the chronology of *Le Lever* and its reception at the Salon of 1850–51.

HONORÉ DAUMIER
Marseille 1808–1879 Valmondois

50 *Le Malade imaginaire* (*The Hypochondriac*), c. 1850

Black chalks, black ink wash, watercolour and touches of bodycolour,
with pen and point of the brush in brown and black-grey ink, on laid paper;
inscribed by the artist in pen and brown and black ink *h* and *h. Daumier*;
slight discolouration towards the edges, localised scratch marks at
lower centre with loss of media
207 × 271 mm

WATERMARK
HUDELIST

Samuel Courtauld Trust, D.1934.SC.113

Daumier's affinities with the seventeenth-century playwright Molière have often been noted – their kinship as moralists grounded, according to Charles Baudelaire, in a shared simplicity and directness.[1] Theatre was a life-long passion for the artist, and Daumier frequently saw Molière's plays in Paris and used elements of them, as well as the formal conventions of the stage, in his drawings, prints and paintings. In particular, the professions of medicine and law were primary targets of Daumier's satirical wit, as they had been for Molière.

In this drawing after Molière's last play, *Le Malade imaginaire*, a bed with drawn-back curtains fills the horizontal dimension and serves as the stage on or in front of which a trio of figures play their roles. Molière's protagonist, M. Argan, lies on the bed in profile facing right. His head and upper body are propped up on pillows, and his torso is swaddled in bedcovers. A bonnet with a large blue bow pulled over his brow completes the image of infantile helplessness and sets off his grotesquely hollow cheeks and open mouth frozen in a grimace.[2] The equally aged Dr Purgon (or possibly Dr Diafoirus) stands erect in the centre of the composition, his head forming the apex of a pyramid. He carries a tome in one hand and raises the other in a rhetorical flourish, as if to underline the gravity of his communication to the obliviously terrified patient. Argan's attention is focused on the slinking figure behind the doctor, the apothecary M. Fleurant, who is dragging an obscenely large clyster for administering an enema to the supposedly dying man.[3]

Daumier's image does not correspond exactly to any one scene in the play.[4] But it does not stray far from the text, which recounts the *folie-à-trois* that emerges as the scheming man of science and his wily assistant profit from the deranged patient in providing him with useless, out-moded procedures – "a small, insinuative clyster, preparative and gentle, to soften, moisten, and refresh the bowels . . . a carminative clyster to cure the flatulence of M. Argan".[5] In Molière's time, the enema had attained the status of a craze and became a frequent source of satire.[6] Although by the nineteenth century its popularity as a

PROVENANCE
Lemaire, Paris; Bignou, Paris; Reid and Lefèvre, London; Samuel Courtauld (1876–1947), acquired from L'Art moderne, Lucerne, March 1929; Samuel Courtauld Gift, 1934

SELECTED LITERATURE
Cooper 1954, pp. 134–35, no. 113; Farr (ed.) 1987, pp. 202–03; Laughton 1996, pp. 88–89

SELECTED EXHIBITIONS
New York 1930, no. 98; Paris 1955, no. 74; Paris 1958, no. 211; London 1959, no. 4; London 1961, no. 165; London 1966, no. 8; Ingelheim am Rhein 1971, no. 38; London 1976, no. 66; Sheffield and elsewhere 1977, no. 5; Marseille 1979, no. 65; London 1983, no. 103; Tokyo and elsewhere 1984, no. 21; London 1994, no. 75; Tokyo, Osaka and Kyoto 1997, no. 55; Toronto 1998, no. 2; Ottawa and elsewhere 1999, no. 206

FIG. 96 Honoré Daumier,
*Esculape se mettant en garde pour
défendre énergiquement sa position*
…(Aesculapius getting ready to
defend his position vigorously),
no. 20 of 'Actualités' in
Le Charivari, 29 March 1859
Lithograph, 230 × 270 mm
San Francisco, The Fine Arts
Museums of San Francisco,
Achenbach Foundation for
Graphic Arts, inv. no.
1963.30.32058

cure-all was largely discredited, the clyster remained in the arts a symbol of medical folly and fad, and often appeared in Daumier's prints (fig. 96).

This superbly crafted drawing is a study in dark on dark tones. Daumier positioned the chain lines of the laid paper in the vertical direction and established the composition in charcoal or black chalk, covering most of the image in a soft grey wash, which he also used as shadows. Certain areas of the white paper were left in reserve, spotlighting the key elements of the narrative – the patient; the doctor's face, jabot and raised hand; and the clyster. The cross-hatching Daumier added over the grey wash in the space between the two medical men modulates the tone with a flickering light. In some areas he applied a viscous substance, perhaps gum Arabic, to saturate the black and to add lustre. The high level of finish in this work suggests that Daumier intended it for sale.[7]

Daumier returned to the story of *Le Malade imaginaire* several times, most notably in a small painting from 1860–63 (fig. 97) and another painting, *Dr Diafoirus*, which has been dated to 1870 (New York, Bakwin collection).[8] While in other treatments of the theme Daumier focused on the psychology of the doctor-patient relationship, in this drawing he exploited Molière's narrative to showcase its underlying human comedy. SGG

FIG. 97 Honoré Daumier, *Scene from
'Le Malade imaginaire', c. 1860–63*
Oil on panel, 27 × 35 cm
Philadelphia Museum of Art: Purchased with the
Lisa Norris Elkins Fund and with funds contributed
by R. Sturgis Ingersoll, George D. Widener, Lessing
J. Rosenwald, Henry P. McIlhenny, Dr. I.S. Ravdin,
Floyd T. Starr, Irving H. Vogel, Mr. and Mrs.
Rodolphe Meyer de Schauenesee, and Mrs. Herbert
Cameron Morris, 1954

NOTES

1 In his essay of 1857 '*Quelques caricaturistes
français*', Baudelaire noted, "*Quant au moral,
Daumier a quelques rapport avec Molière.
Comme lui, il va droit au but*": cited by Henri
Loyrette in Ottawa and elsewhere 1999,
p. 357.

2 The bow could also be construed as a set of
horns; if so, the invalid is cuckolded by his
second wife.

3 Laughton 1996, p. 89: "The joke about the
clyster is pure ham, of course, and was part
of the stock and trade of all cartoonists –
Daumier had used it in satirical prints since
the 1830s." For examples of the clyster in
Daumier's lithographs from 1859 and 1867,
see fig. 1 and Adhémar 1966, no. 43.

4 Ottawa and elsewhere 1999, p. 357.

5 Molière, *Le Malade imaginaire,* Act 1, Scene 1,
in Wall 1879, vol. 3, pp. 407–08.

6 *Time* 1946: "The 17th Century was the Golden
Age of the enema, or clyster as it was then
called. The crude instruments of yesteryear
– tubes of bone or wood attached to animal
bladders or silk bags – were replaced by a
formidable piston-and-cylinder device."

7 Ottawa and elsewhere 1999, p. 357. In New
York 1992, p. 10, Colta Ives notes that when
Daumier's contract with *Le Charivari* ended
in the early 1860s, when some scholars
have dated this work, he began producing
watercolours intended for collectors, their
finish and careful construction representing

a "surrender of his naturally unadorned
draughtsmanship to the prejudices of
current fashion".

8 Farr (ed.) 1987, p. 202. Other works related to
Molière's *Malade imaginiare* include a sketch
for the Philadelphia painting, drawings in
pen, ink and wash in the Yale University
Art Gallery and a private collection (Ottawa
and elsewhere 1999, no. 205, fig. 1, no. 207
and no. 208), as well as a lost watercolour
of Dr Diafoirus and Argan and its studies
(Maison 1968, vol. 2, nos. 476, 475, and IV).

ÉDOUARD MANET
Paris 1832–1883 Paris

51 *La Toilette*, 1860

Red chalk, incised along the contours for transfer, on laid paper; some incised lines cut through the paper; slight overall discolouration and staining.

Verso: localised brown staining and repairs to cut incised lines; inscribed in graphite *19 large*
290 × 208 mm

WATERMARK
NF

Samuel Courtauld Trust, D.1948.SC.140

In the late 1850s and early 1860s Manet wanted to find a new way to represent the nude – the most enduring subject in the history of art. To his friend Antonin Proust he famously remarked, "It seems I'll have to paint a nude. Very well then, I'll paint a nude for them."[1] The culmination of five drawings of the nude dating from 1858–60,[2] *La Toilette* was central to the artist's preoccupations at this moment.

The figure is neither nude nor clothed, neither bathing nor drying herself, but suspended somewhere in between. While a servant behind her appears to gather up clothes, she sits on a pouf with a round basin at her feet. When something or someone outside the frame of the picture catches her eye, she pulls back and throws out a wary glance, shielding her body with the towel while her shoulders, arms, legs and feet remain exposed to view. Whereas the focus of the viewer-voyeur's attention – the bather – is drawn in firm, simplified outlines, the maid, not yet aware of the prying eyes, is represented in a looser manner. Her bending form seen from behind is lightly blocked out, and a tangle of lines suffices to indicate the clothing she is retrieving.

The Courtauld drawing is a preparatory sketch for an etching of the same name that was published in 1862 (fig. 98) and even bears the physical evidence of the

FIG. 98 Édouard Manet, *La Toilette*, 1862
Etching, 284 × 224 mm
London, The Courtauld Gallery, G.1935.SC.188

transfer process from paper to copperplate. Laying the drawing face down on the plate, Manet pressed on the outlines of the bather to transfer the chalk to the prepared surface. In certain places, the point of the stylus cut through the figure's contours, breaking the paper.[3] With

PROVENANCE
Marcel Guiot (known 1920–60), Paris; Leicester Galleries, London; Samuel Courtauld (1876–1947), August 1928; Samuel Courtauld Bequest, 1948

SELECTED LITERATURE
Meier-Graefe 1912, fig. 19; Guérin 1944, no. 26; Cooper 1954, no. 140; Mathey 1961, vol. 1, p. 15, no. 53; Leiris 1969, no. 185 and pp. 57–59; Wilson-Bareau 1986, no. 13 and pp. 32–34; Ligo 2006, vol. 1, pp. 135–36

SELECTED EXHIBITIONS
Brussels and elsewhere 1949, no. 183; London 1954, no. 18; Paris 1955, no. 83; London 1959, no. 47; London 1966, no. 46; London 1976, no. 70; Ingelheim am Rhein 1977, no. Z/7; Sheffield and elsewhere 1977, no. 34; London 1983, no. 109; Tokyo and elsewhere 1984, no. 51; Oxford and elsewhere 1986, no. 34; London 1994, no. 82; Tokyo, Osaka, and Kyoto 1997, no. 61; Toronto 1998, no. 12

FIG. 99 Jean-Antoine Watteau, *La Toilette*, c. 1717–19
Oil on canvas, 45.2 × 37.8 cm
London, The Wallace Collection

Manet may have cropped or considered cropping his canvas".[5]

Manet continued to exploit the drama of a figure or figures reacting to the gaze of a presumed viewer or voyeur in his *Nymphe surprise* of 1861 (Buenos Aires, Museo Nacional de Bellas Artes) and *Le Dejeuner sur l'herbe* of 1863 (Paris, Musée d'Orsay).[6] This strategy was most memorably used by Diego Velázquez in *Las Meninas*, a work that Manet greatly admired, and harks back to the long tradition of bathing nudes – Dianas and Bathshebas – interrupted by a voyeur. Manet's vow to Proust to "paint a nude for them" already anticipates the viewer-critic who will evaluate his work in the context of a long art historical succession. Various references for this work have been suggested, from Watteau's *La Toilette* in the Wallace Collection (fig. 99) to Tintoretto's *Susannah bathing* in the Louvre, though there is no known direct precedent.[7]

If the subject combines multiple references to past masters, Manet's use of sanguine evokes similar reverberations. The association of sanguine with the academy and the classical drawing tradition and the combination of finished and unfinished areas give this work the look of an Old Master study sheet. Compared with Manet's earlier drawings of nymphs and bathers from the 1850s, all of which were executed in delicate pencil lines,[8] the Courtauld sanguine is more simplified and direct in manner with an emphasis on contours. Yet, while the boldness of execution may be accounted for primarily by the function of the drawing as a preparatory study to be transferred to a copperplate, the sheet fits in with Manet's desire to find a new way to represent a nude. Here, the pose the figure assumes is a result of the viewer's intrusive presence, a force that counters the classical composure of the bather and throws it into disarray. SGG

the bather transferred (in reverse) to the plate, Manet continued to develop the image. He augmented the sense of surprise by spotlighting the bather within an almost totally dark interior. The maid, veiled in shadow, now faces front and appears to acknowledge the viewer beyond the space of the picture. The different position of the maid and the greater development of the background in the print have prompted scholars to propose that it may be after a lost painting.[4] The framing lines cutting through the bather's knees in the sanguine (red-chalk) drawing show that Manet debated converting the full-length into a half-length seated figure – suggesting that, as Michael Parke-Taylor writes, "if a related painting once existed,

NOTES

1 Proust 1897: *"Il paraît qu'il faut que je fasse un nu. Eh bien je vais leur faire un nu".*

2 London 1994, p. 206. These five drawings, along with a mica sheet made from one of them and the print made from the Courtauld sheet, are discussed in Wilson-Bareau 1986, pp. 32–34.

3 London 1994, p. 206.

4 Wilson-Bareau 1986, p. 34, states that the "final design" of this image "most probably existed at one time as a painting", noting that most of Manet's prints were after his paintings, and that Proust recorded a painting entitled *La Toilette*, unknown today. If that is the case, the Courtauld drawing may be a study for the figure in that painting.

5 Toronto 1998, p. 32.

6 Parke-Taylor in Toronto 1998, p. 32, emphasises the relationship of this drawing to the *Nymph surprise* and *Le Déjeuner sur l'herbe* on the basis of their shared voyeuristic theme.

7 Cooper in London 1954, p. 13, was the first to make the comparison to *La Toilette*. Leiris 1969, p. 58, makes the connection to Tintoretto.

8 Examples include Rouart and Wildenstein 1975, vol. 2, p. 60, no. 71, *Femme nue assise* after an unidentified master; p. 66, no. 100, *Baigneuse*; and p. 70, no. 119, *Silhouette de femme nue assise*.

PAUL CÉZANNE

Aix-en-Provence 1839–1906 Aix-en-Provence

52 *Hortense Fiquet (Madame Cézanne) sewing, c. 1880*

Graphite, on wove paper, with laid and chain lines, laid down;
overall slight discolouration and undulation; minor losses and tears at edges
472 × 309 mm

WATERMARK
INGRES and *P L BAS* imitated mechanically

Samuel Courtauld Trust, D.1978.PG.239

This female figure – a woman of fairly stout build with
a roundish head and her hair up – appears in many
drawings by Cézanne, especially in the 1870s and 1880s.
Appearing primarily in his sketchbooks, the drawings
were at first of a private nature but increasingly came to
form the basis of paintings. The sitter is Hortense Fiquet,
the artist's partner from 1869, the mother of his son
(born in 1872) and his wife from 1886.

Careful consideration of this restrained, rather
muted image discloses specific characteristics of
Cézanne's manner of draughtsmanship. The impression
conveyed by the drawing as a whole, its overall organisation within the narrow vertical format, is dominated by
the balance between linear activity and blank sections and
by a constantly redefined tension between the centre and
the outer areas. The woman's upright pose as she sits
at an angle on the chair is echoed by the chairback, the
bedpost and the bedside table, all of them summary
indications of a private interior densely furnished but
by no means cramped.

At first sight the woman sewing appears to represent
nothing more than an ordinary, everyday subject. Yet her
intense absorption in her activity and the sense of privacy
this generates at once draw in and distance the viewer.
Cézanne clearly took his cue from images created by
artists of the previous generation, by the Realists Gustave
Courbet and François Bonvin (see fig. 100) and by Camille

FIG. 100 François Bonvin, *Woman knitting*, 1881
Oil on canvas, 54 × 40 cm
Private collection

Corot. All were familiar with seventeenth-century
Dutch genre painting, but Cézanne, more than any other,
eschewed allegorical, let alone sexual, allusion. Instead, he
used compositional and other formal means to encourage
the viewer to engage and identify with what we see.

PROVENANCE
Ambroise Vollard collection (1865–1939), Paris;
Simon Meller, Munich, December 1933; Paul
Cassirer, Amsterdam; Paul Cassirer, London,
9 February 1941; Count Antoine Seilern
(1901–1978), acquired from Paul Cassirer,
15 February 1941; Princes Gate Bequest, 1978

SELECTED LITERATURE
Vollard 1914, p. 177; Meier-Graefe 1918, p. 37;
Venturi 1936, no. 1466; Seilern 1961, p. 105,
no. 239; Andersen 1970, no. 67; Chappuis 1973,
no. 729; Venturi 1978, p. 76

SELECTED EXHIBITIONS
Paris 1939, no. 44; Newcastle and London 1973,
no. 66; London 1981, no. 133; London 1983,
no. 99; London 1988, no. 5; London 2008, no. 11

A close look reveals that Cézanne did not outline and model each form step by step but proceeded in such a way as to prompt viewers to complete things in their mind's eye that are described only in part in the drawing. As a result, the eye is guided by the disposition of blank areas in relation to what is omitted and what is more clearly delineated. This is obvious in the diagonal seated pose and, most notably, in the complementary relationship between the woman's arms and hands. The viewer sees that she is sewing, but without being shown what and how. Cézanne the draughtsman suggests movement through the interaction of line, space and plane. By contrast, he largely expunged movement from his paintings of the same subject,[1] in which he depicted the woman's upper body, her hands and the fabric as elements juxtaposed statically with one another, using the physical substance of the paint to order and clarify the various volumes. Ambroise Vollard thus displayed remarkable understanding of Cézanne's art when he chose to reproduce the present drawing, rather than a painting, as the frontispiece of the book on the artist he published in 1914.[2]

From the outset, Cézanne's drawing was characterised by the modest technical means (pencil of medium softness on plain paper), the confident exploitation of the potential of those means, and an aesthetic concerned less with superficial virtuosity than with conveying relationships between constitutive elements. In all probability, the decisive artistic influence on Cézanne's work as a draughtsman, not just as a painter, came from Eugène Delacroix. The several thousand works on paper – watercolours, drawings, prints – that formed part of Delacroix's estate sale in February 1864 were previously known only to a few of his friends and revealed to the public completely new aspects of his important oeuvre. Idiosyncratic and anti-academic, they must have appealed instantly to the twenty-five-year-old Cézanne, who was staying in Paris at the time, and he seems to have returned to them repeatedly throughout his career. Delacroix's drawings (see fig. 101) are fundamentally characterised by a rejection of pure outlines in favour of concentrations of line with an intense dynamism of their own; a striking sense of corporeality; an approach to volume from the inside out, resulting in unity between the interior and the exterior; and the identity of line and colour. These features also dominate Cézanne's work on paper. Testifying to this are not only such examples from the 1880s as the present *Hortense Fiquet sewing* but also drawings and watercolours from his late period, including the still life *Apples, bottle and chairback* (cat. no. 57). MS

FIG. 101 Eugène Delacroix,
Three studies of a cat, 1843
Graphite on paper, 247 × 381 mm
Paris, Musée du Louvre, RF 32262

NOTES
1 For example, *Hortense Fiquet (Madame Cézanne) sewing*, c. 1877, Stockholm, Nationalmuseum; see London 2008, p. 112, fig. 62.
2 See *ibid.*, p. 110, fig. 61.

EDGAR DEGAS
Paris 1834–1917 Paris

53 *Woman adjusting her hair, c. 1884*

Charcoal, chalk and pastel, on two sheets of buff-coloured laid paper,
joined horizontally in the area of the figure's head; laid down on wove paper;
overall slight undulation and discolouration; abrasion around the edges;
some compressed creases along the bottom edge
630 × 599 mm

Samuel Courtauld Trust, D.1948.SC.115

The theme of the milliner's shop appears frequently in
Degas's pastels and oils in the 1880s.[1] The intimate space
of the shop, with its mirrors, windows, reflections and
fanciful hats, provided a perfect venue for Degas's interest
in pictorial experimentation and distillations of modern
life. The bending and twisting of elegantly attired women
trying on hats also offered an array of spontaneous poses
seen at odd angles that appealed to the artist (see, for
example, fig. 102). Taken out of context, as in the study
of a single figure in the Courtauld pastel, such poses
often acquire an expressive power that goes beyond the
realist subject-matter and verges on the bizarre.

In this pastel on brown paper, Degas focuses on a seated
woman seen from behind, pivoting forwards at the hips.
With hands raised to her head, she adjusts either a hat
or her hair.[2] Her body rises in a diagonal line, as if pulled
by some magnetic force from the lower left to the upper
centre of the sheet. Along this line, the drawing decreases
in finish. In the lower left-hand corner, Degas drew the
subject's olive green skirt in precise angular folds that
catch the light. His style in this area of the drawing has
been compared with the treatment of drapery by Northern

FIG. 102 Edgar Degas,
*Women in conversation at
the milliner's, c. 1884*
Pastel on cardboard, 630 × 840 mm
Berlin, Staatliche Museen,
Nationalgalerie, A I 552

PROVENANCE
Edgar Degas (1834–1917; L. 658); second Degas
sale, Paris, 11 December 1918, lot 94; Nunès
et Fiquet, Paris (known 1917–21); Samuel
Courtauld (1876–1947), acquired from Leicester
Galleries, 1923; Samuel Courtauld Bequest, 1948

SELECTED LITERATURE
Lemoisne 1946, vol. 3, no. 781; Cooper 1954,
no. 115; Russoli and Minervino 1970, no. 620;
Farr (ed.) 1987, pp. 204–05; Boggs and
Maheux 1992, no. 43

SELECTED EXHIBITIONS
London 1948, no. 92; Paris 1955, no. 75;
London 1959, no. 45; Manchester 1962, no. 58;
London 1966, no. 43; Nottingham 1969, no. 20;
London 1976, no. 19; London 1983, no. 105;
Tokyo and elsewhere 1984, no. 25; Cleveland
and elsewhere 1987, no. 9; London 1994, no. 176;
Tokyo, Osaka and Kyoto 1997, no. 62; Toronto
1998, no. 19

European artists, such as Albrecht Dürer or Lucas Cranach, whose works he had copied.[3] A few touches of orange-red suggest the seat of a chair, and more emphatic strokes convey the colour of the wall. Degas models the figure's long, tapered torso sheathed in a tight black jacket, enhancing the vitality of the body's thrust. The bent arms propel the figure upwards and balance the wide skirt below.

In the process of drawing, Degas made adjustments to accommodate his "organically ascending design":[4] he added a strip of paper to the top of the sheet, and, to quicken the sense of forward movement, he revised the contours of the figure – increasing the curve of the hip, tapering the waist, moving the shoulders up. A haze of smudged black chalk behind the head and arms creates a sense of atmospheric depth, though it may simply be the result of rubbing out while Degas adjusted the figure's position. On the added strip, the artist redrew the left forearm and the top of the head, leaving a margin of space above it, and in the upper right-hand corner he made a note of a mirror, or possibly the figure's reflection in one. With these revisions, Degas increased the dynamism of the seated figure's thrusting movement and left evident on the sheet the process of his thinking.

The relationship of the pastel to an oil painting in the former Viau collection (fig. 103) has been discussed at length.[5] Noting that the pastel was originally considered by André-Paul Lemoisne as a study for the painting, William Bradford and Helen Braham, and later John House, argue convincingly that the relation was more complex. Bradford and Braham suggest that the painting may have been made "concurrently or possibly after" the pastel,[6] while

FIG. 103 Edgar Degas,
Woman adjusting her hat, c. 1884
Oil on canvas, 61 × 74 cm
Private collection

House claims that, if the pastel began as a study for the oil, Degas probably returned to revise it after completing the painting.[7]

Overall, the composition of the oil is more static than that of the pastel. The figure, clearly adjusting a hat, is more upright and centred within a horizontal format, her head brushing against the upper edge of the canvas. With the added segment, Degas gives his figure room to extend her body more forcefully towards the mirror. In the pastel, Degas's composition evolves in the direction of greater sleekness of form and dynamism. It seems unlikely that the awkwardness of the figure in the canvas could have followed a drawing of such power and freedom. SGG

NOTES

1 See, for example, pastels such as *At the Milliner's* (1882; New York, The Metropolitan Museum of Art), and paintings such as *The Milliners* (c. 1882; Los Angeles, J. Paul Getty Museum).

2 Following Lemoisne, Douglas Cooper (Cooper 1954) refers to the figure as coiffing herself but in Paris 1955, he titles the drawing *Woman trying on a hat*. From then on, the figure is referred to as adjusting her hat, until London 1983, in which Bradford and Braham call the work *A Woman adjusting her hair*.

Thereafter, the figure has consistently been referred to as coiffing or adjusting her hair.

3 Tokyo and elsewhere 1984 is the first to make this comparison, indicating (p. 77) that Degas copied works by the Northern Renaissance masters between 1859 and 1864. On Degas's copies Reff 1963 is fundamental.

4 Nottingham 1969, no. 20.

5 See especially Bradford and Braham in London 1983, p. 98, and House in London 1994, p. 194. These authors also point out affinities to other works. Bradford and

Braham assert that the pose of the figure in the pastel is close to that in a pastel in the Thyssen-Bornemisza Collection (Lemoisne 729). House makes a connection to the pose of a dancer in a drawing included in the fourth sale of the artist's atelier, 2–4 July 1919, lot 140a.

6 London 1983, p. 98. Russoli and Minervino 1970 go so far as to write that the painting is a study for the drawing. See their nos. 621 and 620.

7 London 1994, p. 194.

GEORGES SEURAT
Paris 1859–1891 Paris

54 *Female nude, c.* 1879–81

Black Conté crayon over preliminary drawing with stumped graphite, on laid paper; sheet untrimmed; overall slight discolouration; losses at bottom corners, tear at lower right edge, repaired.

Verso: inscribed by Félix Fénéon in pencil *de Georges Seurat/ fel F*; with red chalk *381* at lower right

632 × 483 mm

WATERMARK
MICHALLET

Samuel Courtauld Trust, D.1948.SC.151

The subject of this sheet distinguishes it from the majority of Seurat's surviving drawings. Since classes at the École des Beaux-Arts in Paris (where he studied between 1876 and 1879) tended to focus on the male body,[1] he produced relatively few female nudes. This sheet was probably produced at one of the city's open studios, or it may have resulted from a private session with a model, arranged by the artist independently. Seurat enjoyed modest financial support from his parents throughout his career, and so would have had various opportunities at his disposal. However, as some of the evident awkwardness in his description of the figure's anatomy suggests, the task presented new challenges at this stage in his career. The persistent contour of the right breast – reiterated several times over – seems a little too angular, and the hands and feet are left incomplete.

Though it is possible that the drawing was made by lamplight – one of Seurat's student friends, Ernest Laurent, remembered that the two of them had adopted this unusual practice in the early 1880s – the muted treatment of the figure in this sheet owes much to methods employed by his contemporaries in the academic milieu.[2] Consequently, though the use of chiaroscuro recalls his work of the early 1880s, it is possible that the drawing dates from about 1879, before Seurat left the École. The laying down of lines, the use of shading and stumping to accentuate curves, and the decision to depict the model at the centre of the sheet, at full length and against a dark background, are traits seen in the work of his successful student peers. This is not to deny the work its particular appeal. Countless authors have noted the extraordinary atmosphere that seems to pervade Seurat's drawings. But it is important to recognise that, in many respects, this early work is a logical development of conventional practice. A faint structural framework – akin to that expounded by Adolphe Yvon, the École des Beaux-Arts drawing master – is evident around the calf area of Seurat's model.[3] The pose, too, is in keeping with those found in Seurat's more typical *académies*, though the suggestion of a chair beneath the model's right knee, supporting her weight, renders the work a little less formal than a comparable early work (fig. 104).

This conventional type of drawing highlights Seurat's distinctive use of his medium all the more forcibly. Vigorous marks in Conté crayon are knit together to form the fabric of the background; they appear to have been

PROVENANCE
? Mme Seurat (mère); ? Félix Fénéon; Samuel Courtauld (1876–1947), acquired from Independent Gallery, July 1928; Samuel Courtauld Bequest, 1948

SELECTED LITERATURE
Kahn 1928, pl. 62 (repr. only); Herbert 1962, pp. 25–26, pl. 23; Thomson 1985, p. 27, pl. 20; Callen 2009; Ireson 2010, pp. 799–803; Ireson 2011, pp. 174–80

SELECTED EXHIBITIONS
Paris 1920, no. 40; Paris 1926, no. 28; London 1975a, no. 76; London 1981a, no. 100; Oxford and elsewhere 1986, no. 73; London 1989a, no. 32; London 1994, no. 83; Tokyo, Osaka, and Kyoto 1997, no. 72; Los Angeles 2007, no cat.; New York 2007, no. 6; Vienna 2012, no. 146

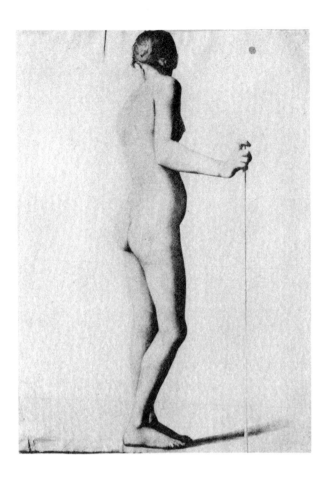

FIG. 104 Georges Seurat,
Female nude (DH 267), *c.* 1877
Location unknown

made from different angles, as if the artist's hand moved freely in this area, liberated from mapping out the contours of the figure. If the drawing gives an overall impression of stillness, here the lines convey an extraordinary sense of energy. The artist made much of the rich texture of the Michallet paper – his preferred choice of support – and seems to have enjoyed the variations created by its prominent laid lines and felt marks. This gives the work a sensuality that almost seems to anticipate the extraordinary softness of his later depiction of his mistress.[4] Given that the paper was most probably far whiter when Seurat made the drawing than it is now, the contrast between the blank paper highlights on the body of the model and the extensively worked backdrop must have been striking.[5]

Though Samuel Courtauld purchased the work as a genuine Seurat (it had been included in the first attempt at a catalogue raisonné of the drawings in 1928),[6] the authenticity of the sheet was questioned in the years to follow. César de Hauke did not include it in his catalogue raisonné of Seurat's work published in 1961, and it was only through the efforts of Robert Herbert (who was then an emerging authority on Seurat's drawings), that a firm attribution was established. In 1956 Herbert had asked Anthony Blunt (then director of the Courtauld Institute) to send a photograph of the work; in January 1960, in a letter to Blunt, Herbert described the drawing as an "unusual Seurat".[7] Ultimately, in his influential 1962 study *Seurat's Drawings*, Herbert reported that he and Blunt had examined the work repeatedly and were convinced of its autograph quality, citing the treatment of the background and the potential influence of Henri Fantin-Latour – who sometimes set his sitters against similarly dark backdrops – as supporting factors. Félix Fénéon's inscription on the verso is equally significant. Similar annotations are visible on other Seurat drawings and, having championed Seurat

FIG. 105 Georges Seurat (?),
Study for a female nude
Dimensions, medium and
whereabouts unknown

before his untimely death in 1891, it was Fénéon who
arranged the first posthumous exhibitions.

Herbert also illustrated what is supposedly a study
for the Courtauld sheet in his book (fig. 105).[8] It shows a
model in a similar pose, her right leg raised, if slightly less
poised than in the polished drawing. However, though the
two may be connected, it is difficult to be certain without
first-hand examination. Notably, de Hauke had excluded
it in 1961, though it appears he had been aware of its
existence.[9] N I

NOTES

1 Ireson 2011, pp. 174–80.

2 Thomson 1985, p. 27; Jamot 1911, p. 177.

3 Ireson 2011, pp. 174–80.

4 Georges Seurat, *Young woman powdering
   herself*, oil on canvas, 95.5 × 79.5 cm,
   London, The Courtauld Gallery.

5 Buchberg in New York 2007, p. 33.

6 Kahn 1928, pl. 62.

7 See object record file for D.1948.SC.151 held
   at The Courtauld Gallery.

8 Herbert 1962, p. 24, fig. 22.

9 See object record file for D.1948.SC.151 held
   at The Courtauld Gallery.

55 *A tile factory*, 1888

Pen and brown ink over graphite (including preliminary ruled construction lines in graphite),
on wove paper; ink heavily faded in the foreground; pinholes in each corner;
overall discolouration with areas of lighter tone; Verso: inscribed in pen and brown ink *174*
256/258 × 348 mm

Samuel Courtauld Trust, D.1948.SC.155

The short and precise marks of pencil and ink that Van Gogh used in this drawing produce effects similar to those he achieved in his paintings. A range of strokes is in evidence, from the small, empty, circular shapes in the central section, suggestive of fallen leaves, to longer diagonal lines that reach towards the foreground, indicating spatial recession. These were probably made with reed pens of different thicknesses, for the density of the lines varies as much as the apparent pressure applied to the nib. The graphite marks play an equally lively role. In addition to situating the buildings and cart with rider, they demarcate the individual planks of wood in the fence and add overall tonal depth.

Beneath such details, visible even to the naked eye, a grid covers the entire sheet. Some of its lines are ruled, others are hand drawn, but all were made with a hard grade of pencil that left a slight indentation (see detail overleaf). This may be evidence of Van Gogh's use of a perspective frame.[1] The image also reveals the influence of artists Van Gogh knew and respected; he had met Georges Seurat in 1887 and admired his pointillist touch. When he made this drawing, the artist was also hopeful that Paul Gauguin – who extolled the virtues of flattening forms with dark outlines – would soon be a guest in his home.

If the artist focused on the formal aspects of drawing at this time, however, it was also to lessen the financial burden he placed on his brother. As he explained in a letter to Theo, in late March or early April 1888, "If there comes a month or a fortnight when you feel pressed, let me know, from then on I'll make drawings, and that will cost us less". The idea did not seem to worry him artistically, since, having just moved to Arles from Paris, he was excited about the pictorial possibilities of working out-doors: "There's so much to do here, all sorts of studies which aren't the same as in Paris, where you can't sit where you would like to. If it happens that a month's a bit tight, so much the better, because the orchards in flower are motifs that there's a chance of selling or exchanging."[2] To justify his efforts as an artist, clearly, Van Gogh was keen for his works to find a market.[3]

Nonetheless, even in its picturesque rural surroundings, the subject of the tile factory was a modern one. Martin Bailey established its exact location in 2002, when he discovered that the only such enterprise in the vicinity of Arles in the 1890s had been located on the Tarasan road (around half a mile from the city centre).[4] This was the route that the artist had taken to arrive in Arles, on 21 February 1888. In transit, he had been struck by how the

PROVENANCE
Theo van Gogh, Paris, 1888; Johanna Gesina van Gogh-Bonger (1862–1925), Amsterdam; Vincent Willem van Gogh (1890–1978), Laren; Samuel Courtauld (1876–1947), acquired from Leicester Galleries, 1927; Samuel Courtauld Bequest, 1948

SELECTED LITERATURE
Cooper 1954, no. 154; Novotny 1953, pp. 35–43, pl. 1; *Lettres de Van Gogh à Bernard* 1911, pl. LXVIII; de la Faille 1970, no. 1500; Hulsker 1996, pp. 308–09, no. 1373

SELECTED EXHIBITIONS
Amsterdam 1905, no. 408; Amsterdam 1914, no. 169; Utrecht and Rotterdam 1923, no. 48; London 1923, no. 37; London 1948, no. 100;

Paris 1955, no. 92; Manchester 1962, no. 21; London 1976, no. 80; Sheffield and elsewhere 1977, no. 77; London 1983, no. 108; Tokyo and elsewhere 1984, no. 99; London 1988, no. 23; Southampton and elsewhere 1995, no. 79; Tokyo, Osaka and Kyoto 1997, no. 70; Arles 2003, pp. 26–27; Edinburgh and Compton Verney 2006, no. 27

245

FIG. 106 Vincent van Gogh, *Landscape with path and pollard trees*, 1888
Pencil, pen and brown ink, 255 × 350 mm
Amsterdam, Van Gogh Foundation, F1499

landscapes flattened out as he neared his destination, and he may have noted this collection of buildings.[5] At that point, the ground had been covered by around sixty centimetres of snow, so he presumably produced this image once the weather had improved. It is comparable to a few other drawings of the area, one of which, *Landscape with path and pollard trees*, is inscribed 'March 1888' (fig. 106), and so it is likely that all were made at around the same time.[6] Vincent had sent Theo a number of small pen drawings by May 1888, and one of them could well have been the present work.[7]

Despite the considerable fading of the medium and the discolouration of the support, the sheet gives a strong sense of Van Gogh's working practice. Perhaps it was a point of reference in the studio; pinholes in the corners show that it was once attached to a wall or easel. When Samuel Courtauld acquired the drawing, it would have

been classified as one from Van Gogh's most stable stage; commentators had tended to read the artist's work in relation to his mental illness. Thus, in the catalogue for the 1923 exhibition at the Leicester Galleries (where the collector probably saw the work), Michael Sadler described this period (about 1888) as one in which the artist had "found himself", before his "overtaxed brain" held sway.[8] However, in later years, the drawing also served as independent evidence of the artist's mental difference. In 1953 Fritz Novotny noted how its "graphic systems" invited thoughts of Japanese and medieval European art – not in stylistic similarity but in a supposed "community of purpose . . . a concentration on the object".[9] Significantly, then, though it relates logically to the broader historical moment of its production, this modest study has also played its part in narratives that set Van Gogh apart from his late nineteenth-century contemporaries. NI

NOTES
1 London 1994, p. 202.
2 *Lettres de Van Gogh à son frère* 1988, p. 358, letter 474F.
3 On the interpretation of Van Gogh's correspondence, see Baker, Jansen, and Luijten in London 2010a, pp. 14–29.
4 Bailey in Edinburgh and Compton Verney 2006, p. 104.
5 *Lettres de Van Gogh à son frère* 1988, pp. 353–54, letter 463F.
6 Hulsker 1996, nos. 1372, 1374, and 1375 (1372 is fig. 1 above).
7 House in London 1994, p. 202.
8 Sadler in London 1923, p. 13.
9 Novotny 1953, p. 39.

HENRI DE TOULOUSE-LAUTREC
Albi 1864–1901 Malromé

56 *Au lit, c.* 1896

Graphite and black chalk, on laid paper; sheet untrimmed at left, right and top;
inscribed by the artist in graphite at lower left *HT Lautrec* (HT interlinked);
overall light discolouration, minor foxing; tear repaired top right corner;
several pinholes

Verso: inscribed *Mr* [illegible name] *55 + 38*
304/309 × 483/479 mm

WATERMARK
PL BAS

Samuel Courtauld Trust, D.1948.SC.154

A woman lies in bed, her legs crossed, her eyes barely open. The sheets around her are in disarray; crumpled and slept in, they fall across her body haphazardly. Scarcely do they cover her sizable feet – seemingly shod or stockinged – whose soles loom large in the foreground. The overall state of dress of the model is debatable. She may be wearing a chemise, but it is impossible to know, since her arms are drawn close to her face beneath the covers. It is likely that she is a prostitute, for Lautrec spent many months depicting women who worked in the brothels of Montmartre, in whose company he lived intermittently in the mid 1890s.[1] This sheet appears to have been based on first-hand study, and, as the searching for the placement of certain lines (particularly around the legs) suggests, the artist may well have worked directly before the model.

Lautrec's approach to executing the image seems as unapologetic as the model's languid pose. The thrust of his lines, confident and quickly done, conveys a sense of vigour and excitement that, given the supposed brothel subject-matter, might suggest his dominance over the sitter. Recent commentators on Lautrec have argued that his images of female sex workers are exploitative – works by an upper-class male who either recognised the commercial appeal of his bedroom subjects or enjoyed control and surveillance of the women he depicted, as he subjected them to representation.[2] However, though such readings do well to align Lautrec with broader issues of class and gender in the late nineteenth century, in this image there is little sense of transaction (either sexual or financial).[3] The model is clearly aware of the artist's presence, but it seems to matter little. Perhaps a sense of collusion is at work: if such women were social outsiders in late nineteenth-century Paris, to an extent so were artists. Thadée Natanson – who knew Lautrec well – claimed that the artist's lesbian models had viewed his regard as fraternal,[4] and, in the eyes of early commentators, Lautrec had a gift for spotting a side of the bohemian world that had escaped his contemporaries, "the side that was restless and tired, bright and dreary, luxuriant and pained".[5] The image is not overtly erotic, the atmosphere one of familiarity rather than seduction or submission.

Close study of the drawing shows that Lautrec used two different mediums to make *Au lit* – a soft black chalk to describe the bed and pillows, the drape of the sheets and the placement of the legs, followed by a harder pencil to emphasise the facial features and crown of the hair.

PROVENANCE
Gustave Pellet (1859–1919), Paris; Claude Sayle (?); Samuel Courtauld (1876–1947), acquired from Leicester Galleries, February 1922; Samuel Courtauld Bequest, 1948

SELECTED LITERATURE
Huyghe 1948, pl. 134; Reynolds 1949, pl. 31; *Art et style* 1950, pl. 48; London 1976, p. 78

SELECTED EXHIBITIONS
London 1932, no. 976; London 1948, no. 121; Brussels and elsewhere 1949, no. 215; London 1952a, no. 156; Kassel 1964, Part 2, *Handzeichnungen Toulouse-Lautrecs*, pl. I; Stockholm 1967, no. 109a; Brussels 1973, no. 37; London 1991c, no. 148; Boston 1992, perhaps without cat.; Southampton and elsewhere 1994, p. 212, no. 85; London 1994, p. 212, no. 85; London 1995a, no. 192; Tokyo, Osaka and Kyoto 1997, no. 71; Toronto 1998, no. 59; Osaka and Tokyo 2000, no. 71; Los Angeles 2007, no catalogue; Vienna 2012, no. 181

Relatively little attention is paid to describing the body; it is the brows and nostrils that are outlined most carefully. The variation of textures, created with different degrees of applied pressure, might indicate that Lautrec had printmaking in mind when he made the image. The transition between the looseness of his sketches and the more definite contours of his lithographs was often worked out through drawings and, in the wider context of his oeuvre, this sheet belongs to the moment when he prepared his portfolio *Elles* (which he exhibited in April 1896). However, *Au lit* does not appear to have been developed for printing purposes; the work is executed on good-quality laid paper and is signed. No printed version

of the work exists and, furthermore, the drawing is relatively unlike many of the studies made for the *Elles* project. Several of those images focus on domestic activity – the acts of dressing or washing, of styling hair or fastening a corset. Others are more obviously involved with the business of prostitution – an encounter with a client, an inviting look or half-dressed exhaustion (fig. 107). None shares quite the same sense of direct nonchalance exhibited in the present work.

Equally, if many of the initial drawings for *Elles* were executed in red chalk (see fig. 108), it was perhaps because the medium recalled the sensuality of eighteenth-century drawings.[6] No doubt this choice was also made in

FIG. 107 Henri Toulouse-Lautrec, *Elles: femme sur le dos – lassitude*, 1896
Colour crayon lithograph, printed in sanguine ink with tint stone in olive green, 395 × 525 mm
London, British Museum, inv. no. 1949,0411.3643

anticipation of the final sanguine lithographs, as, on a practical level, red chalk allowed Lautrec to achieve similar effects. Perhaps, with his combination of chalk and pencil, the artist invited a more contemporary regard. However, though the model may have been a woman he knew – Mlle Pauline or 'Popo', who is thought to appear in a handful of the *Elles* prints[7] – it is unlikely that she would have been widely recognisable. Instead, it is the woman's unkempt hair and crossed legs, together with the audacity of Lautrec's lines, which render her so unmistakably of her time. This startling drawing would become one of Courtauld's earliest acquisitions of modern French art, purchased from the Leicester Galleries in 1922.[8] N I

FIG. 108 Henri Toulouse-Lautrec,
Elles: femme au tub, 1896
Red chalk on wove paper,
390 × 508 mm
Minneapolis Institute of Arts,
Bequest of Putnam Dana
McMillan, inv. no. 61.36.2

NOTES

1 Jourdain and Adhémar 1952, pp. 73–74.
2 Pollock 1999, pp. 88–89.
3 As Richard Thomson (in London 1991c, p. 17) has argued, Lautrec's images of prostitutes suggest a range of attitudes.
4 Natanson 1951, p. 58.
5 Alexandre in Paris 1902, p. 9: "… *le coté agité et fatigué, brilliant et morne, volupteux et grimaçant*".
6 Thomson in London 1991c, p. 437.
7 *Elles: femme au plateau – petit déjeuner*, 1896, colour crayon lithograph with scraper, printed in sanguine ink, 403 × 522 mm, London, British Museum, 1949-4-11-3637.
8 Bowness in London 1976.

PAUL CÉZANNE
Aix-en-Provence 1839–1906 Aix-en-Provence

57 *Apples, bottle and chairback, c.* 1904–06

Graphite and watercolour, on wove paper; pinholes at upper left and right; minor tears repaired at lower right and upper left; the sheet unevenly torn, at bottom, and right, at right apparently to ruled pencil line.

Verso: numbered in blue crayon in lower left corner *13*
458/462 × 604 mm

BLIND-STAMPED
ANC^NE MANUF^RE CANSON ET MONTGOLFIER VIDALON LES ANNONAY (reversed, recto)

Samuel Courtauld Trust, D.1948.SC.111

Together with a number of comparable works,[1] this watercolour dating from about 1904–06 forms an impressive conclusion to Cézanne's oeuvre in a medium that is animated by the interaction of line and colour.

The impression of painterly finished work arises not only from the fact that the surface of the paper is covered almost completely but, more notably, from the masterly organisation of the picture plane. This is defined principally by the horizontals of the two table edges and by the bold vertical formed on the left by the bottle and tall wineglass, the colours of which are echoed in the background on the right. The background testifies to Cézanne's sure sense of proportion, of the relative importance of each area: with the centre emphasised by a curved chairback, it is structured in sections arranged in the ratio 1:2:1. The pictorial space is dominated by the deep reds and browns of the table and chairback, which provide an effective foil for the yellow, red and orange of the apples in the blue-ornamented faience dish in the centre. On its own, the carefully balanced arrangement of the apples in the centre might well recall paintings by Jean-Siméon Chardin, but towards the right the apples seem to tumble off

horizontally until brought to a halt by the right edge of the image, as though by (well-judged) chance. This arrangement recurs in the *Still life with apples and pears* in Washington (fig. 110). The light, entering at the upper left and from the centre front, enhances this effect.[2]

The compelling sense of assurance with which the compositional elements in this watercolour are placed resulted from a more or less deliberate working process. Resembling an architectural element in space, the Baroque-style chairback frames a view of flowered wallpaper and, in doing so, effects a transition to another section of the background. Several drawings by Cézanne, pages from sketchbooks as well as independent sheets, show him using such elements – chairbacks, table edges, beds – to clarify spatial relationships in the context of the objects' surroundings (see fig. 109).[3]

The pencil drawing in this watercolour, as delicate as it is sharply focused, both abets colour and works against it. As Elisabeth Reissner has shown, drawing of this kind not only functions as preliminary notation but also interacts closely and dynamically with colour to generate movement and definition.[4]

PROVENANCE
Paul Cézanne fils, Paris (b. 1872); Justin K. Thannhauser (1892–1976), Berlin and Lucerne; Wildenstein Galleries, Paris, London and New York; Samuel Courtauld (1876–1947), September 1937; Samuel Courtauld Bequest, 1948

SELECTED LITERATURE
Venturi 1936, no. 1155; Cooper 1954, no. 111; Koschatzky 1969, p. 10; Wechsler 1975, fig. 19;

Rewald 1983, no. 643; Farr (ed.), London 1987, p. 214; Kendall 1988, p. 255

SELECTED EXHIBITIONS
Philadelphia 1934, no. 55; London 1939, no. 73; London and elsewhere 1946, no. 56; London 1948, no. 86; London 1959, no. 14; Vienna 1961, no. 81; Aix-en-Provence 1961, no. 38; Newcastle and London 1973, p. 21, no. 98; New York and

elsewhere 1977, no. 77 (no. 34 in French edn); Tübingen and Zurich 1982, no. 93; London 1983, no. 102; London 1988, no. 10; London 1994, no. 73; Tokyo, Osaka and Kyoto 1997, no. 67; London 1999, no. 34; Los Angeles 2004, no. 7; London 2006, no. 40; London 2008, no. 17

FIG. 109 Paul Cézanne,
Chairback, *c.* 1879–82
Watercolour, 177 × 127 mm
Private collection

FIG. 110 Paul Cézanne, *Still life
with apples and peaches*, *c.* 1905
Oil on canvas, 81 × 100.5 cm
Washington, National Gallery
of Art, Gift of Eugene and
Agnes E. Meyer

Direct observation – working in front of the motif –
was of fundamental importance to Cézanne, yet mental
processes also performed an essential role in his work.
They might involve memories of things seen or experi-
enced in other artists' work, for instance, or consideration
of fellow artists' written statements. Thus, the art of
two great figures of the past played a major part in the
genesis and realisation of the present watercolour.

One of these artists was Eugène Delacroix. In particular,
Cézanne emulated his systematic combination of the
primary colours, red, yellow and blue, with their comple-
mentaries, green, violet and orange, to invest both oils
and watercolours with conceptual, constructional and
emotional presence.[5] The sale of Delacroix's estate early
in 1864, the memorial exhibition shown at the Sociéte
Nationale des Beaux-Arts the same year, the large retrospective mounted at the École des Beaux-Arts in Paris in
1885, and, not least, the publication in the 1880s and 1890s
of his articles on various artists, his correspondence and

his diary prompted Cézanne repeatedly to confront the
work and personality of Delacroix. Support for his observations came from the writings of Charles Baudelaire – to this
day, essential reading – which define in exemplary fashion
Delacroix's characteristic combination of intellectual
understanding, psychological sensitivity and exceptional
creative energy. Baudelaire described an artistic existence
that clearly served Cézanne as confirmation and led
him on 13 September 1906, shortly before his death,
to recommend Baudelaire as reading for his son.[6]

The second artistic point of reference evident in the
present watercolour is the work of Paolo Veronese.
Cézanne may have been encouraged in his enthusiasm
for the Venetian by his preoccupation with Delacroix,
who likewise admired him. Veronese's art could be studied
extensively in the Louvre, and, early in his career, Cézanne
made drawings of details from Veronese's *The Marriage at
Cana*, and he later referred repeatedly to the Venetian
painter.[7] Cézanne's experiences and memories of such

works may be responsible for the impression conveyed by the Courtauld still life of a festive banquet (though without guests) rather than a calmly contemplative bourgeois ambience.

In their almost alarming conjunction of sensuous physical appearances with conceptual discipline, Cézanne's watercolours represent a synthesis of his entire oeuvre. Their juxtaposition of bold volumes and vibrant transparency, of material description and systematic colour, demand of the viewer intense observation and considerable imaginative power. In no other area of Cézanne's work does the spectator have such an immediate sense of witnessing the creative process itself. Retracing the sequence of inception, development and conclusion, the viewer becomes aware that the original, deeper meaning of still life as a subject is being conveyed in a new way. The potential inherent in a work on paper is here unfolded to create an image fully equal in significance to an oil painting. MS

NOTES
1 Rewald 1983, nos. 643, 610, 572.
2 Rewald 1996, no. 936.
3 Chappuis 1973, nos. 336–40, and Rewald 1983, no. 188.
4 Reissner in London 2008, pp. 49–71.
5 For a recent in-depth discussion of this procedure, see Dittmann 2005, pp. 45ff.
6 Rewald (ed.) 1984, p. 323.
7 Chappuis 1973, nos. 169, 170; see also Buck in London 2008, p. 132.

PABLO PICASSO
Málaga 1881–1973 Mougins

58 *Female nude with her arm resting on a chair*, 1920–21
Verso: *Female nude with her arm resting on a chair*

Charcoal, on wove paper; inscribed by the artist in graphite at lower left: *Picasso*; overall slight undulation and discolouration; pinhole at upper centre.

Verso: inscribed in graphite *582*
315/320 × 246 mm

Samuel Courtauld Trust, D.1978.PG.265

© 2012 Estate of Pablo Picasso/Artists Rights Society (ARS), New York

CAT. NO. 58 VERSO

The recto of this sheet features a standing nude leaning on the back of a chair drawn in a classicising style, while on the verso a faint image of one or two figures in an interior in a linear Cubist mode can be discerned.[1] The sheet was first assigned to 1920–21 by Anthony Blunt on the basis of style and its relation to a group of similar drawings.[2] Large bathers, such as the figure seen here, as well as images of a woman in an interior – often in the likeness of the artist's wife Olga Kokhlova – appear frequently in Picasso's art in the early 1920s in both naturalistic and more abstract modes.

The monumental character of this nude's body is in keeping with Picasso's contemporaneous Neoclassical bathers, who are often shown on the seashore either nude or in classical garb. A distinctive trait of the figure in the present drawing is the unusual arrangement of the legs. The woman stands on her left foot, and the lower half of the right leg disappears behind the left, giving the illusion that below the knee the legs taper into one. The serpentine, one-legged pose of the figure in the present drawing can also be seen in a bathing figure at the right in the pastel drawing *Group of female nudes*, of 1921 (fig. 111).

PROVENANCE
Count Antoine Seilern (1901–1978), acquired from Alfred Scharf (1900–1965), 16 March 1941; Princes Gate Bequest, 1978

SELECTED LITERATURE
Seilern 1961, no. 265

SELECTED EXHIBITION
London 1981, no. 141

The chair, as well, relates to other works that Picasso completed around this time. An armless tapestry-covered chair appears prominently in paintings and drawings of Olga in 1917, shortly after the couple met, and served as a signature of sorts of their new abode in Montrouge, outside Paris.[3] In this drawing, the overall shape of the chair is similar, although the seat is round rather than rectangular and has no patterning. This chair may be a schematic version of the elegant tapestry chair, thus associating the drawing with Olga. A few stray lines on the left of the sheet suggest a curtain, the presence of which would make the surrounding space a domestic interior.

At first glance, the towering figure that fills the sheet in the vertical dimension seems out of scale with the chair and the presumed room in which it is situated. On closer inspection, however, it can be seen that the figure was initially smaller and perhaps partially draped, and thus more in keeping with the scale of the chair. Contained within the contours of the nude are another set of shoulders and arms, a neck and an outline of a head, all drawn in a more tentative fashion. Over the shoulders are suggestions of the straps of a shift or classical garb, which also feature in such works as the pencil sketch *Draped woman standing* of January 1921 (fig. 112), in which the woman leans against a pedestal, and in a painting, *Woman and Child*, of 1922–23.[4] The emphatic curved horizontal strokes of chalk over the figure's vulva in the Courtauld sheet do not appear in Picasso's classical nudes of this period and may be vestiges of drapery from his initial sketch.

Whether in the initial process of putting charcoal to paper or at a later date, Picasso revised the contours of the nude's upper body, raising them on the sheet to create a more massive figure. He then reinforced the new contours with bold, broken charcoal lines, re-established the outlines of the right arm and hand and made adjustments

FIG. 111 Pablo Picasso,
Group of Female Nudes, 1921
Pastel on paper, 243 × 299 mm
Staatsgalerie Stuttgart,
Graphische Sammlung,
C 1959/915

© 2012 Estate of Pablo Picasso/
Artists Rights Society (ARS),
New York

FIG. 112 Pablo Picasso,
Draped woman standing, 1921
Red chalk, 290 × 220 mm
Paris, private collection

© 2012 Estate of Pablo Picasso/
Artists Rights Society (ARS),
New York

across the figure's midsection. The legs, however, seem
not to have been changed. By lightly smudging the
friable charcoal on the textured surface of the laid paper,
Picasso modelled the figure, giving it a pronounced
sense of volume.

On this sheet the evolution of Picasso's figure remains
visible. The drawing is a testament to the fluidity of the
artist's thinking on paper, in which themes are inter-
changeable in the process of making, and distinctly
different styles can cohabit on opposite sides of a single
sheet. SGG

NOTES

1 Seilern 1961, fig. 62, titles the verso
   Abstract Construction.

2 *Ibidem*, p. 153. Seilern accepts the date on
   the basis of comparison of the drawing with
   Zervos 1942–78, IV, no. 6, and *ibidem*, VI,
   no. 1400. See also London 1981, p. 103, in
   which the work is dated to the same years.

3 The classic example is the oil painting *Olga
   in an Armchair* (1917; Paris, Musée Picasso),

Zervos 1942–78, III, no. 83. The chair
appears in a photograph by Picasso on which
the painting was based: Olga Picasso in the
studio at 22, avenue Victor-Hugo, Montrouge,
November 1917. Paris, Musée Picasso,
Picasso Archives.

4 Zervos 1942–78, IV, no. 455.

HENRI MATISSE
Le Cateau-Cambrésis (now Le Cateau) 1869–1954 Nice

59 *Seated woman*, 1919

Graphite, on wove paper; inscribed by the artist in graphite at top right *Henri-Matisse*; three holes along top edge (possibly sewing holes).

Verso: inscribed with blue crayon *1A* and with graphite, partially erased
34 s x … and *46 x 35 s …*
355 × 254 mm

WATERMARK
1912 ENGLAND (may be Whatman)

Samuel Courtauld Trust, D.1935.SC.142

© 2012 Succession H. Matisse/Artists Rights Society (ARS), New York

This drawing is a study for the figure in Matisse's canvas *The black table* (fig. 113), painted at his studio in Issy-les-Moulineaux, near Paris, in the summer of 1919.[1] In the drawing, the model is presented in three-quarter length, seated on a wicker chair, her head and body strictly frontal. Her Moorish costume includes a long-sleeved, transparent blouse edged with tiny buttons, a sleeveless embroidered vest and a flowing skirt or harem pants. A tight scarf covering most of her hair and her forehead draws attention to the pure oval of her head and her large, slightly misaligned eyes. The vertical slats of the chair-back provide the only deviation from the predominantly arabesque lines of the drawing. At bottom left, the edge of a table bisects the corner of the sheet – a small detail that anchors the figure to the space of an imagined room.

The model, nineteen-year-old Antoinette Arnoux, began posing for Matisse in Nice during the winter of 1918–19, and when the artist left for Issy-les-Moulineaux that summer she accompanied him.[2] Arnoux's impact on Matisse is evident in the prolific body of work he carried out with her at this time, including a celebrated series of drawings and paintings in which she wears a plumed hat,

designed for her by the artist.[3] The model's youth and versatility, along with the surrounding environment of the Riviera and the general postwar revival of classicism, contributed to a new direction in Matisse's drawing. As John Elderfield wrote, in the works of this period Matisse's drawing shifted from "'difficult' and avant garde" to "accessible, traditional and, technically, extraordinarily accomplished".[4] In 1920, on the occasion of his fiftieth birthday, Matisse published a book of fifty recent drawings, *Cinquante dessins*, in which Arnoux is featured prominently – a homage to her effect on his evolving draughtsmanship.[5]

The Courtauld sheet shares the technical virtuosity of the works of the Plumed Hat series, many of which were included in *Cinquante dessins*. In this sheet, however, Matisse's response to his model is more directly sensual. Two related studies for *The black table* show Arnoux seated in the same wicker chair; in one she appears nude (fig. 114) and in the other in the same costume, although recessed in space and alongside the table.[6] In the Courtauld drawing the figure is pushed up to the picture plane and, because of the model's direct rapport with the viewer, the drawing

PROVENANCE
Samuel Courtauld (1876–1947), acquired from Leicester Galleries, 1928; Samuel Courtauld Gift, 1935

SELECTED LITERATURE
Cooper 1954, no. 142

SELECTED EXHIBITIONS
Paris 1955, no. 84; London 1959, no. 53; London 1966, no. 25; London 1976, no. 71; Marseille 1974, no. 25; Sheffield and elsewhere 1977, no. 45; London and New York 1984, no. 53; Tokyo, Osaka and Kyoto 1997, no. 81; Toronto 1998, no. 75; Düsseldorf and Riehen/Basel 2006, no. 81

shares – though to a lesser degree – the frank sensuality of the nude study, while the iconic frontality of the figure injects the sense of distance of the other sketch.

Unlike the related compositions, however, the present drawing diminishes the role of the table, emphasising the prominence of the arabesque when the garments and body are presented close-up. Indeed, Matisse wrote that his time in Nice provoked a desire to create works in which "the supremacy of the arabesque would be assured".[7] In this sheet, the soft, flowing contours of the figure and clothing create a dynamic sense of movement and an almost abstract play of line. The model's right arm appears disembodied, a mere arrangement of wispy strokes. At the same time, the overall patterning of light and shadow, made up of areas of untouched paper and fine, disciplined hatching lines, restores the figure's solidity. With its integration of sinuous line and surface detail with solid form, Matisse's drawing is reminiscent of the technique of Ingres, whose reputation as a draughtsman reached new heights in the nationalistic postwar return-to-order movement.[8] At this moment, Matisse and his longtime rival Picasso both drew in different ways from the French master's legacy and competed for his mantle, as they had earlier in the century.[9] SGG

FIG. 114 Henri Matisse,
Nude in an armchair, 1919
Pencil, 330 × 230 mm
Private collection

© 2012 Succession H. Matisse/
Artists Rights Society (ARS),
New York

NOTES

1 The drawing also relates to *Woman in Oriental Dress*, July 1919, a smaller painting (Glasgow, Kelvingrove Art Gallery).

2 See entry by Bourguignon in Jiminez and Banham (eds.) 2001, p. 51.

3 Eight of the Plumed Hat drawings, mainly in pencil, but some in ink, are reproduced in Schneider 1984, pp. 498–99. Paintings from the series include *The White Plumes* (Minneapolis Institute of Art) and *The Plumed Hat* (Washington, DC, National Gallery of Art). For more paintings featuring Arnoux, see Jiminez and Banham (eds.) 2001, p. 51.

4 London and New York 1984, p. 76.

5 *Ibid.*, p. 75. *Cinquante dessins* included at least one drawing related to *The Black Table*, though not the Courtauld sheet.

6 *Odalisque in an armchair*, 1919, pencil, reproduced in Schneider 1984, opposite p. 496.

7 Matisse, quoted *ibid.*, p. 496.

8 Louis Aragon compared Matisse's attention to detail and the finished quality of his drawings at this time with Ingres's: see Aragon 1972, vol. 2, pp. 103–09. Ingres remained popular in France at the beginning of the twentieth century. An important exhibition of his work, including many preparatory drawings for *The Turkish Bath*, was shown in 1905 at the Salon d'Automne, where Matisse also exhibited.

The Galeries Georges Petit held another major Ingres show in 1911, which included some 450 drawings. Ingres's work became more popular with the national resurgence of interest in classicism during and after World War I. See Silver 1989, pp. 244–63.

9 See, for example, *Portrait of Madame Georges Wildenstein*, 1918, private collection (not in Zervos). The competition between Matisse and Picasso in their explorations of naturalism and figuration at this time was captured in their 1918 joint exhibition at the Galerie Paul Guillaume in Paris, organised by Guillaume Apollinaire.

Bibliography

A Brief Chronological Description 1871
A Brief Chronological Description of a Collection of Original Drawings and Sketches ... Formed and Belonging to Mr Mayor, London, 1871

ACHILLES 1982
Katrin Achilles, 'Indianer auf der Jagd: Der neue Kontinent in den *Venationes* des Johannes Stradanus', in Karl-Heinz Kohl (ed.), *Mythen der Neuen Welt*, Berlin, 1982, pp. 161–72

ADELAIDE 1968
Master Drawings of the 17th Century from the Witt Collection, exh. cat., Art Gallery of South Australia, Adelaide, 1968

ADHÉMAR 1966
Jean Adhémar, *Les gens de médecine dans l'œuvre de Daumier*, Paris, 1966

AIX-EN-PROVENCE 1961
Exposition Cézanne: Tableaux–Aquarelles–Dessins, exh. cat., Pavillon de Vendôme, Aix-en-Provence, 1961

ALBERTI (SINISGALLI) 2011
Rocco Sinisgalli, ed. and trans., *Leon Battista Alberti: On Painting, A New Translation and Critical Edition*, Cambridge, 2011

ALSTEENS AND SPIRA 2012
Stijn Alsteens and Freyda Spira, *Dürer and Beyond: Central European Drawings in The Metropolitan Museum of Art, 1400–1700*, New York, 2012

AMES-LEWIS 1981
Francis Ames-Lewis, *Drawing in Early Renaissance Italy*, New Haven and London, 1981

AMSTERDAM 1905
Michael E. Sadler, *Vincent Van Gogh*, exh. cat., Stedelijk Museum, Amsterdam, 1905

AMSTERDAM 1914
Vincent Van Gogh Teekeningen uit de verzameling mevr. J. van Gogh Bonger en V.W. van Gogh, exh. cat., Stedelijk Museum, Amsterdam, 1914

AMSTERDAM 1936
Catalogus van de tentoonstelling twee eeuwen engelsche kunst, exh. cat., Stedelijk Museum, Amsterdam, 1936

ANANOFF 1961–70
Alexandre Ananoff, *L'œuvre dessiné de Jean-Honoré Fragonard (1732–1806): Catalogue raisonné*, 3 vols., Paris, 1961–70

ANDERSEN 1970
W. Andersen, *Cézanne's Portrait Drawings*, Cambridge, MA, and London, 1970

ANN ARBOR 1976
Clifton C. Olds, Ralph G. Williams and William R. Levin (eds.), *Images of Love and Death in Late Medieval and Renaissance Art*, exh. cat., The University of Michigan Museum of Art, Ann Arbor, 1976

ANTWERP 2002
F. Koreny et al., *Early Netherlandish Drawings from Jan van Eyck to Hieronymus Bosch*, exh. cat., Rubenshuis, Antwerp, 2002

ANTWERP 2004
Kristin Belkin, Fiona Healy, with an introductory essay by Jeffrey M. Muller, *A House of Art: Rubens as Collector*, exh. cat., Rubenshuis, Antwerp, 2004

ANZELEWSKY 1971
F. Anzelewsky, *Albrecht Dürer. Das malerische Werk*, Berlin, 1971

ARAGON 1972
Louis Aragon, *Henri Matisse*, trans. Jean Stewart, 2 vols., London, 1972

ARLES 2003
Van Gogh at Arles, exh. cat., Fondation Van Gogh, Arles, 2003

ARMSTRONG 1902
W. Armstrong, *Turner*, Manchester and Liverpool, 1902

Art et style 1950
Art et style, no. 14, 1950, pl. 48

AUCKLAND 1960
Philip Troutman, *Old Master Drawings from the Witt Collection*, exh. cat., Auckland City Art Gallery, Auckland, 1960

BAILLIE-GROHMAN 1899
W.A. Baillie-Grohman, 'Arts and Crafts in the Sixteenth Century, Part III', *Nash's Pall Mall Magazine*, ed. Lord Frederic Hamilton, 21, May–August 1900, pp. 158–66

BAJOU 1999
Valérie Bajou, *Monsieur Ingres*, Paris, 1999

BALLON 1999
Hillary Ballon, *Louis Le Vau: Mazarin's Collège, Colbert's Revenge*, Princeton, 1999

BARNARD CASTLE 1962
Tony Ellis, *Neapolitan Baroque and Rococo Painting*, exh. cat., The Bowes Museum, Barnard Castle, 1962

BARONI 1980
Jean-Luc Baroni, *Old Master Drawings*, London, June 1980

BATH 1969
Masters of the Water-colour: Watercolours from the Spooner Collection, exh. cat., Holburne of Menstrie Museum, Bath, 1969

BAZIN 1987
Germain Bazin, *Théodore Géricault: Étude critique, documents et catalogue raisonné*, 7 vols., Paris, 1987

BEAN AND GRISWOLD 1990
J. Bean and W. Griswold, *18th Century Italian Drawings in the Metropolitan Museum of Art*, New York, 1990

BECKETT (ED.) 1962–68
R.B. Beckett (ed.), *John Constable's Correspondence*, 6 vols., London, 1962–68

BELL AND GIRTIN 1934–35
C.F. Bell and T. Girtin, 'The Drawings and Sketches of J.R. Cozens', *Walpole Society*, vol. 23, 1934–35

BÉNARD 1810
Cabinet de M. Paignon Dijonval, rédigé par M. Bénard, peintre et graveur, Paris, 1810

BENESCH 1954–57
Otto Benesch, *The Drawings of Rembrandt*, 6 vols., London, 1954–57

BENISOVICH 1956
Michel N. Benisovich, 'The Drawings of Stradanus (Jan Van der Straeten) in the Cooper Union Museum for the Arts of Decoration, New York', *Art Bulletin* 38, no. 4, December 1956, pp. 249–51

BERENSON 1938
Bernard Berenson, *The Drawings of the Florentine Painters*, 3 vols., Chicago, 1938

BERENSON 1961
Bernard Berenson, *I disegni dei pittori fiorentini*, 3 vols., Milan, 1961

BERGER 1966
Robert W. Berger, 'Antoine Le Pautre and the Motif of the Drum-without-Dome', *Journal of the Society of Architectural Historians*, vol. 25, no. 3, October 1966, pp. 165–80

BERLIN 1910
L'art français au XVIIIe siècle, exh. cat., Royal Academy of Arts, Berlin, 1910

BERLIN 1975
Fedja Anzelewsky, Peter Dreyer, et al. (eds.), *Pieter Bruegel d. Ä. als Zeichner: Herkunft und Nachfolge*, exh. cat., Staatliche Museen Preussischer Kulturbesitz, Kupferstichkabinett, Berlin, 1975

BERLIN 1996
H.-Th. Schulze Altcappenberg, *Giovanni Battista Tiepolo (1696–1770) und sein Atelier. Zeichnungen und Radierungen im Berliner Kupferstichkabinett*, exh. cat., Kupferstichkabinett, Berlin, 1996

BERN 1960
Bestände aus den Sammlungen des Fürsten von Liechtenstein. Beiträge aus schweizerischen und überseeischen Privatsammlungen, sale cat., Klipstein und Kornfeld, Bern, 1960

BERNT 1979
Walther Bernt, *Die niederländischen Maler und Zeichner des 17. Jahrhunderts*, Munich, 1979

BESANÇON 2006
Pierre Rosenberg, *Les Fragonard de Besançon*, exh. cat., Musée des Beaux-Arts et d'Archéologie de Besançon, 2006

BIERMANN 1928
G. Biermann (ed.), *Albrecht Dürer. Festschrift der Internationalen Dürer-Forschung*, Leipzig, 1928

BIRKE AND KERTÉSZ 1992–97
V. Birke and J. Kertész, *Die italienischen Zeichnungen der Albertina. Generalverzeichniss*, 4 vols., Vienna, Cologne, and Weimar, 1992–97

BIRMINGHAM 1829
Birmingham Society of Artists, *Modern Works of Art*, exh. cat., Birmingham, 1829

BIRMINGHAM 1993
Michael Liversidge and Jane Farrington (eds.), *Canaletto's England*, exh. cat., Birmingham Gas Hall, Birmingham, 1993

BIRMINGHAM 2003
James Hamilton, *Turner's Britain*, exh. cat., Birmingham Museums and Art Gallery, 2003

BJURSTRÖM 1984
Per Bjurström, *French Drawings: Eighteenth Century*, Stockholm, 1984

BLUNT 1953
Anthony Blunt, *Art and Architecture in France 1500 to 1700*, London, 1953

BOECKL 2000
Christine M. Boeckl, *Images of Plague and Pestilence: Iconography and Iconology*, Kirksville, MO, 2000

BOGGS AND MAHEUX 1992
Jean Sutherland Boggs and Anne Maheux, *Degas Pastels*, New York, 1992

BOK-VAN KAMMEN 1977
Welmoet Bok-van Kammen, 'Stradanus and the Hunt', PhD diss., Baltimore, The Johns Hopkins University, 1977

BOLOGNA 1969
Denis Mahon, *Il Guercino (Giovanni Francesco Barbieri, 1591–1666). Catalogo critico dei disegni*, exh. cat., Pinacoteca, Bologna, 1969

BOLTEN 2007
Jaap Bolten, *Abraham Bloemaert: The Drawings*, Leiden, 2007

BOMBE 1933
W. Bombe, 'Pintorrichio', in *Thieme-Becker. Allgemeines Lexikon der bildenden Künstler von der Antike bis zur Gegenwart*, ed. by Hans Vollmer, Leipzig, 1933, vol. 27, p. 65

BORDEAUX 1984
J.-L. Bordeaux, *François Le Moyne and His Generation (1688–1737)*, Neuilly-sur-Seine, 1984

BORGHINI (ELLIS) 2007
Lloyd H. Ellis, ed. and trans., *Raffaello Borghini, Il Riposo*, Toronto, 2007

BOSKOVITS AND BROWN 2003
Miklós Boskovits and David Alan Brown, *Italian Paintings of the Fifteenth Century, The Collections of the National Gallery of Art, Washington, Systematic Catalogue*, Washington, DC, 2003

BOSTON 1992
Henri de Toulouse-Lautrec, exh. cat., Museum of Fine Arts, Boston, 1992

BOTTARI 1757
Giovanni Bottari, *Raccolta di lettere*, Florence, 1757

BRESC-BAUTIER 2008
Geneviève Bresc-Bautier, *The Louvre: A Tale of a Palace*, Paris, 2008

BRETT 1949
Gerard Brett, 'The Seven Wonders of the World in the Renaissance', *Art Quarterly* 12, 1949, pp. 346–58

BRINCKMANN 1925
A.E. Brinckmann, *Michelangelo Zeichnungen*, Munich, 1925

BRISTOL 1973
English Watercolours: The Spooner Collection and Bequest, exh. cat., City Art Gallery, Bristol, 1973

BROWN 1972
Jonathan Brown, 'Notes on Princeton Drawings 6: Jusepe de Ribera', *Record of the Art Museum, Princeton University*, vol. 31, no. 2, 1972, pp. 2–7

BRUSSELS 1929
Exposition retrospective de peinture anglaise (XVIII & XIX siècles), exh. cat., Musée Moderne, Brussels, 1929

BRUSSELS 1973
Toulouse-Lautrec, exh. cat., Musée d'Ixelles, Brussels, 1973

BRUSSELS 1980
Philippe Roberts-Jones, Fritz Grossmann, Konrad Oberhuber, et al. (eds.), *Bruegel: Une dynastie de peintres*, exh. cat., Palais des Beaux-Arts, Brussels, 1980

BRUSSELS AND ELSEWHERE 1949
Le Dessin français de Fouquet à Cézanne, exh. cat., Palais des Beaux-Arts, Brussels; Museum Boymans, Rotterdam; and Orangerie des Tuileries, Paris, 1949

BUCK 2001
S. Buck, *Die niederländischen Zeichnungen des 15. Jahrhunderts im Berliner Kupferstichkabinett. Kritischer Katalog*, Turnhout, 2001

BUCK 2003
S. Buck, 'The Impact of Hugo van der Goes as a Draftsman', *Master Drawings*, vol. 41, no. 3, 2003, pp. 228–39

BUDAPEST AND LUXEMBOURG 2006
I. Takács (ed.), *Sigismundus rex et imperator. Kunst und Kultur zur Zeit Sigismunds von Luxemburg, 1387–1437*, exh. cat., Szépművészeti Múzeum, Budapest, and Musée National d'Histoire et d'Art, Luxembourg, 2006

BUONANNI 1716
Filippo Buonanni et al., *Histoire du clergé seculier et regulier. des congregations de chanoines & de clercs, & des ordres religieux de l'un & de l'autre sexe …*, 4 vols, Amsterdam, 1716

BURKE 2004
Jill Burke, *Changing Patrons: Social Identity and the Visual Arts in Renaissance Florence*, London, 2004

BYAM SHAW 1976
James Byam Shaw, *Drawings by Old Masters at Christ Church, Oxford*, Oxford, 1976

BYAM SHAW 1983
James Byam Shaw, *The Italian Drawings of the Frits Lugt Collection*, 3 vols., Paris, 1983

CALAIS 1961
L'Aquarelle romantique en France et Angleterre, exh. cat., Musée des Beaux-Arts, Calais, 1961

CALLEN 2009
Anthea Callen, 'Hors-d'oeuvre: Edges, Boundaries and Marginality, with particular reference to Seurat's drawings', in Paul Smith (ed.), *Seurat Re-viewed*, Pennsylvania 2009, pp. 24–26

CALMANN 1976
Hans M. Calmann, 'Dealer in Old Master Drawings', manuscript autobiography, 1976

CAMBRIDGE, MA 1949
A. Mongan (ed.), *One Hundred Master Drawings*, exh. cat., Fogg Museum of Art, Cambridge, MA, 1949

CAMBRIDGE, MA, AND ELSEWHERE 1991
David M. Stone, *Guercino, Master Draftsman: Works from North American Collections*, exh. cat., Arthur M. Sackler Museum, Cambridge, MA; National Gallery of Canada, Ottawa; and The Cleveland Museum of Art, 1991

CAMPBELL 1985
Lorne Campbell, *The Early Flemish Pictures in the Collection of Her Majesty the Queen*, London, 1985

CARPI 2009
Manuela Kahn-Rossi, *Ugo da Carpi, l'opera incisa. Xilografie e chiaroscuri da Tiziano, Raffaello e Parmigianino*, exh. cat., Palazzo dei Pio, Loggia di Primo Ordine, Carpi, 2009

Carteggio 1965–83
P. Barocchi and R. Ristori (eds.), *Il Carteggio di Michelangelo*, 5 vols., Florence, 1965–83

CAVIGLIA-BRUNEL 2004
Susanna Caviglia-Brunel, 'Des finalités du dessin chez Charles-Joseph Natoire', *Revue de l'art*, vol. 143, 2004, pp. 35–48

CHANTELOU (BLUNT) 1985
Paul Fréart de Chantelou, *Diary of the Cavaliere Bernini's Visit to France*, trans. Margery Corbett, ed. Anthony Blunt, Princeton, 1985

CHAPMAN AND FAIETTI 2010
Hugo Chapman and Marzia Faietti, *Fra Angelico to Leonardo: Italian Renaissance Drawings*, London, 2010

CHAPPUIS 1973
A. Chappuis, *The Drawings of Paul Cézanne: A Catalogue Raisonné*, 2 vols., Greenwich, CT, and London, 1973

CHRISTIANSEN 2009
Keith Christiansen, 'The Genius of Andrea Mantegna', *Metropolitan Museum of Art Bulletin*, vol. 67, no. 2, 2009

CLAPP 1914
Frederick Mortimer Clapp, *Les Dessins de Pontormo. Catalogue raisonné, précédé d'un étude critique*, Paris, 1914

CLARK 1973
T.J. Clark, *The Absolute Bourgeois: Artists and Politics in France, 1848–1851*, London, 1973

CLAYTON AND PRICE 1988
Peter A. Clayton and Martin J. Price, *The Seven Wonders of the Ancient World*, London and New York, 1988

CLÉMENT 1867
Charles Clément, 'Géricault, étude biographique et critique, avec le catalogue raisonné de l'oeuvre du maître', *Gazette des beaux-arts*, vol. 2, October 1867, pp. 354–72

CLEVELAND AND ELSEWHERE 1987
Impressionist and Post-Impressionist Masterpieces: The Courtauld Collection, The Cleveland Museum of Art; The Metropolitan Museum of Art, New York; Kimbell Art Museum, Fort Worth; The Art Institute of Chicago; and The Nelson-Atkins Museum of Art, Kansas City, MO, 1987

COCKE 1984
Richard Cocke, *Veronese's Drawings*, London, 1984

COLOGNE 2002
J.M. Plotzek et al. (eds.), *Ars Vivendi–Ars Moriendi: Die Kunst zu leben, Die Kunst zu sterben; Die Handschriftensammlung Renate König*, exh. cat., Erzbischöftliches Diözesanmuseum, Cologne, 2002

COLVIN 1897
Sidney Colvin, 'Über einige Zeichnungen des Carpaccio in England', *Jahrbuch der Königlich Preussischen Kunstsammlungen*, vol. 18, 1897, pp. 193–204

CONISBEE (ED.) 2007
Philip Conisbee (ed.), *French Genre Painting in the Eighteenth Century* (Studies in the History of Art, National Gallery of Art), Washington, DC, 2007

CONISBEE 2009
Philip Conisbee, *French Paintings of the Fifteenth through the Eighteenth Century, The Collections of the National Gallery of Art, Washington, Systematic Catalogue*, Washington, DC, 2009

CONSTABLE 1927
W.G. Constable, 'Canaletto in England: Some Further Work', *Burlington Magazine*, vol. 50, 1927, pp. 16–19

CONSTABLE 1962
W.G. Constable, *Canaletto*, 2 vols., Oxford, 1962

CONSTABLE (LINKS) 1976
W.G. Constable (revised by J.G. Links), *Canaletto*, 2 vols., Oxford, 1976

COOPER 1954
Douglas Cooper, *The Courtauld Collection*, London, 1954

COPENHAGEN 1992
C. Fischer, *Det døende Venezia, Lommebog 57*, exh. cat., Den Kgl Kobberstiksamling, Statens Museum for Kunst, Copenhagen, 1992

CORBOZ 1978
André Corboz, *Peinture militante et architecture révolutionnaire: À propos du thème du tunnel chez Hubert Robert*, Basel, 1978

COSTAMAGNA 1994
Philippe Costamagna, *Pontormo*, Milan, 1994

COSTAMAGNA 2005
Philippe Costamagna, 'The Formation of Florentine Draftsmanship: Life Studies from Leonardo and Michelangelo to Pontormo and Salviati', *Master Drawings*, vol. 43, no. 3, October 2005, pp. 274–91

COURTAULD INSTITUTE OF ART 1956
Courtauld Institute of Art, *Hand-List of the Drawings in the Witt Collection*, London, 1956

COX-REARICK 1964
Janet Cox-Rearick, *The Drawings of Pontormo*, Cambridge, MA, 1964

COX-REARICK 1981
Janet Cox-Rearick, *The Drawings of Pontormo: A Catalogue Raisonné with Notes on the Paintings*, 2 vols., 2nd ed., New York, 1981

CRAIG-MCFEELEY 2002
Julia Craig-McFeeley, 'The Signifying Serpent: Seduction by Cultural Stereotype in Seventeenth-Century England', in Phyllis Austern (ed.), *Music, Sensation, and Sensuality*, New York, 2002

CROWE AND CALVACASELLE 1914
J.A. Crowe and G.B. Calvacaselle, *A History of Painting in Italy*, ed. by Tancred Borenius, 6 vols., London, 1914

CUST 1898
Lionel Cust, *The Master E.S. and the 'Ars Moriendi': A Chapter in the History of Engraving during the XVth Century*, Oxford, 1898

DAHLBERG (ED.) 1971
C. Dahlberg (ed.), *The Romance of the Rose by Guillaume de Lorris and Jean de Meun*, Princeton, 1971

DAVIS 1996
A. Davis, 'Ruskin, Turner, and the Crescent Moon', *Turner Society News*, vol. 72, March 1996, pp. 10–12

DAVIS 2009
A. Davis, 'Sunrise or Sunset? New Light on the Moon in *Dawn after the Wreck*', *Turner Society News*, vol. 112, August 2009, pp. 6–11

DAY 1975
H. Day, *John Constable, R.A., 1776–1837: Drawings, the Golden Age*, Eastbourne, 1975

DE BOSIO 2008
Giovanni Romano, Stefano de Bosio and Siverio Salamon, *Andrea Mantegna. Catalogo dell'opera grafica*, Turin, 2008

DE LA FAILLE 1970
J.-B. de la Faille, *The Works of Vincent van Gogh: His Paintings and Drawings*, rev. ed., Amsterdam, 1970

DELLA CHIESA 1968
A.O. Della Chiesa, *L'opera completa di Dürer*, Milan, 1968

DE MARIA 2010
Blake de Maria, *Becoming Venetian: Immigrants and the Arts in Early Modern Venice*, New Haven and London, 2010

DHANENS 1998
Elizabeth Dhanens, *Hugo van der Goes*, Antwerp, 1998

DITTMANN 2005
Lorenz Dittmann, *Die Kunst Cézannes. Farbe, Rhythmus, Symbolik*, Cologne, Weimar, and Vienna, 2005

DOERING 1896
Oscar Doering, *Des Augsburger Patriciers Philipp Hainhofer Beziehungen zum Herzog Philipp II. von Pommern-Stettin. Correspondenzen aus den Jahren 1610–1619 im Auszuge mitgetheilt und commentiert von Dr. Oscar Doering*, Vienna, 1896

DOERING 1901
Oscar Doering, *Des Augsburger Patriciers Philipp Hainhofer Reisen nach Innsbruck und Dresden*, Vienna, 1901

DOOSRY 2003
Y. Doosry, *In den hellsten Farben. Aquarelle von Dürer bis Macke*, Nuremberg, 2003

DRESDEN 1862
Sammlung Rietschel, Auctionskatalog, Dresden, 17ff. March 1862

DRESDEN 2002
Zwischen den Zeiten, exh. cat., Stadtmuseum Bautzen, Dresden, 2002

DROST 1957
W. Drost, *Adam Elsheimer als Zeichner*, Stuttgart, 1957

DUCLAUX 1981
Lise Duclaux, 'Dessins de Martin van Heemskerck', *Revue du Louvre et des Musées de France* 30–31, nos. 5–6, December 1981, pp. 375–80

DUMAS 1996
Ann Dumas, 'Degas as Collector', *Apollo*, vol. 144, no. 414, August 1996, pp. 3–70

DÜSSELDORF AND RIEHEN/BASEL 2006
Figure Color Space: Henri Matisse, exh. cat., K20 Kunstsammlung, Nordrhein-Westfalen, Düsseldorf, and Fondation Beyeler, Riehen/Basel, 2006

DUSSLER 1959
Luitpold Dussler, *Die Zeichnungen des Michelangelo*, Berlin, 1959

ECHINGER-MAURACH 2009
C. Echinger-Maurach, 'Michelangelo begegnet Dürer. Zu Entwürfen für zwei Schächer und einen Hl. Sebastian', *Mitteilungen des Kunsthistorischen Institutes in Florenz*, vol. 53, 2009, pp. 251–84

EDINBURGH 1984
H. MacAndrew, *Dutch Church Painters*, exh. cat., National Gallery of Scotland, Edinburgh, 1984

EDINBURGH 1994
Timothy Clifford, John Dick and Aidan Weston-Lewis, *Raphael: The Pursuit of Perfection*, exh. cat., National Gallery of Scotland, Edinburgh, 1994

EDINBURGH AND COMPTON VERNEY 2006
Martin Bailey, *Van Gogh and Britain: Pioneer Collectors*, National Gallery of Scotland, Edinburgh, and Compton Verney, Warwickshire, 2006

EDINBURGH AND LONDON 1964
Delacroix: An Exhibition of Paintings, Drawings, and Lithographs, exh. cat., Royal Scottish Academy, Edinburgh, and Royal Academy of Arts, London, 1964

EDINBURGH AND LONDON 2001
J. Lloyd-Williams et al., *Rembrandt's Women*, exh. cat., National Gallery of Scotland, Edinburgh, and Royal Academy of Arts, London, 2001

EDWARDS 1808
E. Edwards, *Anecdotes of Painters Who Have Resided or Been Born in England: With Critical Remarks on Their Productions*, London, 1808

EIDELBERG 1977
Martin P. Eidelberg, *Watteau's Drawings: Their Use and Significance*, New York, 1977

EISLER 1989
Colin Eisler, *The Genius of Jacopo Bellini: The Complete Paintings and Drawings*, New York, 1989

EKSERDJIAN 2006
David Ekserdjian, *Parmigianino*, New Haven and London, 2006

ELAM 1986
J.F. Elam, *St Mary's Church Bergholt: A Building and Its History*, Ipswich, 1986

ELLIS 1990
C.S. Ellis, 'Two Drawings by Fra Bartolommeo', *Paragone*, nos. 479–81, 1990, pp. 3–19

EMISON 1985
Patricia Anne Emison, 'Invention and the Italian Renaissance Print, Mantegna to Parmigianino', PhD diss., Columbia University, 1985

Encyclopédie 1751–65
Denis Diderot and Jean Le Rond d'Alembert, *Encyclopédie; ou Dictionnaire raisonné des sciences, des arts et des métiers*, 17 vols., 1751–65

EXETER AND NOTTINGHAM 1995
The Perfection of England: Artist Visitors to Devon, c. 1750–1870, exh. cat., Royal Albert Memorial Museum, Exeter, and Djanogly Art Gallery, University of Nottingham, 1995

FARR (ED.) 1987
Dennis Farr (ed.), *100 Masterpieces: Bernardo Daddi to Ben Nicholson; European Paintings and Drawings from the 14th to the 20th Century, Courtauld Institute Galleries*, London, 1987

FERINO PAGDEN 1987
Silvia Ferino Pagden, 'Perugino's Use of Drawings: Conventions and Invention', in W. Strauss and T. Felker (eds.), *Drawings Defined*, New York, 1987, pp. 77–102

FILEDT KOK 2006
J.P. Filedt Kok, *De heilige Lucas tekent en schildert de Madonna*, Amsterdam, 2006

FINALDI 1995
Gabriele Finaldi, 'Aspects of the Life and Work of Jusepe de Ribera (1591–1652)', 2 vols., PhD diss., Courtauld Institute of Art, London, 1995

FINBERG 1909
A.J. Finberg, *A Complete Inventory of the Drawings of the Turner Bequest: with which are included the Twenty-three Drawings bequeathed by Mr Henry Vaughan*, 2 vols., London, 1909

FINBERG 1961
A.J. Finberg, *The Life of J.M.W. Turner, R.A.*, 2nd ed., Oxford, 1961

FIOCCO 1958
Giuseppe Fiocco, 'Postille al mio Carpaccio', *Arte Veneta*, vol. 12, 1958, pp. 228–30

FISCHEL 1917
Oskar Fischel, *Die Zeichnungen der Umbrer*, Berlin, 1917

FISCHER 1989
Chris Fischer, 'Fra Bartolommeo's Landscape Drawings', *Mitteilungen des Kunsthistorischen Institutes in Florenz*, vol. 33, 1989, pp. 301–42

FISCHER 2007
Chris Fischer, 'Reflektion og redelighed. En landskabstegning af Fra Bartolommeo', in L. Bonde and M. Fabricius Hansen (eds.), *Hvorfor Kunst*, Copenhagen, 2007

FLECHSIG 1928–31
E. Flechsig, *Albrecht Dürer. Sein Leben und seine künstlerische Entwicklung*, 2 vols., Berlin, 1928–31

FLEMING-WILLIAMS 1990
Ian Fleming-Williams, *Constable and His Drawings*, London, 1990

FLEMING 1958
John Fleming, 'Mr Kent, Art Dealer, and the Fra Bartolommeo Drawings', *Connoisseur*, vol. 141, 1958, p. 227

FLETCHER 2001
Jennifer Fletcher, 'Carpaccio at the Courtauld', *British Art Journal*, vol. 2, 2001, pp. 71–74

FLORENCE 1956
Mario Salmi and Luciano Berti, *Mostra del Pontormo e del primo manierismo fiorentino*, exh. cat., Palazzo Strozzi, Florence, 1956

FLORENCE 1980
Luciano Berti et al. (eds.), *Il primato del disegno*, exh. cat., Palazzo Strozzi, Florence, 1980

FLORENCE 1986
Chris Fischer, *Disegni di Fra Bartolommeo e della sua scuola*, exh. cat., Gabinetto disegni e stampe degli Uffizi, Florence, 1986

FLORENCE 1996
A. Cecchi (ed.), *L'Officina della Maniera*, exh. cat., Galleria Nazionale degli Uffizi, Florence, 1996

FLORENCE 2010
Carlo Falciani and Antonio Natali (eds.), *Bronzino: Artist and Poet at the Court of the Medici*, exh. cat., Palazzo Strozzi, Florence, 2010

FORSTER 1998
Carter Forster, 'Jean-Bernard Restout's Sleep-figure Study: Painting and Drawing from the Life at the French Académie of Painting and Sculpture', *Cleveland Studies in the History of Art*, vol. 3, 1998, pp. 48–85

FRANKFURT AM MAIN 2009
M. Sonnabend, *Michelangelo: Zeichnungen und Zuschreibungen / Drawings and Attributions*, exh. cat., Städel Museum, Frankfurt am Main, 2009

FRANKFURT AND ELSEWHERE 1989
F. Vivian, *The Consul Smith Collection: Masterpieces of Italian Drawings from the Royal Library, Windsor Castle, Raphael to Canaletto*, exh. cat., Schirn Kunsthalle, Frankfurt; Kimbell Art Museum, Fort Worth; Virginia Museum of Fine Arts, Richmond; and National Gallery of Scotland, Edinburgh, 1989 (Italian ed., 1990)

FREY 1909-11
K. Frey, *Die Handzeichnungen Michelagniolos Buonarroti*, 3 vols., Berlin, 1909-11

FRIEDLÄNDER 1896
Max J. Friedländer, 'Dürer's Bildnisse seines Vaters', *Repertorium für Kunstwissenschaft*, vol. 19, 1896, pp. 9-19

FRIEDLÄNDER 1935
Max J. Friedländer, 'Eine Zeichnung von Hugo van der Goes', *Pantheon*, vol. 15, 1935, pp. 99-104

FRIEDLÄNDER 1942
Max J. Friedländer, *On Art and Connoisseurship*, London, 1942

FRIEDLÄNDER 1969
M.J. Friedländer, *Early Netherlandish Painting*, 14 vols., New York, 1969

GABILLOT 1895
C. Gabillot, *Hubert Robert et son temps. Les artistes célèbres*, Paris, 1895

GAGE 1987
J. Gage, *J.M.W. Turner: 'A Wonderful Range of Mind'*, New Haven and London, 1987

GASSIER 1972
Pierre Gassier, *Une Source inédite de dessins de Goya en France au XIXe siècle*, Paris, 1972

Gazette des beaux-arts 1970
Gazette des beaux-arts, 6th per., vol. 75, year 112, January 1970

GEBAROWICZ AND TIETZE 1929
M. Gebarowicz and H. Tietze, *Albrecht Dürers Zeichnungen im Lubomirskimuseum in Lemberg*, Vienna, 1929

GIBSON 2000
Walter S. Gibson, *Pleasant Places: The Rustic Landscape from Bruegel to Ruisdael*, Berkeley, 2000

GIBSON 2006
Walter S. Gibson, *Pieter Bruegel and the Art of Laughter*, Berkeley, 2006

GIOSEFFI 1959
D. Gioseffi, *Canaletto. Il quaderno delle Gallerie Veneziane e l'impiego della camera ottica*, Trieste, 1959

GIRTIN AND LOSHAK 1954
Thomas Girtin and David Loshak, *The Art of Thomas Girtin*, London and New York, 1954

GLÜCK 1937
Gustav Glück, *Pieter Bruegel*, Paris and New York, 1937

GNANN 2007
Achim Gnann, *Parmigianino. Die Zeichnungen*, 2 vols., Petersberg, 2007

GODFREY 1978
R.T. Godfrey, *Printmaking in Britain*, Oxford, 1978

GOLDNER 1993
George Goldner, 'Review: *Andrea Mantegna*, exhibition catalogue by Suzanne Boorsch et al., 1992', *Master Drawings*, vol. 31, no. 2, Summer 1993, pp. 172-76

GOLDNER 2004
George Goldner, 'Bellini's Drawings', in Peter Humfrey (ed.), *The Cambridge Companion to Giovanni Bellini*, Cambridge, 2004, pp. 226-55

GOLDSCHEIDER 1951
L. Goldscheider, *Michelangelo Drawings*, London, 1951

GOMBRICH 2000
E.H. Gombrich, 'Sleeper Awake! A Literary Parallel to Michelangelo's Drawing of "The Dream of Human Life"', in A. Gnann and H. Widauer (eds.), *Festschrift für Konrad Oberhuber*, Milan, 2000, pp. 130-32

GONCOURT 1856-75
Edmond de Goncourt and Jules de Goncourt, *L'Art du dix-huitième siècle*, Paris, 1856-75, trans. R. Ironside (as *French Eighteenth-Century Painters*), London, 1958

GOTTI 1875
Aurelio Gotti, *Vita di Michelangelo Buonarroti*, 2 vols., Florence, 1875

GRASSELLI 1987
Margaret Morgan Grasselli, 'The Drawings of Antoine Watteau: Stylistic Development and Problems of Chronology', PhD diss., Harvard University, Cambridge, MA, 1987

GRASSELLI 2001
Margaret Morgan Grasselli, 'Review: Pierre Rosenberg and Louis-Antoine Prat, *Antoine Watteau 1684-1721. Catalogue raisonné des dessins*', *Master Drawings*, vol. 39, no. 3, Autumn 2001, pp. 310-34

GRONAU 1957
C. Gronau, *Drawings of Landscapes and Trees by Fra Bartolommeo Sold at Auction on Wednesday the 20th November ... at Sotheby's & Co.*, London, 1957

GUÉRIN 1715
Nicolas Guérin, *Description de l'Académie royale des arts de peinture et de sculpture*, Paris, 1715

GUÉRIN 1944
Marcel Guérin, *L'œuvre gravé de Manet*, Paris, 1944

GUICCIARDINI 1567
Lodovico Guicciardini, *Description de tout le Païs bas*, Antwerp, 1567

GUSTIN-GOMEZ 2006
Clémentine Gustin-Gomez, *Charles de La Fosse: 1636-1716*, Dijon, 2006

GUTHKE 1999
Karl S. Guthke, *The Gender of Death: A Cultural History in Art and Literature*, Cambridge, 1999

HAARLEM 1986
Eddy de Jongh, *Portretten van Echt en Trouw*, exh. cat., Frans Halsmuseum, Haarlem, 1986

HADELN 1921
Detlev Freiherr von Hadeln, 'Zeichnungen des Tintoretto', *Jahrbuch der Preussischen Kunstsammlungen*, vol. 42, 1921, pp. 82-103

HADELN 1929
Detlev Freiherr von Hadeln, *Die Zeichnungen von Antonio Canal, genannt Canaletto*, Vienna, 1929

HALL 2005
James Hall, *Michelangelo and the Reinvention of the Human Body*, London, 2005

HALL 2007
Michael Hall, 'Gianlorenzo Bernini's Third Design for the East Façade of the Louvre of 1665, Drawn by Mattia de Rossi', *Burlington Magazine*, vol. 149, no. 1252, July 2007, pp. 478-82

HAMBURG 1976
W. Hoffman, A. Wilton and S. Hosten, *William Turner und die Landschaft seines Zeit (Kunst um 1800)*, exh. cat., Hamburger Kunsthalle, Hamburg, 1976

HAMBURG 2011
Annemarie Stefes, *Hamburger Kunsthalle, Kupferstichkabinett: Niederländische Zeichnungen 1450-1850*, Cologne, Weimar, and Vienna 2011

HARDIE 1966
M. Hardie, *Water-colour Painting in Britain*, 3 vols., London, 1966

HARROGATE 1968
English Watercolours: Memorial Exhibition to William Wycliffe Spooner, exh. cat., Corporation Art Gallery, Harrogate, 1968

HÄRTER 2006
K. Härter, 'Aachen-Frankfurt-Nürnberg-Regensburg. Politische Zentren des Reiches zwischen 1356 und 1806', in B. Heidenreich and F.-L. Kroll (eds.), *Wahl und Krönung*, Frankfurt am Main, 2006, pp. 175-88

HÄRTH 1960
I. Härth, 'Zu Landschaftzeichnungen Fra Bartolommeos und seines Kreises', *Mitteilungen des Kunsthistorischen Institutes in Florenz*, vol. 9, 1960, pp. 125-30

HARTT 1971
Frederick Hartt, *The Drawings of Michelangelo*, London, 1971

HATTORI 2001
Cordélia Hattori, 'De Charles de la Fosse à Antoine Watteau. Les *Saisons Crozat*', *Revue du Louvre: La Revue des musées de France*, vol. 51, no. 2, 2001, pp. 56-65

HAVERKAMP BEGEMANN 1961
Egbert Haverkamp Begemann, review of Otto Benesch, *The Drawings of Rembrandt*, *Kunstchronik*, 1961, pp. 3–30

HAYES 1970
John Hayes, *The Drawings of Thomas Gainsborough*, 2 vols., New Haven and London, 1970

HAYES 1970a
John Hayes, 'Gainsborough and the Gaspardesque', *Burlington Magazine*, vol. 112, no. 806, May 1970, pp. 308–11

HELLER 1827
J. Heller, *Das Leben und die Werke Albrecht Dürer's*, 1827

HÉLYOT 1714–19
Pierre Hélyot, *Histoire des ordres monastiques, religieux et militaires, et des congregations seculieres de l'un & l'autre sexe, qui ont esté establies jusque'à present....*, 8 vols., Paris, 1714–19

HERBERT 1962
Robert Herbert, *Seurat's Drawings*, New York, 1962

HERRMANN 1990
Luke Herrmann, *Turner Prints: The Engraved Work of J.M.W. Turner*, Oxford, 1990

HESELTINE 1913
J.P. Heseltine, *Original Drawings by Old Masters of the Italian School*, London, 1913

HILLAIRET 1997
Jacques Hillairet, *Dictionnaire historique des rues de Paris*, 2 vols., Paris, 1997

HOLLSTEIN 1949–2004
F.W.H. Hollstein et al., *Dutch and Flemish Etchings, Engravings and Woodcuts, c. 1450–1700*, 64 vols., Amsterdam and elsewhere, 1949–2004

HÜLSEN AND EGGER 1913
Christian Hülsen and Hermann Egger, *Die römischen Skizzenbücher von Marten van Heemskerck im Königlichen Kupferstichkabinett zu Berlin*, Berlin, 1913

HULSKER 1996
Jan Hulsker, *Complete Van Gogh: Paintings, Drawings, Sketches*, Philadelphia, 1996

HUYGHE 1948
René Huyghe, *Le Dessin français au XIXième siècle*, Lausanne, 1948

Illustrated Bartsch 56 (Dolders) 1987
Arno Dolders (ed.), *The Illustrated Bartsch*, vol. 56, *Netherlandish Artists: Philips Galle*, New York, 1987

Illustrated Bartsch 10 (Strauss) 1980–81
Walter L. Strauss (ed.), *The Illustrated Bartsch*, vol. 10, *Sixteenth-Century German Artists: Albrecht Dürer*, 2 vols., New York, 1980–81

INGAMELLS 1997
J. Ingamells, *A Dictionary of British and Irish Travellers in Italy, 1701–1800, Compiled from the Brinsley Ford Archive*, New Haven and London, 1997

INGELHEIM AM RHEIN 1971
Honoré Daumier: Gemälde, Zeichnungen, Lithographien, Skulpturen, exh. cat., Villa Schneider, Ingelheim am Rhein, 1971

INGELHEIM AM RHEIN 1977
Édouard Manet: Das graphische Werk, exh. cat., Villa Schneider, Ingelheim am Rhein, 1977

INGENHOFF-DANHÄUSER 1984
Monika Ingenhoff-Danhäuser, *Maria Magdalena. Heilige und Sünderin in der italienischen Renaissance. Studien zur Ikonographie der Heiligen von Leonardo bis Tizian*, Tübingen, 1984

IRESON 2010
Nancy Ireson, 'The Pointillist and the Past', *Burlington Magazine*, vol. 152, no. 1293, December 2010, pp. 799–803

IRESON 2011
Nancy Ireson, 'Seurat and the Cours de M. Yvon', *Burlington Magazine*, vol. 153, no. 1296, March 2011, pp. 174–80

JACKSON 1798
William Jackson, *The Four Ages: Together with Essays on Various Subjects*, London, 1798

JAFFÉ 1989
M. Jaffé, *Catalogo completo, Rubens*, Milan, 1989

JAFFÉ 2010
David Jaffé, 'Rubens's Lost "Pocketbook": Some New Thoughts', *Burlington Magazine*, vol. 152, no. 1283, 2010, pp. 94–98

JAMOT 1911
P. Jamot, 'Artistes contemporains. Ernest Laurent', *Gazette des beaux-arts*, pér. 3, vol. 50, March 1911, pp. 173–203

JANSEN 1999
Katherine Ludwig Jansen, *The Making of the Magdalen: Preaching and Popular Devotion in the Late Middle Ages*, Princeton, 1999

JEAN-RICHARD 1978
Pierrette Jean-Richard, *L'Œuvre gravé de François Boucher dans la collection Edmond de Rothschild*, Paris, 1978

JENNI 2006
Ulrike Jenni, 'Das Porträt Kaiser Sigismunds in Wien und seine Unterzeichnung. Bildnisse Kaiser Sigismunds in Wien und seine Unterzeichnung', in M. Pauly and F. Reinert (eds.), *Sigismund von Luxemburg. Ein Kaiser in Europa. Tagungsband des internationalen historischen und kunsthistorischen Kongresses in Luxemburg, 8.–10. Juni 2005*, Mayence, 2006, pp. 285–300

JIMINEZ AND BANHAM (EDS.) 2001
Jill Berk Jiminez and Joanna Banham (eds.), *Dictionary of Artist's Models*, Chicago, 2001

JOANNIDES 1983
Paul Joannides, *The Drawings of Raphael: With a Complete Catalogue*, Oxford, 1983

JOHNSON 1986
Lee Johnson, *The Paintings of Eugène Delacroix: A Critical Catalogue*, 6 vols., Oxford, 1986

JONES 1990
Pamela M. Jones, 'Bernardo Luini's *Magdalene* from the Collection of Federico Borromeo', *Studies in the History of Art. National Gallery of Art, Washington*, vol. 24, 1990, pp. 67–72

JOURDAIN AND ADHÉMAR 1952
Francis Jourdain and Jean Adhémar, *Henri de Toulouse-Lautrec*, Paris, 1952

Journal 2009
Michèle Hannoosh (ed.), *Journal d'Eugène Delacroix*, Paris, 2009

JUSTI 1909
Carl Justi, *Michelangelo. Neue Beiträge zur Erklärung seiner Werke*, Berlin, 1909

JUZWENKO 2004
A. Juzwenko (ed.), *The Fate of the Lubomirski Dürers: Recovering the Treasures of the Ossoliński National Institute*, Wrocław, 2004

KAHN 1928
Gustave Kahn, *Les Dessins de Georges Seurat*, 2 vols., Paris, 1928

KASSEL 1964
Documenta III, exh. cat., Alte Galerie, Museum Fridericianum, Orangerie, Kassel, 1964

KAVALER 1999
Ethan Matt Kavaler, *Pieter Bruegel: Parables of Order and Enterprise*, Cambridge, 1999

KEMP AND BARONE 2010
Martin Kemp and Juliana Barone, *I disegni di Leonardo da Vinci e della sua cerchia nelle collezioni della Gran Bretagna*, Florence, 2010

KENDALL 1988
Richard Kendall, *Cézanne by Himself: Drawings, Paintings, Writings*, London, 1988

KERRICH 1829
Thomas Kerrich, *A Catalogue of the Prints Which Have Been Engraved after Martin Heemskerck: or Rather, an Essay towards Such a Catalogue*, London, 1829

KÉRY 1972
B. Kéry, *Kaiser Sigismund. Ikonographie*, Vienna, 1972

KING'S LYNN 1985
French Drawings of the 17th and 18th Century, exh. cat., Fermoy Art Gallery, King's Lynn, 1985

KITSON 1961
Michael Kitson, 'Claude's Books of Drawings from Nature', *Burlington Magazine*, vol. 103, no. 699, June 1961, pp. 252–57

KITSON 1969
Michael Kitson, *Rembrandt*, London, 1969

KNOX 1975
G. Knox, *Catalogue of the Tiepolo Drawings in the Victoria and Albert Museum*, London, 1975

KÖNIG 1992
E. König, *Die Liebe im Zeichen der Rose. Die Hand-schriften des Rosenromans in der Vatikanischen Bibliothek*, Stuttgart and Zurich, 1992

KOERNER 1993
Joseph L. Koerner, *Dürer and the Moment of Self-Portraiture in German Renaissance Art*, Chicago, 1993

KOERNER 2004
Joseph L. Koerner, 'Unmasking the World: Bruegel's Ethnography', *Common Knowledge*, vol. 10, no. 2, 2004, pp. 220–51

KOERNER 2006
Joseph L. Koerner, *Dürer's Hands*, New York, 2006

KOSCHATZKY 1969
W. Koschatzky, *Das Aquarell*, Vienna and Munich, 1969

KOSCHATZKY AND STROBL 1971
W. Koschatzky and A. Strobl, *Die Dürerzeichnungen der Albertina*, Salzburg, 1971

KRAMER 1966
Margia C. Kramer, 'Martin van Heemskerck's *Seven Wonders of the World and the Coliseum*', MA thesis, New York University, Institute of Fine Arts, 1966

KUHRMANN 1964
D. Kuhrmann, *Über das Verhältnis von Vorzeichnung und ausgeführtem Werk bei Albrecht Dürer*, PhD diss., Berlin, 1964

LA MALFA 2009
Claudia La Malfa, *Pintoricchio a Roma. La seduzione dell'antico*, Milan, 2009

LANDAU AND PARSHALL 1994
David Landau and Peter Parshall, *The Renaissance Print, 1470–1550*, New Haven and London, 1994

LAUGHTON 1996
Bruce Laughton, *Honoré Daumier*, New Haven and London, 1996

LAUNAY 1991
Élisabeth Launay, *Les Frères Goncourt: Collectionneurs de dessins*, Paris, 1991

LAUTS 1962
Jan Lauts, *Carpaccio: Paintings and Drawings; Complete Edition*, London, 1962

LEBEER 1949
Louis Lebeer, *Miscellanea Leo van Puyvelde*, Brussels, 1949

LEBEER 1969
Louis Lebeer, *Catalogue raisonné des estampes de Bruegel*, Brussels, 1969

LEBEUF 1867
Jean Lebeuf, *Histoire de la ville et de tout le diocèse de Paris*, vol. 3, Paris, 1867

LEIRIS 1969
Alain de Leiris, *The Drawings of Édouard Manet*, Berkeley and Los Angeles, 1969

LEMOISNE 1946
Paul-André Lemoisne, *Degas et son œuvre*, 4 vols., Paris, 1946

Lettres de Van Gogh à Bernard 1911
Ambrose Vollard (ed.), *Lettres de Vincent Van Gogh à Emile Bernard*, Paris, 1911

Lettres de Van Gogh à son frère 1988
Lettres de Vincent van Gogh à son frère Théo, trans. Louis Roëlandt, Paris, 1988

LEUSCHNER 1997
E. Leuschner, *Persona, Larva, Maske. Ikonologische Studien zum 16. bis frühen 18. Jahrhundert*, Frankfurt am Main, 1997

LICHTENSTEIN 1976
Sara Lichtenstein, 'Delacroix Emblematicus: His Unknown Studies after Bonasone', *Journal of the Warburg and Courtauld Institutes*, vol. 39, 1976, pp. 275–80

LIGO 2006
Larry L. Ligo, *Manet, Baudelaire, and Photography*, 2 vols., Lewiston, NY, 2006

LINCOLN 1993
Evelyn Lincoln, 'Mantegna's Culture of Line', *Art History*, vol. 1, no. 1 (March 1993): 33–59

LINCOLN 2000
Evelyn Lincoln, *The Invention of the Italian Renaissance Printmaker*, New Haven and London, 2000

LINKS 1982
J.G. Links, *Canaletto*, Oxford, 1982

LIPPMANN 1927
F. Lippmann et al., *Zeichnungen von Albrecht Dürer in Nachbildungen*, 7 vols., Berlin, 1927

LIVERPOOL 1910
M. Conway, *The Art of Albrecht Dürer (1471–1528): A Collection of Reproductions of His Paintings, Engravings, Drawings and Woodcuts*, exh. cat., Walker Art Gallery, Liverpool, 1910

LONDON 1829
An Exhibition of Turner Watercolours of the Picturesque Views in England and Wales, exh. cat., Egyptian Hall, London, 1829

LONDON 1833
Drawings by J.M.W. Turner, R.A., Expressly Made for His Work … of 'Views in England and Wales', exh. cat., Moon, Boyes and Graves Gallery, London, 1833

LONDON 1880
The Collection of Mrs (Anna) Charles Golding Constable, exh. cat., South Kensington Museum, 1880

LONDON 1891
Water-colour Drawings Illustrating the Progress of the Art of Water Colour in England, exh. cat., Royal Academy of Arts, London, 1891

LONDON 1892
An Exhibition of Old Masters and by Deceased Masters of the British School … Water-colour Drawings, Studies, and Sketches from Nature, exh. cat., Royal Academy of Arts, London, 1892

LONDON 1913
Water-Colour Drawings by J.M.W. Turner, exh. cat., Thomas Agnew, London, 1913

LONDON 1923
Vincent van Gogh, exh. cat., Leicester Galleries, London, 1923

LONDON 1924
Annual Exhibition of Water-Colour Drawings, exh. cat., Thomas Agnew, London, 1924

LONDON 1927
Exhibition of Flemish and Belgian Art, 1300–1900, exh. cat., Royal Academy of Arts, London, 1927

LONDON 1930
Exhibition of Italian Art, 1200–1900, exh. cat., Royal Academy of Arts, London, 1930

LONDON 1931
Lord David Lindsay Balniel and Kenneth Clark, *A Commemorative Catalogue of the Exhibition of Italian Art*, exh. cat., Royal Academy of Arts, London [1930], Oxford, 1931

LONDON 1932
French Art, exh. cat., Royal Academy of Arts, London, 1932

LONDON 1934
C. Johnson (ed.), *Commemorative Catalogue of the Exhibition of British Art, c. 1000–1860*, exh. cat., Royal Academy of Arts, London, 1934

LONDON 1936
Sir Philip Sassoon, *Gainsborough Exhibition*, exh. cat., 45 Park Lane (Gallery), London, 1936

LONDON 1936a
Catalogue of an Exhibition of Pictures, Drawings, Furniture, and Other Objects of Art, exh. cat., Burlington Fine Arts Club, London, 1936

LONDON 1937
Exhibition of Drawings of the Bolognese School, exh. cat., W. Gersheim, London, 1937

LONDON 1938
A Century of French Drawings, from Prud'hon to Picasso, exh. cat., Matthiesen Gallery, London, 1938

LONDON 1939
John Rewald, *Homage to Paul Cézanne*, exh. cat., Wildenstein Galleries, London, 1939

LONDON 1939a
Exhibition of Venetian Paintings and Drawings, exh. cat., Matthiesen Gallery, London, 1939

LONDON 1948
Samuel Courtauld Memorial Exhibition, exh. cat., Tate Gallery, London, 1948

LONDON 1950
Old Master Drawings of the Eighteenth Century, exh. cat., Matthiesen Gallery, London, 1950

LONDON 1951
Centenary Loan Exhibition of Water-Colour Drawings by J.M.W. Turner, R.A., exh. cat., Thomas Agnew, London, 1951

LONDON 1952
Leonardo Quincentenary, exh. cat., Royal Academy of Arts (Diploma Gallery), London, 1952

LONDON 1952a
French Drawings from Fouquet to Gauguin, exh. cat., Arts Council Gallery, London, 1952

LONDON 1953
K.T. Parker and James Byam Shaw, *Drawings by Old Masters*, exh. cat., Royal Academy of Arts, London, 1953

LONDON 1953a
Loan Exhibition of Water-Colour Drawings by Thomas Girtin, exh. cat., Thomas Agnew, London, 1953

LONDON 1954
Manet and His Circle, exh. cat., Tate Gallery, London, 1954

LONDON 1958
Hans M. Calmann, *Dealer in Old Master Drawings*, exh. cat., Davies Street, London, 1958

LONDON 1958a
Drawings from the Witt Collection, exh. cat., Courtauld Institute Galleries, London, 1958

LONDON 1959
Drawings and Engravings from the Courtauld Collection, exh. cat., Courtauld Institute Galleries, London, 1959

LONDON 1961
Daumier: Paintings and Drawings, Tate Gallery, London, 1961

LONDON 1962
A Selection of Drawings from the Witt Collection: French Drawings, c. 1600–c. 1800, exh. cat., Courtauld Institute Galleries, London, 1962

LONDON 1963
Goya and His Times, exh. cat., Royal Academy of Arts, London, 1963

LONDON 1965
English Landscape Drawings from the Witt Collection, exh. cat., Courtauld Institute Galleries, London, 1965

LONDON 1966
Drawings and Engravings from the Courtauld Collection, exh. cat., Courtauld Institute Galleries, London, 1966

LONDON 1968
William Spooner Collection and Bequest, exh. cat., Courtauld Institute Galleries, London, 1968

LONDON 1968a
Denys Sutton, *France in the Eighteenth Century*, exh. cat., Royal Academy of Arts, London, 1968

LONDON 1968b
Royal Academy Bicentenary, exh. cat., Royal Academy of Arts, London, 1968

LONDON 1969
Michael Kitson, *The Art of Claude Lorrain*, exh. cat., Hayward Gallery, London, 1969

LONDON 1971
The Graphic Work of Albrecht Dürer: An Exhibition of Drawings and Prints in Commemoration of the Quincentenary of His Birth, British Museum, London, 1971

LONDON 1973
Leslie Parris, *Landscape in Britain*, exh. cat., Tate Gallery, London, 1973

LONDON 1974
William Spooner Collection and Bequest, exh. cat., Courtauld Institute Galleries, London, 1974

LONDON 1974a
M. Kitson, *Watercolours by J.M.W. Turner from the Sir Stephen Courtauld Collection,* exh. cat., Courtauld Institute Galleries, London, 1974

LONDON 1975
Drawings by Michelangelo in the Collection of Her Majesty the Queen at Windsor Castle, The Ashmolean Museum, The British Museum and Other English collections, exh. cat., British Museum, London, 1975

LONDON 1975a
The Nude, exh. cat., Morley Gallery, London, 1975

LONDON 1976
Alan Bowness, *Samuel Courtauld's Collection of French 19th Century Paintings and Drawings: A Centenary Exhibition to Commemorate the Birth of Samuel Courtauld*, exh. cat., Courtauld Institute of Art, London, 1976

LONDON 1976a
Leslie Parris, Ian Fleming-Williams and Conal Shields, *Constable Paintings, Watercolours and Drawings*, exh. cat., Tate Gallery, London, 1976

LONDON 1977
Flemish Drawings from the Witt Collection, exh. cat., Courtauld Institute Galleries, London, 1977

LONDON 1977a
English Landscape Drawings and Watercolours, exh. cat., Courtauld Institute Galleries, London, 1977

LONDON 1977b
Drawings by Guercino and Other Baroque Masters, exh. cat., Courtauld Institute Galleries, London, 1977

LONDON 1978
Philip Troutman, *Spanish Drawings from the Witt Collection*, exh. cat., Courtauld Institute of Art, London, 1978

LONDON 1979
English Landscape Drawings and Watercolours, exh. cat., Courtauld Institute Galleries, London, 1979

LONDON 1979a
Turner's Picturesque Views in England and Wales, exh. cat., Thomas Agnew, London, 1979

LONDON 1980
[Oliver Millar], *Canaletto Paintings and Drawings*, exh. cat., The Queen's Gallery, London, 1980

LONDON 1980a
William Bradford and Philip Troutman, *Turner, Prout, Steer: Three Bequests to the Courtauld Institute of Art*, exh. cat., Courtauld Institute Galleries, London, 1980

LONDON 1981
Helen Braham, *The Princes Gate Collection*, exh. cat., Courtauld Institute Galleries, London, 1981

LONDON 1981a
Susan Lambert, *Drawing: Technique and Purpose*, exh. cat., Victoria and Albert Museum, London, 1981

LONDON 1983
William Bradford and Helen Braham, *Mantegna to Cézanne: Master Drawings from the Courtauld; A Fiftieth Anniversary Celebration*, exh. cat., British Museum, London, 1983

LONDON 1983a
Helen Braham, *Drawings by Rembrandt in the Princes Gate Collection*, exh. cat., Courtauld Institute Galleries, London, 1983

LONDON 1987
Helen Braham, *Parmigianino: Paintings, Drawings, Prints*, exh. cat., Courtauld Institute Galleries, London, 1987

LONDON 1988
William Bradford, *Impressionist, Post-Impressionist and Related Drawings from the Courtauld Collections*, exh. cat., Courtauld Institute Galleries, London, 1988

LONDON 1989
Julius Held and Helen Braham, *Rubens Paintings, Drawings, Prints in the Princes Gate Collection*, exh. cat., Courtauld Institute of Art, London, 1989

LONDON 1989a
Drawing: Technique and Purpose, exh. cat., Victoria and Albert Museum, London, 1989

LONDON 1991
William Bradford and Helen Braham, *Master Drawings from the Courtauld Collections*, exh. cat., Courtauld Institute Galleries, London, 1991

LONDON 1991a
Leslie Parris and Ian Fleming-Williams, *Constable*, exh. cat., Tate, London, 1991

LONDON 1991b
Nicholas Turner and Carol Plazzotta, *Drawings by Guercino from British Collections*, exh. cat., British Museum, London, 1991

LONDON 1991c
Henri de Toulouse-Lautrec, exh. cat., Hayward Gallery, London, 1991

LONDON 1991d
Gillian Kennedy and Anne Thackray, *French Drawings XVI–XIX centuries*, exh. cat., Courtauld Institute Galleries, London, 1991

LONDON 1994
John House, *Impressionism for England: Samuel Courtauld as Patron and Collector*, exh. cat., London, 1994

LONDON 1995
Judy Egerton, *Turner: The Fighting Temeraire*, exh. cat., The National Gallery, London, 1995

LONDON 1997
Ed. A. Lyles and R. Hamlyn, *British Watercolours from the Oppé Collection*, exh. cat., Tate Gallery, London, 1997

LONDON 1997a
Eric Shanes, *Turner's Watercolour Explorations*, exh. cat., Tate Gallery, London, 1997

LONDON 1998
Material Evidence, exh. cat., Courtauld Gallery, London, 1998

LONDON 1999
Christopher Green (ed.), *Art Made Modern: Roger Fry's Vision of Art*, exh. cat., Courtauld Gallery, London, 1999

LONDON 2000
Robert Hewison, Ian Warrell and Stephen Wildman, *Ruskin, Turner, and the Pre-Raphaelites*, exh. cat., Tate Gallery, London, 2000

LONDON 2001
Juliet Wilson-Bareau, *Goya: Drawings from His Private Albums*, exh. cat., Hayward Gallery, London, 2001

LONDON 2002
Giulia Bartrum, *Albrecht Dürer and His Legacy: The Graphic Work of a Renaissance Artist*, exh. cat., British Museum, London, 2002

LONDON 2002a
Thomas Girtin: The Art of Watercolour, exh. cat., Tate Gallery, London, 2002

LONDON 2002b
A Passion for Drawings: Collectors at the Courtauld, exh. cat., Courtauld Gallery, London, 2002

LONDON 2004
Hugo Chapman, Tom Henry and Carol Plazzotta, *Raphael: From Urbino to Rome*, exh. cat., The National Gallery, London, 2004

LONDON 2005
Timothy Wilcox, *Francis Towne and His Friends*, exh. cat., John Spink at Colnaghi, London, 2005

LONDON 2005a
Elizabeth McGrath et al., *Rubens: A Master in the Making*, exh. cat., The National Gallery, London, 2005

LONDON 2006
Anna Robbins et al., *Cézanne in Britain*, exh. cat., The National Gallery, London, 2006

LONDON 2008
Stephanie Buck, John House, Ernst Vegelin van Claerbergen and Barnaby Wright (eds.), *The Courtauld Cézannes*, exh. cat., The Courtauld Gallery, London, 2008

LONDON 2010
Stephanie Buck (ed.) with the assistance of Tatiana Bissolati, *Michelangelo's Dream*, exh. cat., Courtauld Gallery, London, 2010

LONDON 2010a
The Real Van Gogh: The Artist and His Letters, exh. cat., Royal Academy of Arts, London, 2010

LONDON 2011
Pierre Rosenberg and Louis-Antoine Prat, *Watteau: The Drawings*, exh. cat., Royal Academy of Arts, London, 2011

LONDON 2011a
The Spanish Line, exh. guide, The Courtauld Gallery, London, 2011

LONDON 2011b
Luke Syson with Larry Keith et al., *Leonardo da Vinci: Painter at the Court of Milan*, exh. cat., The National Gallery, London, 2011

LONDON AND FLORENCE 2010
Hugo Chapman and Marzia Faietti (eds.), *Fra Angelico to Leonardo: Italian Renaissance Drawings*, exh. cat., British Museum, London, and Galleria degli Uffizi, Florence, 2010

LONDON AND GRASMERE 2008
Joanna Selborne, *Paths to Fame: Turner Watercolours from The Courtauld Gallery*, exh. cat., Courtauld Gallery, London, and Wordsworth Trust, Grasmere, 2008

LONDON AND LEEDS 1997
Timothy Wilcox, *Francis Towne*, exh. cat., Tate Gallery, London, and Leeds City Art Gallery, 1997

LONDON AND NEW YORK 1984
The Drawings of Henri Matisse, exh. cat., Hayward Gallery, London, and The Museum of Modern Art, New York, 1984

LONDON AND NEW YORK 1992
Jane Martineau (ed.), *Andrea Mantegna*, exh. cat., Royal Academy of Arts, London, and The Metropolitan Museum of Art, New York, 1992

LONDON AND NEW YORK 2000
Carmen C. Bambach, Hugh Chapman, Martin Clayton and George Goldner, *Correggio and Parmigianino: Master Draughtsmen of the Renaissance*, exh. cat., British Museum, London, and The Metropolitan Museum of Art, New York, 2000

LONDON AND TORONTO 1994
Constable: A Master Draughtsman, exh. cat., Dulwich Picture Gallery, London, and Art Gallery of Ontario, Toronto, 1994

LONDON AND ELSEWHERE 1946
Kenneth Clark (Arts Council), *Paul Cézanne, Exhibition of Watercolours*, exh. cat., Tate Gallery, London; Museum and Art Gallery, Leicester; and Graves Art Gallery, Sheffield, 1946

LONDON AND ELSEWHERE 1953
Arts Council, *Drawings from the Witt Collection at the Courtauld Institute of Art*, exh. cat., Courtauld Institute Galleries, London; City Art Gallery, York; and the Art Gallery, Peterborough, 1953

LONDON AND ELSEWHERE 1999
Gary Tinterow and Philip Conisbee, *Portraits by Ingres: Image of an Epoch*, exh. cat., The National Gallery, London; National Gallery of Art, Washington, DC; and The Metropolitan Museum of Art, New York, 1999

LONDON AND ELSEWHERE 2005
Michael Broughton, William Clarke and Joanna Selborne, *The Spooner Collection of British Watercolours*, exh. cat., Courtauld Institute Gallery, London; The Wordsworth Trust, Grasmere; and The Huntington Library, Art Collections and Botanical Gardens, San Marino, CA, 2005

LOS ANGELES 1961
French Masters: Rococo to Romanticism, exh. cat., University of California, Los Angeles, 1961

LOS ANGELES 2004
Carol M. Armstrong, *Cézanne in the Studio: Still Life in Watercolors*, exh. cat., J. Paul Getty Museum, Los Angeles, 2004

LOS ANGELES 2007
Defining Modernity: European Drawings, 1800–1900, exh. cat., J. Paul Getty Museum, Los Angeles, 2007

LOS ANGELES 2010
Holm Bevers et al., *Drawings by Rembrandt and His Pupils: Telling the Difference*, exh. cat., J. Paul Getty Museum, Los Angeles, 2010

LOS ANGELES AND LONDON 2003
Thomas Kren and Scot McKendrick (eds.), *Illuminating the Renaissance: The Triumph of Flemish Manuscript Painting in Europe*, exh. cat., J. Paul Getty Museum, Los Angeles, and Royal Academy of Arts, London, 2003

LOS ANGELES AND LONDON 2006
Julian Brooks, *Guercino: Mind to Paper*, exh. cat., J. Paul Getty Museum, Los Angeles, and Courtauld Institute Galleries, London, 2006

LOS ANGELES AND ELSEWHERE 1971
Géricault, exh. cat., Los Angeles County Museum of Art, The Detroit Institute of Arts, and Philadelphia Museum of Art, 1971

LÜTHY 1985–86
Hans A. Lüthy, 'Review: Master Drawings by Géricault', *Master Drawings*, vols. 23–24, no. 4, 1985–86, pp. 563–67

LYKIARDOPOULOS 1981
Amica Lykiardopoulos, 'The Evil Eye: Towards an Exhaustive Study', *Folklore*, vol. 92, no. 2, January 1, 1981, pp. 221–30

LYON 2006
Géricault. La Folie d'un monde, exh. cat., Musée des Beaux-Arts, Lyon, 2006

MACK 2005
Charles R. Mack, *Looking at the Renaissance: Essays toward a Contextual Appreciation*, Ann Arbor, MI, 2005

MAHON AND TURNER 1989
Denis Mahon and Nicholas Turner, *The Drawings of Guercino in the Collection of Her Majesty the Queen at Windsor Castle*, Cambridge, 1989

MAHONEY 1965
Michael Mahoney, *The Drawings of Salvator Rosa*, London, 1965

MAISON 1968
K.E. Maison, *Honoré Daumier: Catalogue Raisonnée of the Paintings, Watercolours, and Drawings*, 2 vols., [Greenwich, CT], 1968

MALRAUX 1947
André Malraux, *Goya: Drawings from the Prado*, trans. Edward Sackville-West, London, 1947

MANCHESTER 1962
Anthony Blunt and Philip Troutman, *Loan Exhibition of Master Drawings from the Witt and Courtauld Collections*, exh. cat., Whitworth Art Gallery, Manchester, 1962

MANCHESTER 1965
F.G. Grossmann (ed.), *Between Renaissance and Baroque: European Art, 1520–1600*, exh. cat., City Art Gallery, Manchester, 1965

MANCHESTER 1988
Francis Hawcroft, *Travels in Italy, 1776–83*, exh. cat., Whitworth Art Gallery, Manchester, 1988

MANCHESTER AND LONDON 1971
Francis Hawcroft, *Watercolours by John Robert Cozens*, exh. cat., Whitworth Art Gallery, Manchester, and Victoria and Albert Museum, London, 1971

MANCHESTER AND LONDON 1975
Francis Hawcroft, *Watercolours by Thomas Girtin*, exh. cat., Whitworth Art Gallery, Manchester, and Victoria and Albert Museum, London, 1975

MANNING AND BYAM SHAW 1960
E. Manning and James Byam Shaw, *Colnaghi's, 1760–1960*, London, 1960

MARABOTTINI 1956
A. Marabottini, 'Il "Sogno" di Michelangelo in una copia sconosciuta', in *Scritti di storia dell'arte in onore di Lionello Venturi*, 2 vols., Rome, 1956, vol. 1, pp. 349–58

MARDER 1997
T.A. Marder, *Bernini's 'Scala Regia' at the Vatican Palace*, Cambridge and New York, 1997

MARDER 1998
T.A. Marder, *Bernini and the Art of Architecture*, London, 1998

MARIETTE 1851–60
P.J. Mariette, *Abecedario et autres notes*, 6 vols., Paris, 1851–60

MARIJNISSEN 1988
Roger H. Marijnissen, *Bruegel: Tout l'œuvre peint et dessiné*, trans. by C. Krings, J. Rossbach, and M. Vincent, Antwerp and Paris, 1988

MARLIER 1969
Georges Marlier, *Pierre Bruegel le Jeune*, Brussels, 1969

MARSEILLE 1974
130 Dessins de Matisse, exh. cat., Musée Cantini, Marseille, 1974

MARSEILLE 1979
Daumier et ses amis républicains, exh. cat., Musée Cantini, Marseille, 1979

MARTENS 1997
D. Martens, 'Entre l'Italie et les Flandres. "La Virgo inter virgines" de Hans Holbein l'Ancien et ses sources', *Revue de l'art*, vol. 117, 1997, pp. 36–47

MARTENS 2002
D. Martens, 'Transmission et métamorphose d'un modéle. La descendance au XVIème siècle de la "Virgo inter virgines" attribuée à Hugo van der Goes', *Annales de la Société Royale d'Archéologie de Bruxelles*, vol. 65, 2002, pp. 105–88

MATHEY 1961
J. Mathey, *Graphisme de Manet. Essai de catalogue raisonné des dessins*, Paris, 1961

MAYNE 1949
Jonathan Mayne, *Thomas Girtin*, London, 1949

MEDER 1923
Joseph Meder, *Die Handzeichnung. Ihre Technik und Entwicklung*, Vienna, 1923

MEDER 1932
Joseph Meder, *Dürer-Katalog. Ein Handbuch über Albrecht Dürers Stiche, Radierungen, Holzschnitte, deren Zustände, Ausgaben u. Wasserzeichen*, Vienna, 1932

MEIER-GRAEFE 1912
Julius Meier-Graefe, *Édouard Manet*, Munich, 1912

MEIER-GRAEFE 1918
Julius Meier-Graefe, *Cézanne und sein Kreis*, Munich, 1918

MERZ 1993
Jörg Martin Merz, 'Review of exhibition *Von Bernini bis Piranesi. Römische Architektur-zeichnungen des Barock*', *Burlington Magazine*, vol. 135, no. 1089, December 1993, pp. 843–44

MIEDEMA 1981
Hessel Miedema, 'Feestende boeren–lachende dorpers. Bij twee recente aanwinsten van het Rijksprentenkabinet', *Bulletin van het Rijksmuseum*, vol. 29, 1981, pp. 191–213

MIELKE 1996
Hans Mielke, *Pieter Bruegel. Die Zeichnungen*, Turnhout, 1996

MILAN 1971
Giambattista Piazzetta e l'accademia. Disegni, exh. cat., Castello Sforzesco, Milan, 1971

MILLER 2000
Peter N. Miller, *Peiresc's Europe: Learning and Virtue in the Seventeenth Century*, New Haven and London, 2000

MIRIMONDE 1958
A.P. Miramonde, 'L'Impromptu du plafond, ou l'apothéose de Saint-Louis par Natoire', *La Revue des arts*, vol. 6, 1958, pp. 279–84

MONBALLIEU 1974
Adolf Monballieu, 'De "Kermis van Hoboken" bij P. Bruegel, J. Grimmer en G. Mostaert', *Jaarboek van het Koninklijk Museum voor Schone Kunsten Antwerpen*, 1974, pp. 139–69

MONBALLIEU 1987
Adolf Monballieu, 'Nog eens Hoboken bij Bruegel en tijdgenoten', *Jaarboek van het Koninklijk Museum voor Schone Kunsten Antwerpen*, 1987, pp. 185–206

MORFORD 1991
Mark Morford, *Stoics and Neo-Stoics: Rubens and the Circle of Lipsius*, Princeton, 1991

MORGANTI 1997
C. Morganti, 'Il "Sogno" di Michelangelo. Una ricognizione iconografica', *Grafica d'arte. Rivista di storia dell'incisione antica e moderna e storia del disegno*, vol. 8, no. 31, 1997, pp. 2–6

MORTIMER 1974
R. Mortimer, *Harvard College Library Department of Printing and Graphic Arts: Catalogue of Books and Manuscripts, Part 2, Italian Sixteenth Century Books*, vol. 1, Cambridge, MA, 1974

MOSCHINI 1963
Vittorio Moschini, *Canaletto*, Milan, 1963

MÜLLER-HOFSTEDE 1979
Justus Müller-Hofstede, 'Zur Interpretation von Pieter Bruegel's Landschaftsbegriff und stoische Weltbetrachtung', in Otto von Simson and Matthias Winner (eds.), *Pieter Bruegel und seine Welt*, Berlin, 1979, pp. 73–142

MÜNZ 1961
Ludwig Münz, *The Drawings of Bruegel*, London, 1961

MULLER 1982
Jeffrey M. Muller, 'Rubens's Theory and Practice of Imitation', *Art Bulletin*, vol. 64, no. 2, June 1982, pp. 229–47

MULLER 1989
Jeffrey M. Muller, *Rubens: The Artist as Collector*, Princeton, 1989

MURARO 1977
Michelangelo Muraro, *I disegni di Vittore Carpaccio*, Florence, 1977

MURDOCH 1997
John Murdoch, 'Review of London and Leeds:
Francis Towne', Burlington Magazine, vol. 139, no.
1135, October 1997, p. 711

MUSPER 1953
H.T. Musper, Albrecht Dürer. Der gegenwärtige
Stand der Forschung, Stuttgart, 1953

MUSPER 1969
H.T. Musper, Dürers Kaiserbildnisse, Vienna, 1969

NAEF 1977–80
Hans Naef, Die Bildniszeichnungen von
J.-A.-D. Ingres, 5 vols., Bern, 1977–80

NATANSON 1951
Thadée Natanson, Un Henri de Toulouse-Lautrec,
Paris, 1951

NESSELRATH 1997
Arnold Nesselrath, Raphael's School of Athens,
Recent Restorations of the Vatican Museums,
vol. 1, Vatican City, 1997

NEW HAVEN 1980
Andrew Wilton, The Art of Alexander and John
Robert Cozens, exh. cat., Yale Center for British Art,
New Haven, 1980

NEW HAVEN 1993
Eric M. Lee, Translations: Turner and Printmaking,
exh. cat., Yale Center for British Art, New Haven,
1993

New Hollstein 1 (VELDMAN) 1994
Ilja M. Veldman (comp.) and Ger Luijten (ed.),
The New Hollstein: Dutch and Flemish Etchings,
Engravings and Woodcuts, 1450–1700, vol. 1,
Maarten van Heemskerck, Roosendaal, the
Netherlands, 1994

New Hollstein 12 (MIELKE) 2004
Ursula Mielke (ed.), The New Hollstein: Dutch and
Flemish Etchings, Engravings, and Woodcuts, 1450–
1700, vol. 12, Pieter van der Borcht, Roosendaal
and Amsterdam, 2004

New Hollstein 15 (ORENSTEIN) 2006
Nadine M. Orenstein (ed.), The New Hollstein:
Dutch and Flemish Etchings, Engravings, and
Woodcuts, 1450–1700, vol. 15, Pieter Bruegel the
Elder, Roosendaal and Amsterdam, 2006

New Hollstein 19 (LEEFLANG) 2008
Marjolein Leesberg (comp.) and Huigen Leeflang
(ed.), The New Hollstein: Dutch and Flemish
Etchings, Engravings and Woodcuts 1450–1700,
vol. 19, Johannnes Stradanus, Ouderkerk aan den
Ijssel, 2008

NEW YORK 1930
Eighth Loan Exhibition: Corot–Daumier, exh. cat.,
The Museum of Modern Art, New York, 1930

NEW YORK 1990
Claude to Corot: The Development of Landscape
Painting in France, exh. cat., Colnaghi,
New York, 1990

NEW YORK 1992
Daumier Drawings, exh. cat., The Metropolitan
Museum of Art, New York, 1992

NEW YORK 1992a
Jusepe de Ribera, 1591–1652, exh. cat., The
Metropolitan Museum of Art, New York, 1992

NEW YORK 1999
Perrin Stein and Mary Tavener Holmes,
Eighteenth-Century French Drawings in New York
Collections, exh. cat., The Metropolitan Museum
of Art, New York, 1999

NEW YORK 2001
Nadine M. Orenstein (ed.), Pieter Bruegel the
Elder: Drawings and Prints, exh. cat., The
Metropolitan Museum of Art, New York, 2001

NEW YORK 2003
Carmen C. Bambach (ed.), Leonardo da Vinci,
Master Draftsman, exh. cat., The Metropolitan
Museum of Art, New York, 2003

NEW YORK 2005
Ann-Marie Logan in collaboration with Michael
Plomp, Peter Paul Rubens: The Drawings, exh. cat.,
The Metropolitan Museum of Art, New York, 2005

NEW YORK 2007
Georges Seurat: The Drawings, exh. cat.,
The Museum of Modern Art, New York, 2007

NEW YORK 2010
Linda Wolk-Simon and Carmen C. Bambach, An
Italian Journey: Drawings from the Tobey Collection;
Correggio to Tiepolo, exh. cat., The Metropolitan
Museum of Art, New York, 2010

NEW YORK 2011
David, Delacroix, and Revolutionary France:
Drawings from the Louvre, exh. cat., The Morgan
Library and Museum, New York, 2011

NEW YORK AND LONDON 1986
Dennis Farr and William Bradford (eds.), The
Northern Landscape: Flemish, Dutch and British
Drawings from the Courtauld Collections, exh. cat.,
The Drawing Center, New York, and Courtauld
Institute Galleries, London, 1986

NEW YORK AND LONDON 2005
Perrin Stein with a contribution by Martin
Royalton-Kisch, French Drawings from the
British Museum: Clouet to Seurat, exh. cat.,
The Metropolitan Museum of Art, New York,
and British Museum, London, 2005

NEW YORK AND ELSEWHERE 1977
William Rubin, Cézanne: The Late Work, exh. cat.,
The Museum of Modern Art, New York;
The Museum of Fine Arts, Houston; and
Grand Palais, Paris, 1977

NEW YORK AND ELSEWHERE 1985
Philippe Grunchec (ed.), Master Drawings by
Géricault, exh. cat., The Morgan Library,
New York; San Diego Museum of Art; and
The Museum of Fine Arts, Houston, 1985

NEWCASTLE AND LONDON 1973
L. Gowing and R.W. Ratcliffe, Watercolour and
Pencil Drawings by Cézanne, exh. cat., Laing
Art Gallery, Newcastle, and Hayward Gallery,
London, 1973

NICHOLS 1999
Tom Nichols, Tintoretto: Tradition and Identity,
London, 1999

NOTTINGHAM 1966
Drawings from the Courtauld Collections, exh. cat.,
University Art Gallery, Nottingham, 1966

NOTTINGHAM 1969
Degas: Pastels and Drawings, Nottingham
University Art Gallery, 1969

NOTTINGHAM 1980
The Golden Age of Spanish Art: From El Greco to
Murillo and Valdés Leal; Paintings and Drawings
from British Collections, exh. cat., Nottingham
University Art Gallery, 1980

NOVOTNY 1953
Fritz Novotny, 'Reflections on a Drawing by
Van Gogh', Art Bulletin, vol. 35, no. 1, March 1953,
pp. 35–43

NUREMBERG 1928
Albrecht Dürer Ausstellung, exh. cat., Germanisches
Nationalmuseum, Nuremberg, 1928

NUREMBERG 1997
K. Löcher, Die Gemälde des 16. Jahrhunderts,
exh. cat., Germanisches Nationalmuseum, 1997

NUREMBERG AND NEW YORK 1986
G. Bott (ed.), Nürnberg, 1300–1550. Kunst der Gotik
und Renaissance, exh. cat., Germanisches Nationalmuseum, Nuremberg, and The Metropolitan
Museum of Art, New York, 1986

NUTTALL 2004
Paula Nuttall, From Flanders to Florence:
The Impact of Netherlandish Painting, 1400–1500,
New Haven and London, 2004

On Benefits (LODGE) 1899
Lucas Annaeus Seneca, On Benefits, trans. by
Thomas Lodge, London, 1899

OPPÉ 1920
A.P. Oppé, 'Francis Towne, Landscape Painter',
Walpole Society, vol. 8, 1920, pp. 95–126

OPPÉ 1925
A.P. Oppé, The Water-colours of Turner, Cox and
de Wint, London, 1925

OPPÉ 1952
A.P. Oppé, Alexander and John Robert Cozens,
London, 1952

OPPENHEIMER 1936
Catalogue of the Famous Collection of Old Master
Drawings Formed by the Late Henry Oppenheimer,
Christie, Manson & Woods, July 10, 13, 14, 1936,
London, 1936

OSAKA AND TOKYO 2000
Toulouse-Lautrec, exh. cat., Suntory Museum,
Osaka, and Tobu Museum, Tokyo, 2000

OTTAWA AND ELSEWHERE 1999
Daumier, 1808–1879, exh. cat., National Gallery of Canada, Ottawa; Galeries Nationales du Grand Palais, Paris; and The Phillips Collection, Washington, DC, 1999

OTTLEY 1823
W.Y. Ottley, *The Italian School of Design: Being a Series of Fac-similes of Original Drawings, by the Most Eminent Painters and Sculptors of Italy; with Biographical Notices of the Artists and Observations on Their Works*, London, 1823

OXFORD 1929
Dutch Drawings XVI to XVIII Century, exh. cat., Oxford Arts Club, Oxford, 1929

OXFORD 1998
J.J.L. Whiteley, *Claude Lorrain: Drawings from the Collections of the British Museum and the Ashmolean Museum*, exh. cat., Ashmolean, Oxford, 1998

OXFORD AND ELSEWHERE 1986
Christopher Lloyd and Richard Thomson, *Impressionist Drawings from British Public and Private Collections*, exh. cat., Ashmolean Museum, Oxford; Manchester City Art Gallery; and Burrell Collection, Glasgow, 1986

OXFORD AND ELSEWHERE 2003
Julian Brooks, with an essay by Catherine Whistler, *Graceful and True: Drawing in Florence c. 1600*, exh. cat., Ashmolean Museum, Oxford; P. & D. Colnaghi, London; and Djanogly Art Gallery, Nottingham, 2003

PALLUCHINI 1960
Rodolfo Palluchini, *La pittura veneziana del Settecento*, Venice and Rome, 1960

PANOFSKY 1939
Erwin Panofsky, 'The Neoplatonic Movement and Michelangelo', in *Studies in Iconology*, New York, 1939, pp. 171–230

PANOFSKY 1943
Erwin Panofsky, *The Life and Art of Albrecht Dürer*, 2 vols., Princeton, 1943

PANOFSKY 1953
Erwin Panofsky, *Early Netherlandish Painting*, 2 vols., Cambridge, MA, 1953

PAOLETTI 1992
J.T. Paoletti, 'Michelangelo's Masks', *Art Bulletin*, vol. 74, no. 3, September 1992, pp. 423–40

PAPA 2007
R. Papa, *Dürer*, Florence, 2007

PARDO 1989
Mary Pardo, 'The Subject of Savoldo's Magdalene', *Art Bulletin*, vol. 71, no. 1, March 1989, pp. 67–91

PARIS 1902
Arsène Alexandre, *Exposition Henri de Toulouse-Lautrec*, exh. cat., Durand-Ruel, Paris, 1902

PARIS 1920
Georges Seurat, exh. cat., Galerie Bernheim-Jeune, Paris, 1920

PARIS 1926
Georges Seurat, exh. cat., Galerie Bernheim-Jeune, Paris, 1926

PARIS 1935
P. Jamot and P. Lambotte (eds.), *De Van Eyck à Bruegel*, exh. cat., Orangerie, Paris, 1935

PARIS 1939
Société des Artistes Indépendants. Centenaire du peintre indépendant Paul Cézanne, exh. cat., Grand Palais, Paris, 1939

PARIS 1955
Douglas Cooper, *Impressionistes de la collection Courtauld de Londres*, exh. cat., Musée de l'Orangerie, Paris, 1955

PARIS 1958
Daumier, le peintre-graveur, exh. cat., Bibliothèque Nationale, Paris, 1958

PARIS 1967
Ingres, exh. cat., Musée du Petit Palais, Paris, 1967

PARIS 1967a
Walter Vitzhum and Catherine Monbeig-Goguel, *Le Dessin à Naples*, exh. cat., Cabinet des Dessins, Musée du Louvre, Paris, 1967

PARIS 1983
Jean Cailleux and Marianne Roland Michel, *Rome, 1760–1770: Fragonard, Hubert Robert et leurs amis*, exh. cat., Galerie Cailleux, Paris, 1983

PARIS 1983a
J. Gage, J. Ziff, N. Alfrey et al., *J.M.W. Turner*, exh. cat., Grand Palais, Paris, 1983

PARIS 1986
D. Cordellier (ed.), *Hommage à Andrea del Sarto*, exh. cat., Musée du Louvre, Paris, 1986

PARIS 1991
Sylvain Laveissière, Régis Michel and Bruno Chenique, *Géricault*, exh. cat., Galeries Nationales du Grand Palais, Paris, 1991

PARIS 1991a
Femmes: Œuvres sur papier de collections privées françaises, réunies dans un cabinet d'amateur, exh. cat., Galerie de la Scala, Paris, 1991

PARIS 2003
R.J.A. te Rijdt, *De Watteau à Ingres. Dessins du XVIIIe siècle du Rijksmuseum Amsterdam*, exh. cat., Fondation Custodia, Paris, 2003

PARIS 2008
Giovanni Agosti and Dominique Thiébaut, eds., *Mantegna*, exh. cat., Musée du Louvre, Paris, 2008

PARIS 2009
L'Académie mise à nu. L'École du modèle à l'Académie Royale de Peinture et de Sculpture, exh. cat., École Nationale Supérieure des Beaux-Arts, Paris, 2009

PARIS 2011
Carel van Tuyll van Serooskerken and Michiel C. Plomp (eds.), *Claude Gellée, dit le Lorrain: Le Dessinateur face à la nature*, exh. cat., Musée du Louvre, Paris, 2011

PARIS AND NEW YORK 1987
Pierre Rosenberg, *Fragonard*, exh. cat., Grand Palais, Paris, and The Metropolitan Museum of Art, New York, 1987

PARKER 1938
K.T. Parker, *Catalogue of the Collection of Drawings in the Ashmolean Museum*, vol. 1, *Netherlandish, German, French and Spanish Schools*, Oxford, 1938

PARKER 1948
K.T. Parker, *The Drawings of Antonio Canaletto in the Collection of His Majesty the King at Windsor Castle*, Oxford and London, 1948

PARRIS, SHIELDS, AND FLEMING-WILLIAMS 1975
Leslie Parris, Conal Shields and Ian Fleming-Williams, *John Constable: Further Documents and Correspondence*, London, 1975

PAVANELLO 1996
G. Pavanello, *Canova collezionista di Tiepolo*, Possagno, 1996

PAYNE 2012
Edward Payne, 'Violence and Corporeality in the Art of Jusepe de Ribera', PhD diss., Courtauld Institute, London, 2012

PECK 2003
J. Peck, 'Daniel Dreaming: A Misnomer Revisited', *Apollo*, vol. 156, no. 491, January 2003, pp. 32–36

PEDRETTI 1973
Carlo Pedretti, *Leonardo: A Study in Chronology and Style*, London, 1973

PERRIG 1991
A. Perrig, *Michelangelo's Drawings: The Science of Attribution*, London, 1991

PERUGIA 2004
Vittoria Garibaldi and F.F. Mancini (eds.), *Perugino, il divin pittore*, exh. cat., Galleria Nazionale dell'Umbria, Perugia, 2004

PERUGIA 2008
Vittoria Garibaldi and Francesco Federico Mancini (eds.), *Pintoricchio*, exh. cat., Galleria Nazionale di Umbria, Perugia, 2008

PESCO 1984
Daniela del Pesco, *Il Louvre di Bernini nella Francia di Luigi XIV*, Florence, 1984

PETHERBRIDGE 2010
Deanna Petherbridge, *The Primacy of Drawing: Histories and Theories of Practice*, New Haven and London, 2010

PEVSNER 1974
Nikolaus Pevsner, *The Buildings of England: Suffolk*, London, 1974

PHILADELPHIA 1934
Cézanne, exh. cat., Philadelphia Museum of Art, Philadelphia, 1934

PIGNATTI 1976
Terisio Pignatti, *Veronese*, Milan, 1976

PIGNATTI 1980–96
T. Pignatti, *Disegni antichi del Museo Correr di Venezia*, 5 vols., Venice, 1980–96

PINTO 1962
Olga Pinto, ed., *Viaggi di C. Federici e G. Balbi alle Indie orientali (Il Nuovo Ramusio IV)*, Rome, 1962

PISANI 1891
Paul Pisani, *La Maison des Carmes*, Paris, 1891

PLINY (BOSTOCK AND RILEY) 1857
John Bostock and H.T. Riley (eds.), *The Natural History of Pliny the Elder*, vol. 6, London, 1857

PLYMOUTH 1821
Sixth Annual Exhibition of Pictures at Plymouth, Plymouth Institution, Plymouth, 1821

POLLOCK 1999
Griselda Pollock, *Differencing the Canon: Feminist Desire and the Writing of Art's Histories*, London and New York, 1999

POPHAM 1935
A.E. Popham, 'Pieter Bruegel the Elder', *Old Master Drawings*, vol. 9, no. 26, March 1935, pp. 64–66

POPHAM 1935a
A.E. Popham, *Catalogue of Drawings in the Collection Formed by Sir Thomas Phillipps, Bart., F.R.S., Now in the Possession of His Grandson, T. Fitzroy Phillipps Fenwick of Thirlestaine House, Cheltenham*, London, 1935

POPHAM 1947
A.E. Popham, 'Disegni veneziani acquistati recentemente dal British Museum', *Arte Veneta*, vol. 1, 1947, pp. 226–29

POPHAM 1956
A.E. Popham in A.N.L. Munby, *The Formation of the Phillipps Library from 1841 to 1872: With an Account of the Phillipps Art Collection by A.E. Popham (Phillipps Studies IV)*, Cambridge, 1956

POPHAM 1971
A.E. Popham, *Catalogue of the Drawings of Parmigianino*, 3 vols., New Haven and London, 1971

PORRAS 2011
Stephanie Porras, 'Producing the Vernacular: Antwerp, Cultural Archaeology and the Bruegelian Peasant', *Journal of the Historians of Netherlandish Art*, vol. 3, no. 1, Winter 2011

POSNER 1984
Donald Posner, *Antoine Watteau*, London, 1984

PRAT 2004
Louis-Antoine Prat, *Ingres*, Paris, 2004

PREBISZ 1911
Leon Prebisz, *Martin van Heemskerck. Ein Beitrag zur Geschichte des Romanismus in der Niederländischen Malerei des XVI. Jahrhunderts*, Leipzig, 1911

PRENDEVILLE 1995
Brendan Prendeville, 'The Features of Insanity, as Seen by Géricault and by Büchner', *Oxford Art Journal*, vol. 18, no. 1, 1995, pp. 96–115

PRINCETON 1973
Jonathan Brown, *Jusepe de Ribera: Prints and Drawings*, exh. cat., The Art Museum, Princeton, 1973

PRINCETON 1977
James Henry Rubin, *Eighteenth-Century French Life-Drawing: Selections from the Collection of Mathias Polakovits*, exh. cat., Art Museum, Princeton University, Princeton, 1977

PROUST 1897
Antonin Proust, 'Édouard Manet, souvenirs', *La Revue blanche*, February 15, 1897, reprint, Caen, 1988

RAUPP 1986
Hans-Joachim Raupp, *Bauernsatiren. Entstehung und Entwicklung des bäuerlichen Genres in der deutschen und niederländischen Kunst, ca. 1470–1570*, Hildesheim, Zurich, and New York, 1986

RAWLINSON 1908–13
W.G. Rawlinson, *The Engraved Work of J.M.W. Turner*, 2 vols., London, 1908–13

REFF 1963
Theodore Reff, 'Degas' Copies of Older Art', *Burlington Magazine*, vol. 105, no. 723, June 1963, pp. 241–51

REITLINGER 1927
H.S. Reitlinger, 'An Unknown Collection of Dürer Drawings', *Burlington Magazine for Connoisseurs*, vol. 50, no. 288, 1927

REMPEL 1997
Lora Rempel, "The Matter of Style: Thomas Gainsborough, the Portrait in the Landscape, and the Mark of a Modern Painter," PhD diss., City University of New York, 1997

REUMONT 1876
Alfred von Reumont, *Lorenzo de' Medici, the Magnificent*, 2 vols., London, 1876

REWALD 1983
John Rewald, *Paul Cézanne: The Watercolors; A Catalogue Raisonné*, Boston, 1983

REWALD 1996
John Rewald, with W. Feilchenfeldt and J. Warman, *The Paintings of Paul Cézanne: A Catalogue Raisonné*, New York and London, 1996

REWALD (ED.) 1984
John Rewald (ed.), *Paul Cézanne: Letters*, New York, 1984

REYNOLDS 1981
C. Reynolds, 'London. Courtauld Institute Galleries: Early Netherlandish Works in the Princes Gate Collection', *Burlington Magazine*, vol. 123, no. 942, 1981, pp. 562–64

REYNOLDS 1949
Graham Reynolds, *Nineteenth Century Drawings, 1850–1900*, London, 1949

REYNOLDS 1984
Graham Reynolds, *The Later Paintings and Drawings of John Constable*, 2 vols., New Haven and London, 1984

REYNOLDS 1996
Graham Reynolds, *Earlier Paintings and Drawings of John Constable*, 2 vols., New Haven and London, 1996

REYNOLDS (WARK) 1975
Sir Joshua Reynolds, *Discourses on Art (1788)*, ed. Robert R. Wark, New Haven and London, 1975

RICCI 1912
Corrado Ricci, *Pintoricchio*, Perugia, 1912

RIDOLFI (HADELN) 1965
Carlo Ridolfi, *Le maraviglie dell'arte* [Venice, 1648], ed. Detlev Freiherr von Hadeln, Rome, 1965

RIEMSDIJK 1888
J.C.M. Riemsdijk, 'De twee eerste musyck-boekskens van Tielman Susato. Bijdrage tot het Nederlandsch Volkslied in de 16de eeuw', *Tijdschrift der Vereeniging voor Noord-Nederlands Muziekgeschiedenis*, vol. 3, no. 2, 1888

RIGGS 1977
Timothy Riggs, *Hieronymus Cock: Printmaker and Publisher*, New York, 1977

RIPA (BUSCAROLI) 1999
Cesare Ripa, *Iconologie* [Paris, 1644], ed. Piero Buscaroli, Dijon, 1999

ROBERTS-JONES 2002
Philippe Roberts-Jones and Françoise Roberts-Jones, *Pieter Bruegel*, New York, 2002

ROBERTSON 2010
Charles Robertson, 'Review of Michelangelo's Dream', *Burlington Magazine*, vol. 152, no. 1286, May 2010, pp. 339–40

ROBERTSON 1968
Giles Robertson, *Giovanni Bellini*, Oxford, 1968

ROLAND MICHEL 1987
Marianne Roland Michel, *Le Dessin français au XVIIIe siècle*, Fribourg, 1987

ROLAND MICHEL 1998
Marianne Roland Michel, 'Review: The Rosenberg-Prat Catalogue of Watteau's Drawings', *Burlington Magazine*, vol. 140, no. 1148, November 1998, pp. 749–54

ROME 1990
Jean-Pierre Cuzin and Pierre Rosenberg, *J.H. Fragonard e H. Robert a Roma*, exh. cat., Accademia di Francia, Villa Medici, Rome, 1990

ROME 2007
Dürer e l'Italia, exh. cat., Scuderie del Quirinale, Rome, 2007

ROME 2008
Mauro Lucco and Giovanni Carlo Federico Villa (eds.), *Giovanni Bellini*, exh. cat., Scuderie del Quirinale, Rome, 2008

ROOSES AND REULENS 1887–1909
Max Rooses and Charles Reulens, *Codex Diplomaticus Rubenianus. Correspondance de Rubens et documents épistolaires concernant sa vie et ses œuvres*, 6 vols., Antwerp 1887–1909

ROSENBERG 1940
Jakob Rosenberg, 'Rembrandt's Technical Means and Their Stylistic Significance', *Technical Studies in the Field of the Fine Arts*, vol. 8, 1940, pp. 193–206

ROSENBERG 1959
Jakob Rosenberg, review of Otto Benesch, *The Drawings of Rembrandt*, Art Bulletin, vol. 41, 1959, pp. 63–119

ROSENBERG 1984
Pierre Rosenberg, *Vies anciennes de Watteau*, Paris, 1984

ROSENBERG AND PRAT 1996
Pierre Rosenberg and Louis-Antoine Prat, *Antoine Watteau, 1684–1721: Catalogue raisonné des dessins*, 2 vols., Paris, 1996

ROSENTHAL 1971
Earl E. Rosenthal, 'Die "Reichskrone", die "Wiener Krone" und die "Krone Karls des Grossen" um 1520', *Jahrbuch der Kunsthistorischen Sammlungen in Wien*, vol. 66, 1971, pp. 37–48

RÖTHLISBERGER 1961
Marcel Röthlisberger, *Claude Lorrain: The Paintings*, 2 vols., New Haven and London, 1961

RÖTHLISBERGER 1962
Marcel Röthlisberger, *Claude Lorraine: The Wildenstein Album*, Paris, 1962

RÖTHLISBERGER 1968
Marcel Röthlisberger, *Claude Lorrain: The Drawings*, 2 vols., Los Angeles, 1968

RÖTHLISBERGER 1991
Marcel Röthlisberger, 'Abraham Bloemaert's Vanitas Representations', *Delineavit et Sculpsit* 26, no. 14, May 1991, pp. 20–25

ROTTERDAM 1990
Chris Fischer, *Fra Bartolommeo: Master Draughtsman of the High Renaissance*, exh. cat., Museum Boymans-van Beuningen, Rotterdam, 1990

ROTTERDAM 1996
Bernard Aikema and M. Tuijn, *Tiepolo in Holland: Works by Tiepolo and His Circle in Dutch Collections*, exh. cat., Museum Boijmans Van Beuningen, Rotterdam, 1996

RÖTTGEN 1995
Herwarth Röttgen, review, *Burlington Magazine*, vol. 137, no. 1108, July 1995, pp. 472–74

ROUART AND WILDENSTEIN 1975
Denis Rouart and Daniel Wildenstein, *Édouard Manet: Catalogue raisonné*, 2 vols., Lausanne, 1975

ROYALTON-KISCH 1992
M. Royalton-Kisch, *Drawings by Rembrandt and His Circle in the British Museum*, London, 1992

ROYALTON-KISCH AND SCHATBORN 2011
M. Royalton-Kisch and P. Schatborn, 'The Core Group of Rembrandt Drawings, II: The List', *Master Drawings*, vol. 49, no. 3, 2011, pp. 323–46

RUGGIERI 1967
U. Ruggieri, *Disegni Piazzeschi. Disegni inediti di raccolte bargamasche (Monumenta Bergomensia-XVII)*, Bergamo, 1967

RUPPRICH 1969
H. Rupprich, *Dürer. Schriftlicher Nachlaß*, vol. 3, Berlin, 1969

RUSKIN (COOK AND WEDDERBURN) 1903–12
E.T. Cook and A. Wedderburn (eds.), *The Works of John Ruskin*, 39 vols., London, 1903–12

RUSSELL 1923
Archibald G.B. Russell, *Drawings by Guercino*, London, 1923

RUSSOLI AND MINERVINO 1970
Franco Russoli and Fiorella Minervino, *L'Opera completa di Degas*, Milan, 1970

RUVOLDT 2003
Maria Ruvoldt, 'Michelangelo's Dream', *Art Bulletin*, vol. 85, no. 1, March 2003, pp. 86–113

SALERNO 1988
Luigi Salerno, *I dipinti del Guercino*, Rome, 1988

SALMON 2006
Dimitri Salmon, *Ingres: La Grande Odalisque*, Paris, 2006

SAN FRANCSICO 1989
Lorenz E.A. Eitner and Steven A. Nash, *Géricault, 1791–1824*, exh. cat., The Fine Arts Museums of San Francisco, 1989

SANDER 1969
M. Sander, *Le Livre à figures italien. Depuis 1467 jusqu'à 1530; Essai de sa bibliographie et de son histoire*, 7 vols., Milan, 1969

SASLOW 1986
J.M. Saslow, *Ganymede in the Renaissance: Homosexuality in Art and Society*, New Haven and London, 1986

SAURMA-JELTSCH 2002–03
L.E. Saurma-Jeltsch, 'Karl der Große im Spätmittelalter. Zum Wandel einer politischen Ikone', *Zeitschrift des Aachener Geschichtsvereins*, vols. 104–05, 2002–03, pp. 443–61

SAYRE 1958
Eleanor Sayre, 'An Old Man Writing: A Study of Goya's Albums', *Boston Museum Bulletin*, vol. 56, 1958, pp. 116–36

SCHATBORN 1981
Peter Schatborn, 'Van Rembrandt tot Crozat', *Nederlandse Kunsthistorisch Jaarboek*, vol. 32, 1981, pp. 1–54

SCHATBORN 1985
Peter Schatborn, *Drawings by Rembrandt in the Rijksmuseum*, Amsterdam, 1985

SCHILLING 1934
E. Schilling, *Altdeutsche Meisterzeichnungen*, Frankfurt, 1934

SCHMID 2006
J.J. Schmid, 'Die Reichskleinodien. Objekte zwischen Liturgie, Kult und Mythos', in Bernd Heidenreich and Frank-Lothar Kroll (eds.), *Wahl und Krönung*, Frankfurt am Main, 2006, pp. 123–49

SCHNEIDER 1984
Pierre Schneider, *Matisse*, London, 1984

SCRASE 1983
David Scrase, 'Drawings at the British Museum, London', *Burlington Magazine*, vol. 125, no. 962, 1983, pp. 307–08

SCHULZ 1978
W. Schulz, 'Tiepolo-Probleme. Ein Antonius-Album von Giandomenico Tiepolo', *Wallraf-Richartz Jahrbuch*, vol. 40, 1978, pp. 63–73

SCHULZE ALTCAPPENBERG 1995
Hein-Th. Schulze Altcappenberg, *Die italienischen Zeichnungen des 14. und 15. Jahrhunderts im Berliner Kupferstichkabinett. Kritischer Katalog*, Berlin, 1995

SCHUMACHER 2007
A. Schumacher, *Michelangelos 'teste divine': Idealbildnisse als Exempla der Zeichenkunst*, Münster, 2007

SCHWARTZ AND BOK 1990
G. Schwartz and M. Bok, *Pieter Saenredam: The Painter and His Time*, London, 1990

SEE 1919
R.R.M. See, 'The Pastel Work of John James Masquerier', *Connoisseur*, vol. 55, September–December 1919, pp. 195–204

SEILERN 1955
Antoine Seilern, *Flemish Paintings and Drawings at 56 Princes Gate, London SW 7*, London, 1955

SEILERN 1959
Antoine Seilern, *Italian Paintings and Drawings at 56 Princes Gate London SW 7*, 4 vols., London, 1959

SEILERN 1961
Antoine Seilern, *Paintings and Drawings of Continental Schools Other than Flemish and Italian*, London, 1961

SEILERN 1969
Antoine Seilern, *Italian Paintings and Drawings at 56 Princes Gate London SW7*, London, 1969

SEILERN 1971
Antoine Seilern, *Corrigenda and Addenda to the Catalogues of Paintings and Drawings at 56 Princes Gate London SW7*, London, 1971

SELLINK 2007
Manfred Sellink, *Bruegel: The Complete Paintings, Drawings and Prints*, Antwerp, 2007

SÉRULLAZ 1984
Maurice Sérullaz, *Inventaire général des dessins école française. Dessins d'Eugène Delacroix, 1798–1863*, 2 vols., Paris, 1984

SHANES 1979
Eric Shanes, *Turner's Picturesque Views in England and Wales, 1825–1838*, London, 1979

SHANES 1990
Eric Shanes, *Turner's Human Landscape*, London, 1990

SHANES 2009
Eric Shanes, 'Turner Right. Ruskin Wrong', *Turner Society News*, vol. 111, March 2009, pp. 8–10

SHEARMAN 1972
John Shearman, 'Review of The Drawings of Pontormo', *Art Bulletin*, vol. 54, no. 2, June 1972, pp. 209–12

SHEFFIELD AND ELSEWHERE 1977
Drawings from the Courtauld, exh. cat., Graves Art Gallery, Sheffield; Wolverhampton Art Gallery; Bolton Museum and Art Gallery; Laing Art Gallery, Newcastle-upon-Tyne; Ferens Art Gallery, Hull; and Portsmouth Museum and Art Gallery, London, 1977

SHELTON 2008
Andrew Carrington Shelton, *Ingres*, New York, 2008

SHOAF TURNER 2006
J. Shoaf Turner, *Dutch Drawings in the Pierpont Morgan Library: Seventeenth to Nineteenth Centuries*, 2 vols., New York, 2006

SHUGER 1994
Debora Kuller Shuger, *The Renaissance Bible: Scholarship, Sacrifice, and Subjectivity*, Berkeley, 1994

SICKEL 2008
L. Sickel, 'Die Sammlung des Tommaso de' Cavalieri und die Provenienz der Zeichnungen Michelangelos', *Römisches Jahrbuch der Bibliotheca Hertziana*, vol. 37, 2006, pp. 163–221

SILVANI 1992–92
V. Silvani, 'Il pittore Antonio del Donnino del Mazziere', PhD diss., Università degli Studi di Firenze, Facoltà di Lettere e Filosofia, 1991–92

SILVER 1989
Kenneth E. Silver, *Esprit de Corps: The Art of the Parisian Avant-Garde and the First World War, 1914–1925*, Princeton, 1989

SLIVE 1964
Seymour Slive, 'Reconsideration of Some Rejected Rembrandt Drawings', *Art Quarterly*, vol. 27, 1964, pp. 274–96

SLIVE 2009
Seymour Slive, *Rembrandt Drawings*, Los Angeles, 2009

SOUTHAMPTON AND ELSEWHERE 1995
Drawing the Line: Reappraising Drawing Past and Present, exh. cat., Southampton City Art Gallery; Manchester City Art Galleries; Ferens Art Gallery, Hull; and Whitechapel Art Gallery, London, 1995

ST PETERSBURG, FL 2001
Abraham Bloemaert (1566–1651) and His Time, exh. cat., Museum of Fine Arts, St Petersburg, FL, 2001

STANGE 1957
Alfred Stange, 'Zwei neuentdeckte Kaiserbildnisse Albrecht Dürers', *Zeitschrift für Kunstgeschichte*, vol. 20, 1957, pp. 1–24

STEIN 2000
Perrin Stein, 'Copies and Retouched Drawings', *Master Drawings*, vol. 38, no. 2, 2000, pp. 167–86

STEPHENS 1996
R. Stephens, 'New Material for Francis Towne's Biography', *Burlington Magazine*, vol. 138, no. 1121, August 1996, pp. 500–05

STOCKHOLM 1967
Toulouse-Lautrec, exh. cat., Stockholm, 1967

STRAUSS 1974
Walter L. Strauss, *The Complete Drawings of Albrecht Dürer*, 6 vols., New York, 1974

STRAUSS 1977
Walter L. Strauss, *Hendrick Goltzius, 1558–1617: The Complete Engravings and Woodcuts*, New York, 1977

STRAUSS AND VAN DER MEULEN 1979
Walter L. Strauss and M. van der Meulen, *The Rembrandt Documents*, New York, 1979

STRIEDER 1973
P. Strieder, 'Albrecht Dürers "Vier Apostel" im Nürnberger Rathaus', in *Festschrift Klaus Lankheit zum 20. Mai 1973*, Cologne, 1973, pp. 151–57

STRIEDER 1981
P. Strieder, *Dürer*, Königstein im Taunus, 1981

STUTTGART 1993
Elisabeth Kieven, *Von Bernini bis Piranesi. Römische Architekturzeichnungen des Barock*, exh. cat., Staatsgalerie, Stuttgart, 1993

SUDBURY 1976
R. McPherson and M. Rosenthal, *Constable's Country*, exh. cat., Gainsborough's House, Sudbury, 1976

SULLIVAN 2010
Margaret Sullivan, *Bruegel and the Creative Process, 1559–1563*, Farnham, Surrey, and Burlington, VT, 2010

SUMMERS 1977
David Summers, 'Contrapposto: Style and Meaning in Renaissance Art', *Art Bulletin*, vol. 59, no. 3, September 1977, pp. 336–61

SUMMERS 1981
David Summers, *Michelangelo and the Language of Art*, Princeton, 1981

SUMOWSKI 1961
W. Sumowski, *Bemerkungen zu Otto Beneschs Corpus der Rembrandtzeichnungen II*, Bad Pyrmont, 1961

SWANSEA 1962
Exhibition of French Master Drawings, exh. cat., Glynn Vivian Art Gallery, Swansea, 1962

SYDNEY 1999
Terence Maloon and Peter Raissis, *Michelangelo to Matisse: Drawing the Figure*, exh. cat., Art Gallery of New South Wales, Sydney, 1999

TALBOT 1971
Charles W. Talbot, *Dürer in America: His Graphic Work*, Washington, DC, 1971

TERNOIS 1999
Daniel Ternois, *Lettres d'Ingres à Marcotte d'Argenteuil (Archives de l'art français, 5)*, Nogent-le-Roi, 1999

TESTA 1979
J.A. Testa, 'The Iconography of the Archers: A Study of Self-Concealment and Self-Revelation in Michelangelo's Presentation Drawings', *Studies in Iconography*, vol. 5, 1979, pp. 45–72

THODE 1908–13
Henry Thode, *Michelangelo. Kritische Untersuchungen über seine Werke*, 3 vols., Berlin, 1908–13

THODE 1912
Henry Thode, *Michelangelo und das Ende der Renaissance*, vol. 3, Berlin, 1912

THOMAS À KEMPIS 1892
Thomas à Kempis, *Meditations on the Life of Christ*, ed. and trans. The Ven. Archdeacon Wright, MA, and The Reverend S. Kettlewell, MA, New York, 1892

THOMSON 1985
Richard Thomson, *Seurat*, Oxford, 1985

TIETZE 1951
Hans Tietze, *Dürer als Zeichner und Aquarellist*, Vienna, 1951

TIETZE AND TIETZE-CONRAT 1928–38
Hans Tietze und Erica Tietze-Conrat, *Kritisches Verzeichnis der Werke Albrecht Dürers*, 2 vols., Augsburg, Basel, and Leipzig, 1928–38

TIETZE AND TIETZE-CONRAT 1944
Hans Tietze and Erica Tietze-Conrat, *The Drawings of the Venetian Painters in the 15th and 16th Centuries*, New York, 1944

TILLEROT 2010
Isabelle Tillerot, *Jean de Jullienne et les collectionneurs de son temps. Un regard singulier sur le tableau*, Paris, 2010

Timaeus (LOEB) 1929
Plato, *Timaeus*, Loeb Classical Library, trans. by R.G. Bury, vol. 7, London and New York, 1929

Time 1946
'Medicine: The Clyster Craze', *Time*, July 1, 1946, accessed online at http://www.time.com/time/magazine/article/0,9171,803783,00.html#ixzz1Vn9DsITB

TOKYO 1978
European Landscape Painting, exh. cat., National Museum of Western Art, Tokyo, 1978

TOKYO 1995
Holm Bevers, S. Leclercq, Yoko Mori, and M. Takahashi (eds.), *The World of Bruegel: The Coppée Collection and Eleven International Musuems*, exh. cat., Tobu Museum of Arts, Tokyo, 1995

TOKYO, OSAKA, AND KYOTO 1997
William Bradford, *The Courtauld Collection: Treasures of Impressionism*, Tokyo, Takashimaya Art Gallery; Osaka, Takashimaya; and Kyoto, Takashimaya, 1997

TOKYO AND ELSEWHERE 1984
The Impressionists and the Post-Impressionists from the Courtauld Collection (Japan) and *The Great Impressionists: Masterpieces from the Courtauld Collection of Impressionist and Post-Impressionist Paintings and Drawings* (Australia), exh. cat., Takashimaya, Tokyo; Takashimaya, Kyoto; Takashimaya, Osaka; and Australian National Gallery, Canberra, 1984

TOLNAI 1925
Karl Tolnai, *Die Zeichnungen Pieter Bruegels*, Munich, 1925

TOLNAY 1935
Charles de Tolnay, *Pierre Bruegel l'ancien*, Brussels, 1935

TOLNAY 1952
Charles de Tolnay, *The Drawings of Pieter Bruegel the Elder*, London, 1952

TOLNAY 1960
Charles de Tolnay, *Michelangelo*, vol. 5, *The Last Period*, Princeton, 1960

TOLNAY 1975
Charles de Tolnay, *Corpus dei disegni di Michelangelo*, 4 vols., Novara, 1975–80

TORONTO 1998
The Courtauld Collection: Masterpieces of Impressionism and Post-Impressionism, exh. cat., Art Gallery of Ontario, Toronto, 1998

TORONTO AND ELSEWHERE 1980
Andrew Wilton, *Turner and the Sublime*, exh. cat., The Art Gallery of Ontario, Toronto; Yale Center for British Art, New Haven; and British Museum, London, 1980

TROUTMAN 1968
Philip Troutman, 'The Evocation of Atmosphere in the English Watercolour', *Apollo*, vol. 88, no. 77, July 1968

TROYES AND ELSEWHERE 1977
Charles-Joseph Natoire. Peintures, dessins, estampes et tapisseries des collections publiques françaises, exh. cat., Musée des Beaux-Arts, Troyes; Musées des Beaux-Arts, Nîmes; and Villa Médicis, Rome, 1977

TRUTTY-COOHILL 1988
Patricia Trutty-Coohill, 'Narrative to Icon: The San Diego Luini and Leonardo's Language of the Dumb', *Achademia Leonardi Vinci: Journal of Leonardo Studies and Bibliography of Vinciana*, vol. 1, 1988, pp. 27–31

TÜBINGEN AND ZURICH 1982
Götz Adriani, *Paul Cézanne, Aquarelle, 1866–1906*, exh. cat., Kunsthalle, Tübingen, and Kunsthaus, Zurich, 1982

TULSA 1998
R.P. Townsend, *J.M.W. Turner: 'That Greatest of Landscape Painters'*, exh. cat., The Philbrook Museum of Art, Tulsa, Oklahoma, 1998

TURNER 1986
Nicholas Turner, *Florentine Drawings of the Sixteenth Century*, exh. cat., The British Museum, London, 1986

UTRECHT 1961
Saenredam, exh. cat., Centraal Museum, Utrecht, 1961

UTRECHT AND ROTTERDAM 1923
Vincent Van Gogh collectie van mevr. J. van Gogh Bonger, exh. cat., Vereiniging Voor de Kunst, Utrecht, and Kunstkring, Rotterdam, 1923

VAN DEN DOEL 2008
M. van den Doel, *Ficino en het voorstellingsvermogen phantasia en imagination in kunst en theorie van de Renaissance*, St Hoofd-Hart-Handen, 2008

VAN DER MEULEN 1994
Marjon van der Meulen, *Rubens Copies after the Antique*, Corpus Rubenianum Ludwig Burchard XXIII, 3 vols., London, 1994

VAN SASSE VAN YSSELT 2002
Dorine van Sasse van Ysselt, 'Una Composizione di Giovanni Stradano identificata: La Pesca delle Perle nel Golfo Persico', in Anton W.A. Boschloo, Edward Grasman, and Gert Jan van der Sman (eds.), *'Aux Quatre Vents': A Festschrift for Bert W. Meijer*, Florence, 2002, pp. 237–42

VANNUCCI 1997
Alessandra Baroni Vannucci, *Jan Van Der Straet detto Giovanni Stradano. Flandrus pictor et inventor*, Milan, 1997

VASARI (BETTARINI) 1966–87
Giorgio Vasari, *Le vite de' più eccellenti pittori, scultori e architettori nelle redazioni del 1550 e 1568*, ed. by R. Bettarini, commentary by P. Barocchi, 6 vols., Florence, 1966–87

VASARI 1996
Giorgio Vasari, *Lives of the Painters, Sculptors and Architects*, trans. by Gaston du C. De Vere, intro. and notes by D. Ekserdjian, 2 vols., London, 1996

VASARI SOCIETY 1916–35
The Vasari Society for the Reproduction of Drawings by the Old Masters, 2nd series, 16 vols., Oxford, 1916–35

VELDMAN 1977
Ilja M. Veldman, *Maarten van Heemskerck and Dutch Humanism in the Sixteenth Century*, trans. by Michael Hoyle, Amsterdam, 1977

VÉLIZ 2011
Zahira Véliz, *Spanish Drawings in the Courtauld Gallery: A Complete Catalogue*, London, 2011

VENICE 1962
K.T. Parker and J. Byam Shaw, *Canaletto e Guardi*, exh. cat., Fondazione Giorgio Cini, Venice, 1962

VENICE 1999
Renaissance Venice and the North: Crosscurrents in the Time of Bellini, Dürer, and Titian, exh. cat., Palazzo Grassi, Venice, 1999

VENTURI 1936
Lionello Venturi, *Cézanne: Son art, son œuvre*, 2 vols., Paris, 1936

VENTURI 1978
Lionello Venturi, *Cézanne*, Geneva, 1978

VERMEYLEN 2003
Filip Vermeylen, *Painting for the Market: Commercialization of Art in Antwerp's Golden Age*, Turnhout, 2003

VIENNA 1961
Fritz Novotny, *Paul Cézanne, 1839–1906*, exh. cat., Belvedere, Vienna, 1961

VIENNA 2003
K.A. Schröder and M. Sternath, *Albrecht Dürer*, exh. cat., Albertina, Vienna 2003

VIENNA 2012
Impressionismus: Pastelle, Aquarelle, Zeichnungen, exh. cat., Albertina, Vienna, 2012

VLIEGHE 1987
Hans Vlieghe, *Portraits II. The Identified Sitters Painted in Antwerp*, Corpus Rubenianum Ludwig Burchard XIX, 2 vols., London, 1987

VOLLARD 1914
Ambroise Vollard, *Paul Cézanne*, Paris, 1914

VON BORRIES 1972
E. von Borries, *Albrecht Dürer. Christus als Schmerzensmann*, Karlsruhe, 1972

WAINWRIGHT 1961
G.A. Wainwright, 'The Earliest Uses of the Mano Cornuta', *Folklore*, vol. 72, 1961, pp. 492–95

WALL 1879
The Dramatic Works of Molière, trans. Charles Heron Wall, New York, 1879

WASHINGTON 1988
William R. Rearick and Terisio Pignatti, *The Art of Paolo Veronese*, exh. cat., National Gallery of Art, Washington, DC, 1988

WASHINGTON AND ELSEWHERE 1978
Eunice Williams, *Drawings by Fragonard in North American Collections*, exh. cat., National Gallery of Art, Washington, DC; Fogg Art Museum, Cambridge, MA; and The Frick Collection, New York, 1978

WASHINGTON AND ELSEWHERE 1984
Margaret Morgan Grasselli and Pierre Rosenberg, *Watteau, 1684–1721*, exh. cat., National Gallery of Art, Washington, DC; Galeries Nationales du Grand Palais, Paris; and Château de Charlottenburg, Berlin, Paris, 1984

WASHINGTON AND NEW YORK 1986
John Oliver Hand (ed.), *The Age of Bruegel: Netherlandish Drawings in the Sixteenth Century*, exh. cat., National Gallery of Art, Washington, DC, and Pierpont Morgan Library, New York, 1986

WASHINGTON AND ELSEWHERE 1996
Paul Joannides, *Michelangelo and His Influence: Drawings from Windsor Castle*, exh. cat., National Gallery of Art, Washington, DC; Kimbell Art Museum, Fort Worth; The Art Institute of Chicago; Fitzwilliam Museum, Cambridge; and The Queen's Gallery, London, 1996

WASHINGTON AND ELSEWHERE 2007
Ian Warrell (ed.), *J.M.W. Turner*, exh. cat., National Gallery of Art, Washington, DC; Dallas Museum of Art; and The Metropolitan Museum of Art, New York, in association with Tate Britain, London, 2007

WECHSLER 1975
J. Wechsler, *Cézanne in Perspective*, London, 1975

WEIL 1922
E. Weil, *Die deutsche Übersetzung der Ars moriendi des Meisters Ludwig von Ulm um 1470*, Munich, 1922

WEINBERGER 1929
M. Weinberger, 'Zu Dürers Lehr- und Wanderjahren', *Münchner Jahrbuch der Bildenden Kunst*, Neue Folge, vol. 6, 1929, pp. 124–46

WELLINGTON AND ELSEWHERE 1976
Exhibition of Drawings and Watercolours from the Spooner and Witt Collections, exh. cat., National Art Gallery of New Zealand, Wellington, and other locations in New Zealand, 1976

WHISTLER 2004
Catherine Whistler, 'Life Drawing in Venice from Titian to Tiepolo', *Master Drawings*, vol. 42, no. 4, 2004, pp. 374–76

WHITE 1964
Christopher White, *Rembrandt and His World*, London, 1964

WHITE 1984
Christopher White, *Rembrandt*, London, 1984

WHITNEY 1997
Wheelock Whitney, *Géricault in Italy*, New Haven and London, 1997

WIEMERS 1996
Michael Wiemers, *Bildform und Werk Genese. Studien zur zeichnerischen Bildvorbereitung in der italienischen Malerei zwischen 1450 und 1490*, Munich and Berlin, 1996

WILDE 1930
Johannes Wilde, 'Ein zeitgenössisches Bildnis des Kaiser Sigismund', *Jahrbuch der Kunsthistorischen Sammlungen in Wien*, vol. 4, 1930, pp. 213–22

WILDE 1953
Johannes Wilde, 'Michelangelo and His Studio', in *British Museum Department of Prints and Drawings, Italian Drawings in the Department of Prints and Drawings in the British Museum*, London, 1953

WILDE 1978
Johannes Wilde, *Michelangelo: Six Lectures by Johannes Wilde*, ed. by J. Shearman and M. Hirst, Oxford, 1978

WILK 1985
Sara Wilk, 'The Cult of Mary Magdalen in Fifteenth Century Florence and Its Iconography', *Studi Medievali*, 3rd ser., vol. 26 (1985), pp. 685–98

WILLIAMSTOWN 2006
Richard Rand, *Claude Lorrain: The Painter as Draftsman*, exh. cat., Sterling and Francine Clark Art Institute, Williamstown, MA, 2006

WILLIAMSTOWN AND ELSEWHERE 2003
Turner: The Late Seascapes, exh. cat., Sterling and Francine Clark Art Institute, Williamstown, MA; Manchester City Art Gallery; and Burrell Collection, Glasgow, 2003

WILSON-BAREAU 1986
Juliet Wilson-Bareau, 'The Hidden Face of Manet', *Burlington Magazine*, vol. 128, no. 997, April 1986, pp. i–v, vii, viii, 1–98

WILTON 1979
Andrew Wilton, *The Life and Work of J.M.W. Turner*, London, 1979

WINKLER 1927
Friedrich Winkler, 'The Collection of Dürer Drawings at Lemberg (Galicia)', *Old Master Drawings*, vol. 2, no. 6, 1927, pp. 15–19

WINKLER 1936–39
Friedrich Winkler, *Die Zeichnungen Albrecht Dürers*, 4 vols., Berlin, 1936–39

WINKLER 1949
Friedrich Winkler, *Albrecht Dürer. 80 Meisterzeichnungen*, Zurich, 1949

WINKLER 1957
Friedrich Winkler, *Albrecht Dürer. Leben und Werk*, Berlin, 1957

WINKLER 1964
Friedrich Winkler, *Das Werk des Hugo van der Goes*, Berlin, 1964

Samuel Courtauld Society

DIRECTOR'S CIRCLE

Anonymous
Andrew and Maya Adcock
Farah and Hassan Alaghband
Apax Partners
IC Carr
Christie's
Coller Capital Ltd
Mark and Cathy Corbett
Nicholas and Jane Ferguson
The Garcia Family Foundation
Sir Nicholas and Lady Goodison
James Hughes-Hallett
Nick Hoffman
Daniella Luxembourg, London
John A. McLaren / AkzoNobel
Charles and Tineke Pugh
Derek and Inks Raphael
Paul and Jill Ruddock
Sotheby's
Nicolai and Katja Tangen
Elke and Michael von Brentano
The Worshipful Company of Mercers
Niklas and Catherine Zennström

PATRONS' CIRCLE

Anonymous
Agnew's
Lord and Lady Aldington
Joan and Robin Alvarez
Felixe Appelbe
Mr Dominique and Ms Brit Axelroud
Jean-Luc Baroni Ltd
Philip and Cassie Bassett
John and Cynthia Beerbower
Douglas Blausten
The Lord Browne of Madingley
Tania Buckrell Pos
Mr Damon Buffini
David and Jane Butter
Julian and Jenny Cazalet
Mr Colin Clark
Jonathan Colchester, GAM
Colnaghi
Samantha Darell
Roger and Rebecca Emery
Eykyn Maclean Ltd
Mr Sam Fogg

David Gibbons
Lucia V. Halpern and John Davies
Dr Paula Henderson
Joanna Hewitt
Jennifer Hicks
Andrew Hochhauser QC
Amanda Hochman
Philip Hudson
Nicholas Jones
Daniel Katz Ltd
James Kelly
Klein Solicitors Ltd
Norman A. Kurland and Deborah A. David
Helen Lee and David Warren
Lefevre Fine Art
Professor Gerald Libby
Stuart Lochhead and Sophie Richard
Mark and Liza Loveday
Dr Chris Mallinson
Janet Martin
Mr Jay Massey
Clare Maurice
The Honourable Christopher McLaren
Lillian McNeila
Chiara Medici-Terzaghi
Norma and Selwyn Midgen
John and Jenny Murray
Mr Morton Neal CBE and Mrs Neal
Mrs Carmen Oguz
Mr Michael Palin
Lord and Lady Phillimore
Marie-Christine Poulain and Read Gomm
Leslie Powell
Charles Rose
Lady Jennifer Rose
Mrs Janice Sacher
Philip Searl
Richard and Susan Shoylekov
William Slee and Dr Heidi Bürklin-Slee
Hugh and Catherine Stevenson
Marjorie Stimmel
Sir Angus Stirling
Mrs Philippa Thorp
Johnny Van Haeften
Erik and Kimie Vynckier
The Rt. Hon. Nicholas & Lavinia Wallop
George and Patricia White
Lynn Woolfson
Anita and Poju Zabludowicz

ASSOCIATES

Mrs Kate Agius
Lord Jeffrey Archer
Rupert and Alexandra Asquith
The Hon Nicholas Assheton CVO, FSA
Mrs James Beery
Sarah Boardman
Dame Diana Brittan
Peter Brooks
Henry and Maria Cobbe
Mr Oliver Colman
Prisca and Andrew Cox
Emma Davidson
Richard Deutsch
Simon C. Dickinson Ltd.
Mr Andrew P. Duffy
Ben Elwes Fine Art
Sibylla Jane Flower
David and Diana Frank
Mrs Katherine Gyngell
Edward Harley
Richard Lambert
Annick Lapôtre
Dr Francine van Looij
Virgina Morck
Philip Mould Ltd
Martin Randall
The Lady Ridley of Liddesdale
Anna Somers Cocks
Rex De Lisle Stanbridge
Mr Robert Stoppenbach
Peter Stormonth Darling
Professor Deborah Swallow
Dr John Sweetman
Yvonne Tan Bunzl
John and Diana Uff
The Ulrich Family
The Weiss Gallery

Index of artists

Photographic credits

Credits are arranged alphabetically by city

CAT. NOS.

© The Samuel Courtauld Trust,
The Courtauld Gallery, London

FIGURES

© Rijksprentenkabinet, Amsterdam fig. 54, 40
© Van Gogh Museum, Amsterdam (Vincent Van Gogh Foundation) fig. 106
© Commune di Bergamo – Accademia Carrara fig. 73
© Besançon, Musée des beaux-arts et d'archéologie – Cliché Pierrre Guénat fig. 70
BPK, Berlin / Kupferstichkabinett, SMB / Jörg P. Anders figs. 20, 38 (Art Resource, NY), 59, 102
© Herzog Anton Ulrich-Museum, Braunschweig. Photo: Museumsfotograf fig. 60
© Cleveland, The Cleveland Museum of Art figs. 44, 47
© Musée des Beaux Arts de Dijon. Photo: François Jay fig. 69
© Soprintendenza Speziale per il Polo Museale Fiorentino, Gabinetto Fotografico figs. 31, 53
© Galleria degli Uffizi, Florence, Italy / Alinari / The Bridgeman Art Library fig. 52
© U. Edelmann – Städel Museum – ARTOTHEK figs. 21, 48
© Municipal Archives, Haarlem fig. 58
BPK, Berlin / Hamburger Kunsthalle, Hamburg, Germany; photo: Christoph Irrgang / Art Resource, NY fig. 45
© The British Library Board figs. 39, 68 (7807.e.3)
© Trustees of the British Museum figs. 23, 28, 33, 37, 46, 56, 57, 61, 74, 76, 77
© The Samuel Courtauld Trust, The Courtauld Gallery, London figs. 1–12, 15, 17, 29, 50, 51, 81, 83, 85, 98
© The National Gallery, London figs. 78, 80
© Tate, London 2012 figs. 84, 86, 87

© By kind permission of the Trustees of the Wallace Collection, London fig. 99
© Minneapolis Institute of Art, Bequest of Putnam Dana McMillan fig. 108
© The Burke Library (Columbia University) at Union Theological Seminary in the City of New York fig. 65
Matt Flynn © Smithsonian Institution / Cooper-Hewitt, National Design Museum, Smithsonian Institution / Art Resource, NY fig. 43
© The Frick Collection, New York fig. 72
© The Metropolitan Museum of Art. Image source: Art Resource, NY figs. 36, 67, 88
© The Pierpoint Morgan Library and Museum, New York fig. 49
© Nuremberg, Germanisches Nationalmuseum and bpk / Litz Braun fig. 25
© RMN (Musée du Louvre) / Gerard Blot fig. 19; / Jean-Gilles Berizzi figs. 24, 94 (Art Resource, NY); / Madeleine Coursaget fig. 95; / Franck Raux fig. 101; figs. 89 (Art Resource, NY), 62, 91
© Narodni Galerie, Prague, Czech Republic / Giraudon / The Bridgeman Art Library fig. 26
© Virginia Museum of Fine Arts. Photo: Travis Fullerton fig. 16
© Stichting Museum Bojmans Van Beuningen Rotterdam fig. 42, 55
© The Fine Arts Museums of San Francisco, Achenbach Foundation for Graphic Arts fig. 96
© Vatican Museums and Galleries, Vatican City, Italy / Alinari / The Bridgeman Art Library fig. 30
© Albertina, Wien fig. 14
© National Gallery of Art, Washington figs. 22, 110; image courtesy of the National Gallery of Art, Washington, DC fig. 13
The Royal Collection © 2012, Her Majesty Queen Elizabeth II fig. 75
© Herzog August Bibliothek, Wolfenbüttel, 7 Xylogr. fig. 32

Erich Lessing / Art Resource, NY fig. 62, 90
Bridgeman-Giraudon / Art Resource, NY fig. 92
© 2012 Photo Researchers, Inc. All Rights Reserved fig. 13, 41
Courtesy of Sotheby's Inc. fig. 103
Image by courtesy of the Witt Library, Courtauld Institute of Art, London figs. 27, 34, 35, 71, 100, 104, 109

Aimee Ng (with the assistance of Michael Bodycomb) fig. 64
Michael Bodycomb fig. 93
© Pam Goodey fig. 79

© 2012 Estate of Pablo Picasso / Artists Rights Society (ARS), New York (111 © Photo: Staatsgalerie Stuttgart) cat. no. 58, figs. 111, 112
© 2012 Succession H. Matisse / Artists Rights Society (ARS), New York (114 photo: Archives H. Matisse) cat. no. 59 figs. 113, 114